QUICK & EASY BOAT MAINTENANCE

2nd EDITION

1,001+ TIME-SAVING TIPS

SANDY LINDSEY

INTERNATIONAL MARINE/MCGRAW-HILL

Camden, Maine • New York • San Francisco Washington, D.C.• Auckland
Bogotá • Caracas • Lisbon • London • Madrid • Mexico City • Milan
Montréal • New Delhi • San Juan • Singapore • Sydney • Tokyo • Toronto

The ***McGraw-Hill*** *Companies*

1 2 3 4 5 6 7 8 9 10 11 12 QFR/QFR 1 11 10 9 8 7 6 5 4 3 2

ISBN 978-0-07-178997-4
MHID 0-07-178997-9

e-ISBN 978-0-07-178996-7
e-MHID 0-07-178996-0

Library of Congress Cataloging-in-Publication Data

Lindsey, Sandy.
Quick & easy boat maintenance: 1,001+ time-saving tips/Sandy Lindsey. —2nd ed.
p. cm.
Includes index.

ISBN-13: 978-0-07-178997-4
ISBN-10: 0-07-178997-9
ISBN-13: 978-0-07-178996-7 (e-book)
ISBN-10: 0-07-178996-0 (ebook)

1. Boats and boating—Maintenance and repair—Handbooks, manuals, etc.
I. Title. II. Title: Quick and easy boat maintenance.

VM322.L56 2012
623.82'020288—dc23 2012003983

All photos courtesy of the author.

McGraw-Hill products are available at special quantity discounts to use as premiums and sales promotions or for use in corporate training programs. To contact a representative, please e-mail us at bulksales@mcgraw-hill.com.

This book is printed on acid-free paper.

To my wonderful husband, Bill, an award-winning editor, who shares the cleaning and maintenance chores on our Edgewater.

To my parents, who stuck me with the family boat cleaning duties early in life, when I was the youngest crew member.

To my dachshunds, who have taught me the benefits of having paw prints on deck.

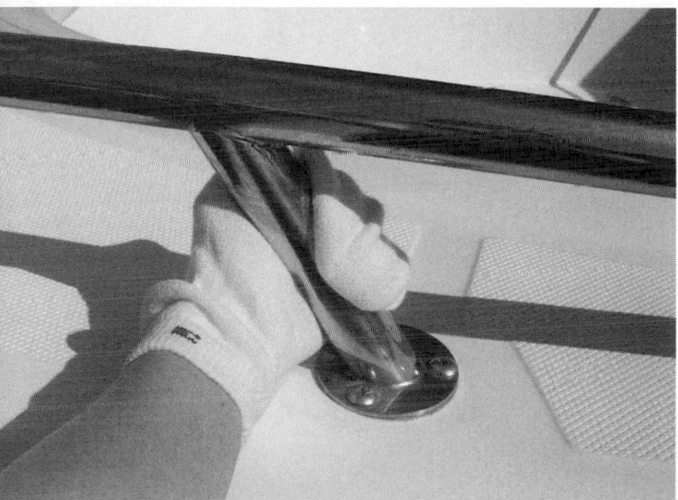

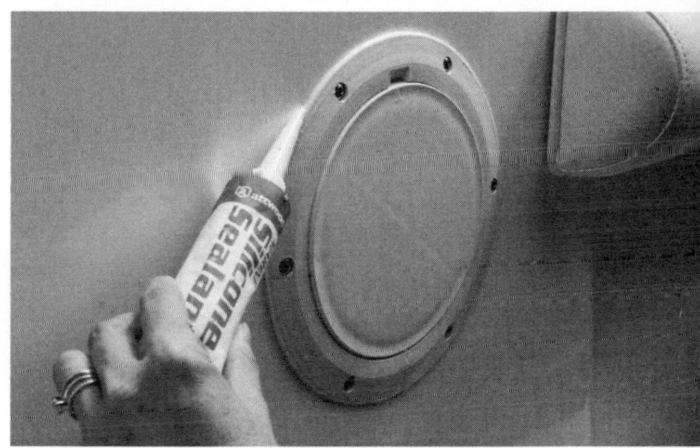
Silicone

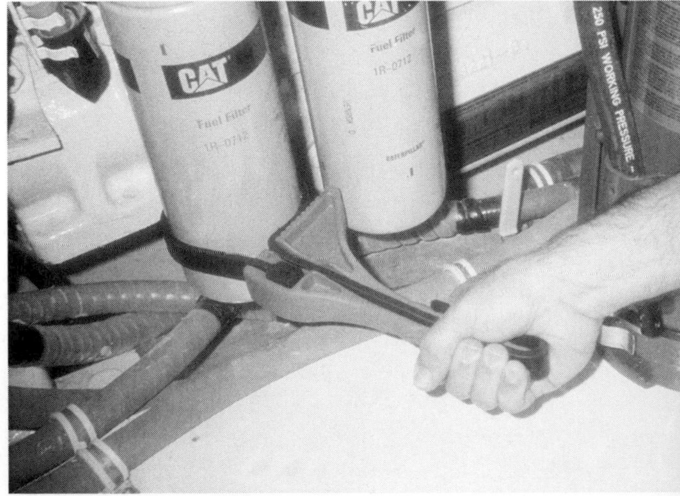
CAT
CAT
250 PSI WORKING PRESSURE

PREFACE

In the original *Quick and Easy Boat Maintenance* we provided quick, effective ways to keep your boat in top shape. This edition has been updated to take into account the many changes we've seen since then. Engines have become a lot more reliable, thanks to four-cycle designs similar to what we find under the hood of our cars. Electronics have made plotting a course as simple as tapping the screen. The gasoline that powers many of our boats now is blended with ethanol biofuel as an eco-friendly replacement for the fuel additive MTBE (methyl tertiary-butyl ether), which was discovered to have carcinogenic properties. A growing number of boat-care products are now formulated to be biodegradable and safe for use while the boat is in or near the water. Batteries are now available that absolutely cannot spill, never need to have water added, and can even be used upside down! However, although the engines have become more reliable, the electronics are more feature-laden, the fuel is better for our planet, the boat soap never smelled better, and our boat batteries now last more than two seasons, we still need to know how to keep all this equipment in operating condition. A large part of that is knowing what to do when all this great new equipment suddenly stops working. Accordingly, we've incorporated this new technology into this edition. However, we have not lost sight of the fact that most boats and the gear on them are more than 10 years old, which is why we have also added even more troubleshooting tips for older boats, engines, and electronics to keep you going out on the water.

We've also added an all-new chapter devoted entirely to the care and maintenance of sailboats. The result is a book that provides a wealth of practical knowledge for the owners of today's most advanced boats as well as for those who own the more "seasoned" vessels that are typically not addressed in most how-to books.

The best way to enjoy boating is to make sure the boat is in good operating condition, meaning that it starts every time and runs smoothly while under way. Part of that process involves recognizing when the boat and its gear are not working or are about to stop working. Preventive maintenance is always better than having to call for a tow when you are 5 miles from shore. At night. In the rain. With grumpy passengers. You can never avoid all mechanical problems, but after reading this expanded edition, you'll be able to avoid most of them and be ready to fix others when and if they do occur.

Boating is all about enjoying the freedom of being out on the water. The best way to do that is in a well-maintained boat. What's funny is that you may well find that maintaining the boat is as enjoyable as using it. It's not that complicated, no matter what your local "dock expert" will have you believe.

In the interest of full disclosure, my husband, Bill, is a vice president of Star brite, a manufacturer of many boat-care products. Star brite has been producing boat-care products for more than 35 years. The various products I mention by name are those I have personal experience with, but it does not mean that they are the only options. There are many fine products available, and I encourage all boaters to discover what works best for them.

ACKNOWLEDGMENTS

Special thanks to Molly Mulhern, Marisa L'Heureux, and all the wonderful people at International Marine/McGraw-Hill, and to Terri Mabe, Katie Mitchell, Jorge Arauz, Lee Braff, Peter Dornau, Greg Dornau, and the little Lindseys—Morgan, Olivia, Casey, and Vicki.

And also thanks to Brian Lipshy, a good friend and great attorney who has the worst luck boating. He has provided me with hours of practical boat maintenance and cleaning projects and has since learned to invite me when he takes his boat out . . . just in case.

ON DECK

Baking soda is an excellent nonabrasive stainless steel polish.

CARING FOR BOAT METAL

The Original Nonabrasive Stainless Steel Polish

If your stainless steel is slightly discolored, but the stains aren't so bad that they require special treatment, you can save some money on conventional nonabrasive stainless polishes by sprinkling baking soda on a sponge instead. Scrub down as you normally would, and rinse thoroughly.

Season Your Stainless to a High Shine

To give stainless steel a long-lasting high shine, rub down railings and other stainless steel with a lemon peel, and then wash as usual. The lemon oil in the peel cuts through grime that other cleaners may miss and restores luster.

If using a lemon peel is too strange for you, you can use the lemon oil that you use on your cabin furniture as an excellent substitute to clean stainless steel.

Rubbing alcohol from your boat's first-aid kit works almost as well on stainless as a lemon peel or lemon oil, and it disinfects.

There's More to Stainless Cleaning than Nevr-Dull

To remove salt buildup on stainless steel, rub on isopropyl rubbing alcohol. Use a 100 percent cotton rag.

To remove rust from stainless steel and most other deck metals, simply sprinkle a little bit of salt on the rust spot, and then squeeze a lime over the salt until it soaks the salt. Leave the mixture on for 2 or 3 hours. Then gently rub the spot with an old toothbrush or a piece of crumpled aluminum foil until the spot disappears.

Railings sticky from a child's gooey hands? Pour vinegar or straight lemon juice onto a sponge and wipe down the goop. Let the vinegar or lemon juice sit for a few minutes to cut through the residue, and then wash off with soap and water.

Drying Is Cleaning, Too

By using a chamois cloth to dry stainless and all other polished metal surfaces after you rinse the boat, you'll need to polish these surfaces only once each season.

Safe Stainless Surgery

When cutting a new section of stainless steel metal railing to size, place a dowel inside the metal tube to help it hold its shape as you saw off the appropriate section.

The Aluminum/Bronze Wool Connection

To remove oxidation from aluminum, wipe down with fine bronze wool or a clean rag dipped in mild laundry detergent such as Wisk. Rinse thoroughly afterward and protect with a fiberglass wax to retard further damage.

If you get bronze wool slivers in your fingers after cleaning the boat's metal, put white school glue over the spot, allow to dry, and then peel off. The glue should take the slivers with it.

For quick removal of tarnish from nonanodized aluminum, rub it with the shiny side of aluminum foil.

Silver Polish and Aluminum

Silver polish makes an excellent aluminum cleaner.

Aluminum Do's

Just like wood, aluminum has a grain. Look closely and you'll see it. Always rub on cleaners and waxes in that direction for better-looking results and an easier job.

Some rusty and tarnished aluminum can be cleaned by rubbing the offending spots with the shiny side of a crumpled piece of aluminum foil.

Use a bottle cork to clean particularly stubborn rust or metal discoloration spots. Dampen the flat edge of the cork first, so that it absorbs some of the metal polish, and then apply more polish and rub away. When you rub the cork over the spot, its flat surface and naturally abrasive properties do the rest, saving you lots of elbow grease.

Aluminum Don'ts

Here's a great way to get out of some boat maintenance work: Don't attempt to shine aluminum rails or fittings when it's cooler than 50°F outside. Aluminum scratches more easily in cold temperatures.

Keep cleaners containing ammonia away from aluminum, because ammonia pits it.

Acid-based teak cleaners and brighteners destroy anodizing on aluminum. For proof, check out the feet of a sportfisherman's tuna tower, where it bolts through the teak cover boards or rubrails. To prevent a purple, black, or whitish stain that's irreversible, use plenty of freshwater when rinsing the teak and stop occasionally to rinse off the hull, transom, vinyl, and any other nonteak materials.

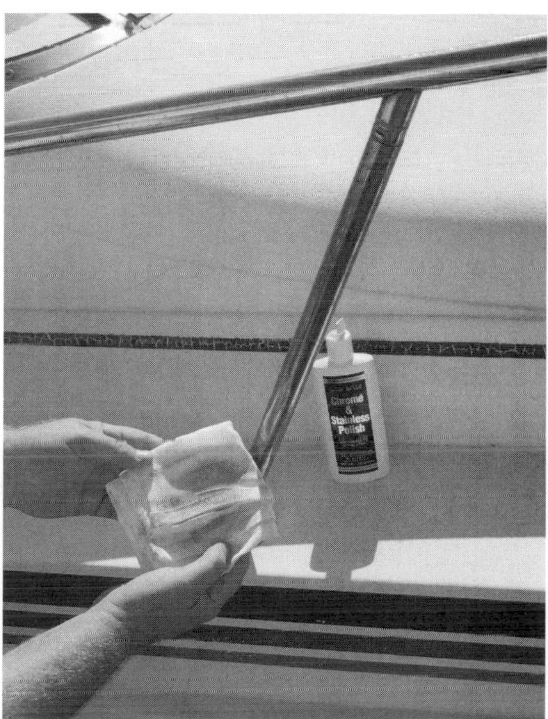

Removing rust from boat metals prevents rust stains from flowing down to the fiberglass below.

Aluminum Painter's Secret

Vinegar can be used to clean and acid-etch aluminum that's about to be painted.

Thrifty Is Nifty When It Comes to Brass

One of the cheapest cleaners for brass can be made at home by mixing 1 tablespoon flour, 1 tablespoon salt, and 1 tablespoon vinegar. Apply the powdered mixture with a clean, damp rag and watch the tarnish wipe off as the shine reappears.

For a quick brass cleanup, slice a lemon in half, dip the cut end in salt, and rub it on all the brass fittings and gear on your boat, working in small sections. Wash with warm, soapy water afterward, and buff dry with a clean rag.

For tough surface discoloration, cut a lemon in half, dust the cut end with baking soda, and rub on small sections at a time; the baking soda adds the necessary mild abrasive to scrub your brass back to life.

Baking Soda ℞

To tell if the baking soda that's made countless voyages with you is still good, put ¼ teaspoon of it in 1 tablespoon vinegar. If it fizzes, it's still fresh.

Simple Brass Protectant

To keep all brass surfaces and hardware looking their best, apply a protective coating of a polymer polish. Cabin brass should be protected with lemon oil.

Restoring Lacquered Brass

To remove chipping lacquer from coated brass, remove the brass fitting and soak it in a mixture of 1 cup baking soda and 1 gallon boiling water. Afterward, you can either relacquer the object or clean and polish it as you would uncoated brass.

Rust Be Gone

A gentle method of removing rust from deck metal is to get out your baking soda paste (1 tablespoon baking soda to 1 teaspoon water) and wipe down deck metal with a clean, damp cloth. Scrub the mixture gently with a small piece of aluminum foil. Buff with a dry paper towel.

To remove tough rust from boat metal, tools left on board, or the bumper of your tow vehicle, dip bronze or stainless steel wool in mineral spirits and rub off the rust. For the highest luster, wipe down afterward with a wadded ball of aluminum foil, shiny side out.

Quick Chrome Cleanups

To clean small polished surfaces such as on instrument gauges or electronics, wet a soft cloth with rubbing alcohol or window cleaner and wipe gently.

For chrome that is tarnished, rub on whitening toothpaste. And while you've got your mother-in-law's toothbrush out . . . whitening toothpaste also works wonders on scratches on Plexiglas windscreens.

You can clean the chrome bumper on your tow vehicle by sprinkling baking soda onto a moist sponge and rubbing it onto the bumper. Let sit for 5 minutes, and then hose off. Applying the baking soda with a moist, synthetic scouring pad works well for difficult spots. Buff dry with a soft rag.

Keep Your Gilt Glittering

To make gilt fittings and fixtures gleam, wipe down with a rag lightly dipped in turpentine.

Gold detailing on boats, which is becoming popular of late, can be cleaned with a mixture of 1 teaspoon cigarette ash (yes, cigarette ash!) or baking soda in just enough water to make it into a paste. Rub on the paste with a clean, soft cloth, rinse with cool water, and then buff it dry with a chamois.

A Pickle a Day . . .

Sweet pickle juice cleans just about everything copper, from dirty ends on electrical wires to galley cooking pans.

Preserve That Pewter

To restore those tarnished old nautical treasures made of pewter, rub down with the outer leaves of a head of cabbage (we're not making this one up!). Buff to a shine with a clean, soft cloth.

Frugal Polishing

To make a canister of powdered metal cleaner last twice as long, tape off half of the shaker holes. This also helps you apply the powdered cleanser only to the areas you wish to scrub.

Let Your Socks Do the Waxing

An easy way to polish tubular railings is to put an old sock over your hand, apply a polymer polish, and get busy. By curving your hand around the railing, you'll be able to cover more area, more completely, in less time.

Stuck Screw Solutions

Cola and other carbonated sodas poured on a rusted screw or bolt help loosen it.

When a stubborn screw refuses to come out, tighten it a tiny bit first to break its hold on the material it's screwed into. If it wasn't screwed in as far as it could go, it should be much easier to remove now.

Prevent Corrosion: The Unwanted Passenger

To keep spare nails, screws, and other small parts from rusting, use an empty face- or hand-cream jar. Not only does it keep the spare parts organized, but the greasy residue in the jar helps prevent rust.

To prevent corrosion on infrequently used tools you carry on board for emergencies, coat

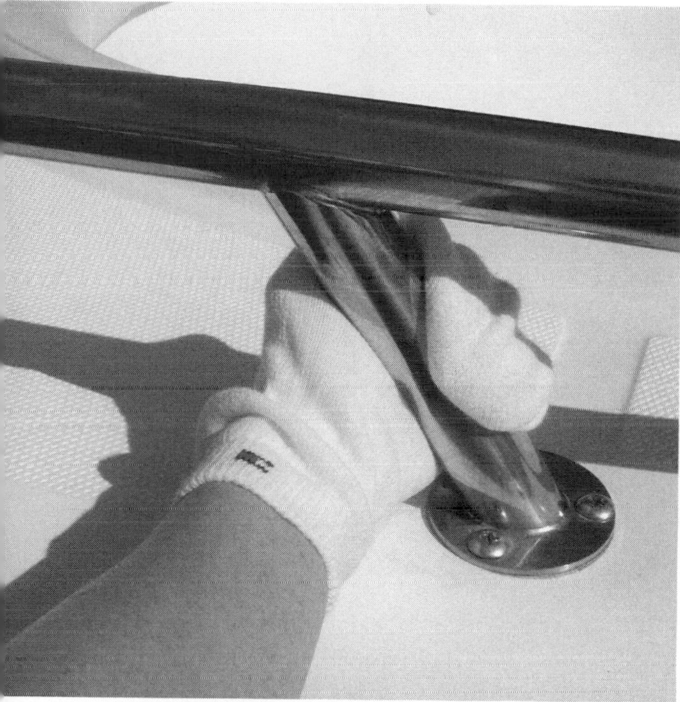

The easiest way to polish tubular railings is to use an old sock slipped over your hand with a quarter-sized amount of a polymer polish.

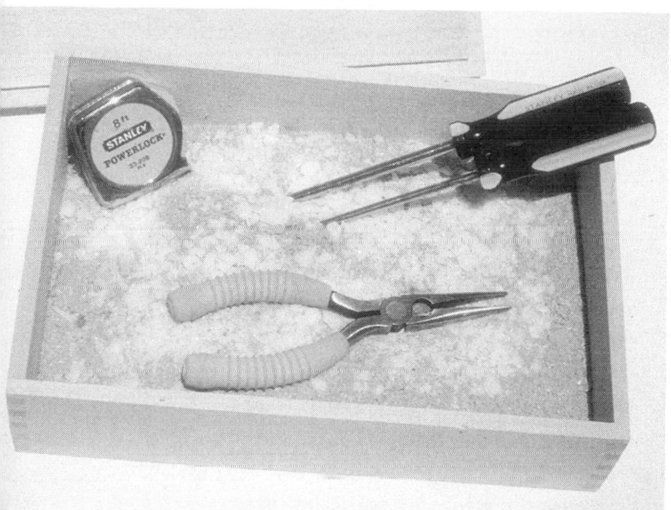

Protect onboard tools from corrosion by storing them in a wooden box with camphor and sawdust.

them with a thin layer of oil and wrap them in plastic wrap. Placing carpenter's chalk in a toolbox helps absorb moisture and also prevents corrosion.

Another effective anticorrosion technique for tools is to store them in a wooden box with camphor and sawdust.

All new boat tools should be protected with the following antirust, anticorrosion coating: ¼ cup lanolin and ¼ cup petroleum jelly. Heat until melted, and stir until blended. While the mixture is still warm (you can reheat it in a microwave for no more than 5 seconds, as needed), paint it on your tools with a cheap paintbrush. Allow to dry.

Quickie Corrosion Cleanup

For a quick cleanup of corroded tools and those with surface rust, lightly dip bronze wool in kerosene and use some elbow grease to rub the offending areas. Then use a balled-up piece of aluminum foil to rub hard. Wipe off the residue with a paper towel, and apply a fine coating of olive oil. ***NOTE:*** Do not work with kerosene near an open flame.

FIBERGLASS CLEANING AND REPAIR, AND GENERAL DECK MAINTENANCE

Pros' Secrets for Showroom Shine Fiberglass

For a quick and gentle gelcoat cleaner that leaves behind a nice shine, mix 1 tablespoon ammonia and 1 cup 70 percent isopropyl alcohol in 1 pint of water. Wash down the boat as usual.

To get a truly glistening showroom shine out of your gelcoat, use grandmother's handy

WHAT IS "GREEN"?

Many marine chemicals are now often labeled as "biodegradable" or "eco-friendly," which certainly seems like a good thing, but it raises the question: what is biodegradable?

In the United States there is no actual, legal definition of "biodegradable," nor are there any standards for compliance. This results in a variety of claims being made that usually cannot be verified by consumers. In Europe, the standard can be applied to materials that will break down into inert substances within six months, but there are no such requirements in the United States.

Biodegradable is most often described as materials that will decompose back into inert materials within a relatively short time. The problem is that many materials will begin to decompose only when exposed to air, moisture, and bacteria.

However, although biodegradability is certainly a good thing, how important is it when choosing marine products? Most waxes or polishes cannot make this claim because of the use of petroleum distillates as a base. Many boat washes use the term, but without a lab analysis there's no easy way to know just how "green" each product may be.

It is not wise to choose a cleaner simply on the basis of its eco-friendly claims. The "greenest" cleaner may be the least effective cleaner. The first objective is to find a cleaner that works well and then to look at its environmental impact. Some cleaners are extremely effective yet dangerous to the user and the environment. Phosphoric acid–based hull cleaners fall into this category. They must be used with care and caution. Waterproofing agents that utilize petroleum distillate bases are very effective, but care must be taken to not breathe the mists or allow overspray into our waters. Look for solvent-free waterproofing sprays or polishes; these products do not seem to work as well as their solvent-based cousins, but they tend to have much less effect on our waterways and aquatic life. When using a traditional polish or wax, do so where the "chaff" (the white residue) will not blow into the water. Most boat washes are essentially biodegradable, but avoid any that contain phosphates or bleaches. These can lead to algae blooms or will harm aquatic life.

Star brite was the first marine chemical manufacturer to offer biodegradable containers. These will decompose into an inert humus within two years of being placed in a landfill. The company's Sea Safe line of cleaners uses many DfE (the EPA's "Designed for the Environment") cleaning agents, but use only when doing so results in an effective, no-compromises product.

remedy of 2 tablespoons cornstarch, ½ cup household ammonia, and ½ cup white vinegar, stirred until dissolved in 1 gallon warm water.

Homemade All-Purpose Boat Cleaners

Pouring ½ cup baking soda, ½ cup white vinegar, and 1 cup ammonia mixed in 1 gallon warm water into a spray bottle creates a handy all-purpose boat cleaner that not only works on fiberglass deck and hull stains but is great for general head cleaning and cabin use.

For a more gentle all-purpose deck and cabin cleaner, mix 1 quart warm water, 1 teaspoon liquid soap, 1 teaspoon borax, and 1 teaspoon

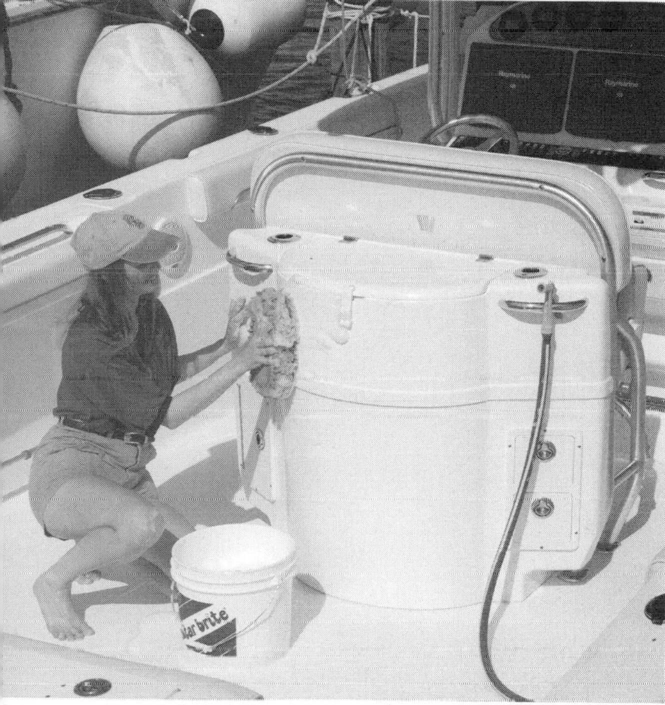

Use proper boat cleaners as common liquid household detergents have a high pH and should not be used on boats.

Learn the pros' secrets for a showroom shine.

vinegar. Store in a spray bottle. It works on fiberglass, metal, the head, cabin walls, floors, countertops, and more.

Leave the Household Cleaners at Home

Household detergents, such as liquid kitchen and laundry soap, should never be used to wash a boat because they have a high pH to cut through stubborn grease. If not washed off thoroughly, this pH can permanently etch your boat's gelcoat.

Rain, Rain, Go Away

Cut through saltwater stains and acid rain buildup on a fiberglass deck with 3 tablespoons ammonia in ¾ cup water.

Sticking with Cleaning

Is the fiberglass area around your helm sticky to the touch? Clean it with a mixture of talcum powder and just enough water to make it into a paste. Rub on with a clean cloth or paper towel, allow to sit for several minutes, and rub off.

Your Deck Deserves a Cool Soda

Rust stains that haven't penetrated the gelcoat of your fiberglass can often be scrubbed away with a mixture of cola and enough salt to make it gently abrasive. Rinse thoroughly. Cola and salt are the enemy of rust discoloration.

Warning: Water Can Be Bad for Your Boat

Want to get rid of hard water deposits on your hull and deck? Wipe it down with full-strength white vinegar, and then clean as usual. Vinegar helps dissolve the hard water spots and make them easier to remove.

Beware of acid rain. Its harmful effects can be activated by dew or fog, as well as rain. If your boat is stored uncovered, rinse and dry it regu-

HANDY EXCUSES FOR NOT CLEANING YOUR BOAT

"I'm conserving water."

"The water restrictions ended two years ago? Really?"

"I've been depressed over what's happening to the sharks."

"My wife insisted that I be present at the birth of our child."

"The EPA keeps banning my boat cleaners."

"I just cleaned the boat yesterday—the dirt you see on it now must be acid rain."

"It was too cold out/hot out/the temperature was so perfect that I decided to go for a cruise."

"My shrink says it's going to take me a while to get over getting my toe stuck in the shower drain while cleaning the head."

"I'm allergic to boat cleaners."

"It's not my turn."

"The Psychic Friends Network said . . . "

"I will never clean the boat again. Last time, my wife tried to use my toupee as a scrubbie."

"There were no good parking spaces at the marina, and you know how my back gets when I have to lug my cleaning bucket too far."

"I lost one of my contact lenses, so the boat looks perfectly fine to me."

"I got so caught up in reading *Quick and Easy Boat Maintenance: 1,001 Time-Saving Tips* that I forgot."

larly, even between washings, to prevent acid rain damage, which occurs when the clean water in the acid rain evaporates and the remaining acidic water eats into the fiberglass or painted surface. The process escalates when the sun heats the droplets and the fiberglass or paint.

Get Rid of Nature's Stains

Bird droppings on deck can be removed by covering them with a rag dipped in cooking oil. Allow to sit until the hardened droppings loosen.

Parking your boat under a tree means you're bound to get some sap drippings on it, but sometimes you don't have a choice. To remove the sap, use the tar remover sold in auto parts stores.

The Immaculate Deck

Black streaks on a fiberglass deck can be removed by rubbing with baking soda paste.

Shoe scuff marks from guests who don't own boat shoes can be easily removed from a fiber-

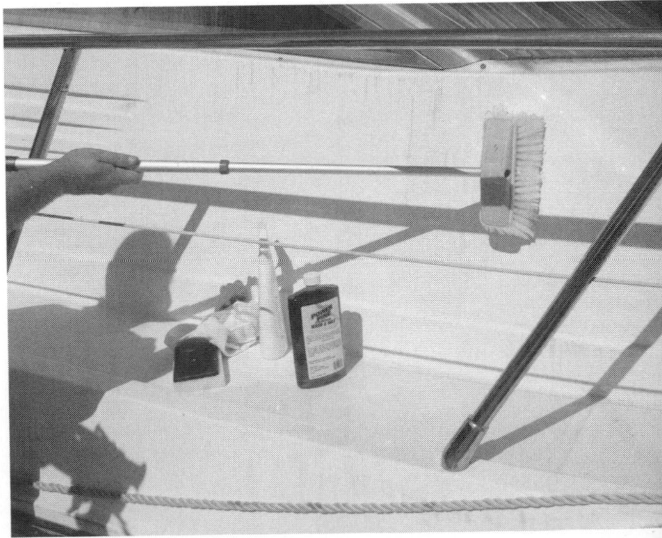

Soft, medium, and hard deck brushes all serve their own particular purpose.

glass deck by rubbing with a pencil eraser or fine, dry bronze wool.

Lemon extract also removes some black scuff marks on a fiberglass deck or hull, as well as some marks on vinyl.

If a careless crew member dropped a cigarette on deck, you can avoid a nasty brown stain by using an oxalic acid—or hydrochloric acid—based cleaner (rust stain remover for fiberglass). If the cigarette left a burn mark, sand down any raised edges around the burned area with 320-grit sandpaper and slowly fill in the burn indentation. Paint over any surrounding sanded area with color-matched gelcoat.

Remove gum from a fiberglass or teak deck or metal railings by placing an ice cube directly on the sticky gum and letting it sit for a few minutes. This makes the gum cold and hard, so it should pop cleanly off the surface, without the need for harsh chemicals. This also works on cabin carpets.

Avoid Cleaning by Keeping It Clean

Want absolutely perfect-looking fiberglass when you're done cleaning? Squeegee your hull and deck area dry.

Carry a Welcome Aboard doormat aboard and put it out every time you dock. Use a gunwale cover when allowing guests to board from the dock. Dirt that isn't brought onto the boat doesn't have to be cleaned off.

Getting Your Money's Worth

When your pump bottles of liquid boat cleaner, engine cleaner, or other liquids get so low that there isn't enough resulting suction for the pump to work, toss some marbles or small, clean stones into the bottle until they raise the liquid level sufficiently to cover the bottom of the intake tube.

You're Only as Good as Your Sponges

A sponge performs best if you dip only one-quarter of it into the cleaner—and we're talking wide side down here. The other three-quarters provides the necessary handhold and additional absorption needed to prevent drips.

Never bleach your sponges, or they'll disintegrate sooner. Flushing them thoroughly with water immediately after cleaning should be sufficient for non-food-service sponges.

The Practical Mopper

Put bicycle hand grips on the back half and midway down the handle of your boat-wash mop or long-handled brush to make it easier to hold and more controllable. The rubber surface also helps hold the mop upright when leaned against a fiberglass cabin or hull. A couple of small nails will hold the handles in place if the fit between the grip and the wooden pole isn't tight enough.

Never wring out your deck mop with your hands. It may have picked up a small sharp object and you might cut your hand. Use a mop wringer or your shoe. But remember, hosing is easier and usually more effective than mopping.

Starting Out Clean

Clean your hands before—not after—cleaning the boat. Rub liquid soap into your hands before washing down your boat and don't rinse it off just yet; the liquid soap protects your hands from dirt and, temporarily, from the drying effects of most cleaning chemicals, and after you're done and rinse off the liquid soap you'll have hands that you can take to a fine restaurant immediately afterward.

Cleaning with hard water is like cleaning with a perpetually dirty rag. Add a water softener such as Calgon to your boat wash bucket before beginning cleaning.

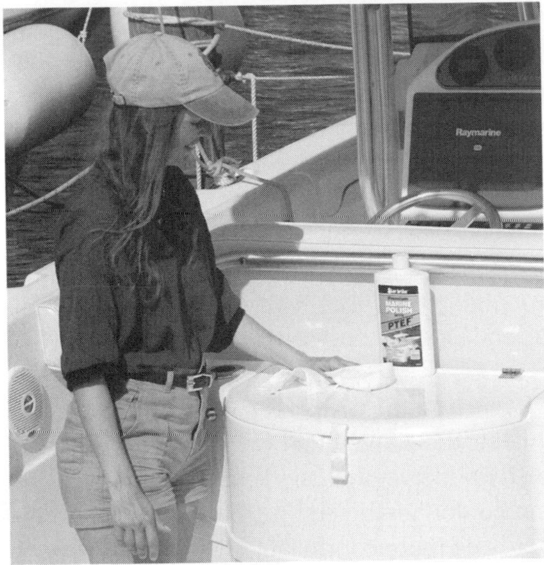

Apply a premium polish to repel future dirt and stains.

The 5-Cent Polish Test

Want to know if it is time to apply a new coat of polish to the boat? Hose down your boat. If the resulting water spots are bigger than a nickel, it's time to apply a fresh coating of a polymer polish.

Clues about Caulk

For professional-looking beads of silicone or other sealants, push—don't pull—the sealant cartridge. Mask both sides of the bead first, and finish the job by smoothing the goop with a wet finger. Misting the goop with water causes it to skin over, allowing you to use the boat sooner.

The can-opener blade of a Swiss Army knife or a Leatherman multitool is the world's best caulk-removing tool. Simply run the can opener along both sides of the bead while applying steady pressure. The dry caulk should come out clean and in long strips.

Don't give in to the temptation to use a cheap off-brand caulk on your boat, especially in the head area. Inexpensive caulk can turn black in less than two years, and no amount of scrubbing undoes the discoloration.

When applying caulk on a sunny, hot day, you may find that your caulk gets runny. If it does, put the caulk tube in the cabin fridge for an hour, after which it is once again ready for use.

To help prevent tubes of 5200, caulk, and other marine repair/sealing products from drying out after they've been opened, store them in a large ziplock bag.

Screwing, Drilling, and Sawing Fiberglass

Rub candle wax on screws before installation to lubricate them and keep potential fiberglass or teak damage to a minimum. The lubricant will make them go in smoother and helps prevent the fiberglass edges from "spidering" and the teak edges from cracking.

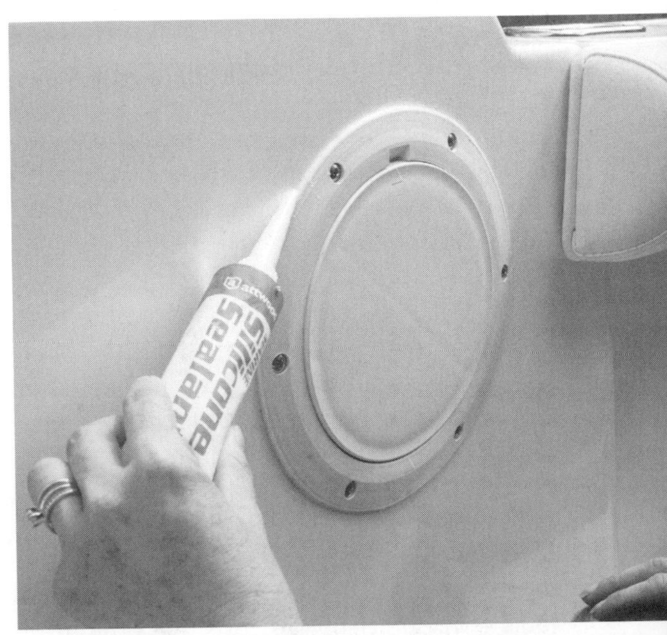

For professional looking beads of silicone, push—don't pull—the sealant cartridge.

Drilling into fiberglass, particularly into nonskid, can cause your gelcoat to chip. To avoid this, and to avoid marring by the drill chuck, place masking tape over the entire area to be drilled. Make sure your bit is sharp and that the drill is on the high-speed setting. When using a holesaw, after your pilot drill bit cuts through, stop before the saw blade hits the gelcoat. Reverse your drill rotation and score the gelcoat before cutting with the blade. These simple procedures virtually eliminate gelcoat chipping.

Even if you drill holes for your self-tapping screws, spider cracks can appear in the gelcoat when you tighten them down. Prevent the cracks by drilling a second, larger hole the same size as the screwhead but through the gelcoat only. Then it won't be stressed when you tighten down the screw.

Another way to prevent damage when drilling or sawing through fiberglass is to place a piece of wood underneath the section to be cut. Tape across the top of the area to lessen and/or completely avoid splintering of the fiberglass.

When drilling holes through fiberglass decks or hulls from the inside out, firmly hold a piece of wood at the drill's exit point to prevent the gelcoat from chipping.

Always lubricate drill bits, especially where there might be even the least bit of corrosion, with a silicone spray to make them go in easier, stay sharp longer, and be less likely to break.

Holes drilled in a boat are usually much shallower than the drill bit itself. Place a cork or two on the drill bit to keep it from accidentally going in too deep.

When sawing fiberglass, metal, or wood, rub a bar of soap or a candlestick over the blade teeth to keep the cut smoother and easier.

Tool Safety at Sea

To protect a handsaw blade (and any children who may be near your work area), slice an old garden hose longitudinally for an instant blade cover. This also protects the teeth of an emergency saw on a rough voyage when it may bounce around against other tools in the hold.

No-Rot Antenna Mount

The last time you made a wood backing plate to hold a rail or antenna mount in place, it rotted away in no time. Before replacing it, place the new piece of wood in front of a space heater for a few hours, rotating it occasionally. This drives out moisture. When you mount it, keep the moisture from returning by painting over the entire piece with fiberglass resin.

Screw Sense

To fill holes in fiberglass, insert a screw through a finishing washer for a finished look. Almost as good as new!

If a stainless-steel tapping screw wallows out of a hole in metal or fiberglass, take a stainless-steel self-tapper the same size or slightly smaller than the loose one, and cut off its head with a pair of electrical wire nippers. Insert the threaded part of the screw into the hole. Then insert the original screw. It should tighten up.

Use a toothbrush to remove wax embedded in screw heads. They'll be cavity-free, too.

For extra torque to remove stubborn screws, use a driver with a square shank, fit an adjustable wrench over the shank, and push down on the screw and turn the wrench at the same time. Use Vise-Grips with round driver shafts.

Pop-Rivet Your Cares Away

A pop-rivet gun is a handy item to have in your emergency toolbox. It can fix everything from plastic to plywood to canvas to sheet metal. It's also handy for attaching objects to thin fiberglass. Use noncorroding stainless steel pop rivets.

Epoxy Advice

You want to bond something on board into place, but you don't have anything to clamp the piece until the epoxy has cured. Epoxy adhesives don't require high clamping pressures, so place some contact cement in various spots along the mating surface. When the contact cement has "tacked," carefully apply the epoxy adhesive to the remainder of the mating surfaces and join the pieces. The contact cement grabs and holds the pieces together until the epoxy cures and provides a permanent, high-strength bond.

Straight white vinegar can be used to remove uncured epoxy from hands and clothing.

Nonslip Paint Prep

How do you sand the textured nonslip pattern on deck if you want to paint it? Wet-sand it with air abrasive grit on a scrub brush. Air abrasive grit is available from professional sandblast supply companies (look in the yellow pages under "abrasives"). Pick a 200-grit that's suitable for marine use. Pour the grit into a plastic container, wet the bristles, and gently scrub. Rinse, dry, and you're ready to paint.

Food Coloring: The Leak Detective

Is water getting into your cabin or overhead electronics box from an unidentified leak? To locate the drip, paint bright red food coloring along the seams and joints. After hosing down the boat, go below or peer into the box and look for the red marks. Wipe red marks off immediately afterward so that they don't stain.

Angled Fiberglass Repairs

Trying to patch a hole in a slanted dashboard? Wet fiberglass resin usually runs to the downhill side of the patch and ends up leaving a gap at the top. To patch the hole evenly, put a strip of masking tape across the hole, leaving a small space at the top. Then pour resin into the hole. Leave on the tape until the resin is tacky, when it is jelled enough to remain even across the hole, but has not solidified against the masking tape yet. Don't touch the area that was covered by tape for several minutes; because it wasn't fully exposed to the air while drying, it'll need extra time.

Updating the Boat Decal

To remove last year's boat registration sticker from fiberglass, swab it down with nail polish remover, or spritz it with WD-40 and wait 10 minutes. It should lift right off.

Unmasking Masking Tape

Cooking oil easily removes masking tape residue from nearly every surface. First peel off any tape that will come off on its own, and smear some cooking oil on the rest. Let sit overnight. Next morning, the tape and adhesive gunk come up easily with a plastic scraper or nonmetallic pot scrubber. Mineral spirits on a rag removes the rest. ***NOTE:*** Mineral spirits can damage plastic, and they are flammable. Do not use mineral spirits while smoking or around any source of sparks or high heat; keep out of the reach of children. Do not use mineral spirits on plastic surfaces. If you do not have cooking oil on board, WD-40 or many other penetrating spray lubricants will work equally well.

All's Quiet On Board

Got a squeaky hinge or fitting but don't want dark oil spots all around it? Use several drops of cooking oil to stop the noise. Be sure to wipe up any excess drips with a clean cloth.

To keep onboard doors from banging and rattling when left open, install heavy-duty Velcro pads near the top and bottom. These hold the doors open, don't make annoying noises when the boat's rolling at a mooring, and if you select a matching color, are hardly noticeable when the doors are closed.

Deck Seating Dilemmas

Deck chairs come with rubber crutch tips on their feet so that you won't have to worry about scratches on your cockpit sole. To prolong their life and preserve your deck, remove the tips when the chair is new, place a small cardboard disc cut to size inside, and then put the tips back on. The cardboard spreads the load from even the heaviest guest and prevents the aluminum tube from cutting through the crutch tip.

At the beginning of the season, you added more on-deck seating by using lightweight plastic garden chairs, but now they look older than your great-grandfather. Use a mixture of 1 part water to 1 part bleach, apply to the chairs thoroughly, and let sit for 5 minutes; then dry with a paper towel until clean. ***CAUTION:*** Wear rubber gloves while working with this mixture.

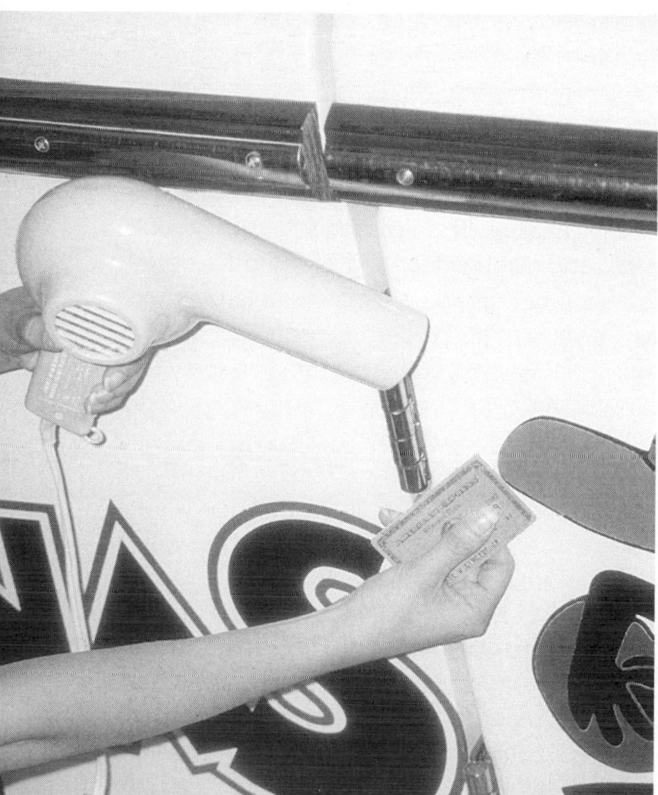

Use a hair dryer to soften the adhesive when removing a vinyl boat name.

Corroded Lock ℞

To lubricate a lightly corroded ignition key slot, rub the key across a graphite pencil, and then slide the key in and out of the key slot several times, until the lubrication is passed into the lock cylinder.

The Correctly Closed Hatch

Hatch covers with through-bolt handles can be hazardous to your toes if the bolt doesn't fall all the way down into the hatch. Even if it sticks up only an eighth of an inch, you could be in for a nasty stubbing. Keep the bolt where it belongs by wrapping a pliable fishing weight around the bottom.

Virtually Instant Nonskid

When painting deck surfaces, to create nonskid surfaces, add a thickening agent, commonly available at most hardware stores, to the paint. Mask off the area you want to cover, and roll on the mixture. The finer the nap on the roller, the finer the nonskid surface. Don't use a thick, fluffy roller, or the job will look like a relief map of the Adirondacks.

Baking soda can also be added to paint to texturize it.

The Name Change Game

To change the vinyl name on your boat, use a hair dryer to first soften the adhesive. Then scrape it clean with an old credit card. Keep the heat source low to prevent damage or burns.

Want to change the painted-on name and registration numbers on the boat you've just inherited? If the boat still has the original gelcoat, spray oven cleaner or barbecue grill cleaner on the painted letters. Wait 10 minutes, and the lettering bubbles up and wipes right off. Thoroughly rinse the area with soap and water when done, before painting or applying new decals.

Want a handy tool for less than a buck? Plastic wall switch covers make great scrapers and can be used on gelcoat, glass, and aluminum. They're especially useful when removing boat names.

Rubrail Renovation

Is your rubber or plastic rubrail all scuffed up? Apply a heavy coat of Armor All or similar vinyl dressing to the scuffed sections, and then wipe the entire rail with a light coat. For best results, don't apply in direct sunlight.

When installing replacement rope or rubber in the channel of your rubrail, leave a few inches hanging on each end. Let sit in the hot sun several days before trimming, because installation often stretches the insert. Sunlight shrinks it back to the intended length, so you can then trim off the excess without coming up short.

The rope popped out of your rubrail and you can't squeeze it back in? Try using a hair dryer to heat the rubber that held the rope. When it's flexible enough, push the rope back in. Hold in place with a C-clamp until the rubber cools down and can hold the rope on its own again.

GLASS AND PLEXIGLAS WINDSCREEN TIPS

Witch's Window Brew

Take 1 gallon warm water, add 2 tablespoons cornstarch, ½ cup white vinegar, and ½ cup ammonia, and what do you have? A homemade, inexpensive version of Windex that gives you high-shine, streak-free glass windows every time.

Erase Those Window Streaks and Stains

To achieve the highest shine and clearest view on glass boat windshields and cabin windows, after washing and drying thoroughly, wipe them down with a clean, dry blackboard eraser.

No-Buffing Window Cleaner

To clean exterior glass, add 1 cup Dawn dishwashing detergent to 2½ gallons water, and use this mixture to wipe down your windows with a sponge. But don't get out the cleaning rag to buff them dry! The good thing about this chemist's combination is that it can be hosed off, and your windows dry streak-free!

The Windshield Washer Alternative

The cheapest glass window washing solution is windshield washer fluid, available from auto supply shops.

Buildup-Free Glass

Windows that feel sticky to the touch should be wiped down with rubbing alcohol first and then cleaned as usual. This also works for cabin mirrors.

For acid rain buildup on glass windshields, mix 2 tablespoons liquid dishwashing detergent such as Dawn, 1 pint 70 percent isopropyl alcohol, and 1 pint water. Put this mixture in a spray bottle, and shake the contents regularly when using.

To remove sea salt spray on glass windows and windshields, sprinkle baking soda generously on a wet sponge and wipe down the cloudy windows. Rinse with a clean sponge, and dry with a chamois or newspaper.

Glass Window Defogger with a Bonus

Glass is made up of microscopic pores. Applying a defogger solution to the glass fills the pores; this not only stops fogging but on windshields gives a mild Rain-X effect. It also makes glass shower doors easier to clean.

Lint-Free Window Cleaning
Don't like to clean your windows with paper towels? Coffee filters are a neat substitute. They make your windows shine without leaving lint behind as paper towels can.

Don't Forget the Corners
To prevent a dirty buildup on glass window corners, clean them regularly with a cotton swab saturated with window cleaner.

Road Grime Removal
Trailer boaters can prevent road grime from making their glass windows opaque by adding a capful of fabric softener to ½ gallon warm water, wiping on the mixture, and then buffing dry with a clean rag.

Tasty Glass Scratch Removal
Got a scratch in your glass windscreen? No problem; you can buff it out with a mixture of white vinegar and dry mustard.

Ice-Free Winter Glass
Another handy window frost preventive method is to saturate your windows with a mixture of ½ cup 70 percent isopropyl alcohol and 1 quart water and allow the mixture to dry on. To stop ice from forming on your boat's windshield during winter storage, put 1 cup white vinegar, ½ cup rubbing alcohol, ½ cup ammonia, and 2 tablespoons cornstarch in 1 gallon warm water and wipe on with a clean rag. This gives your windows a final cleaning and shine at the same time.

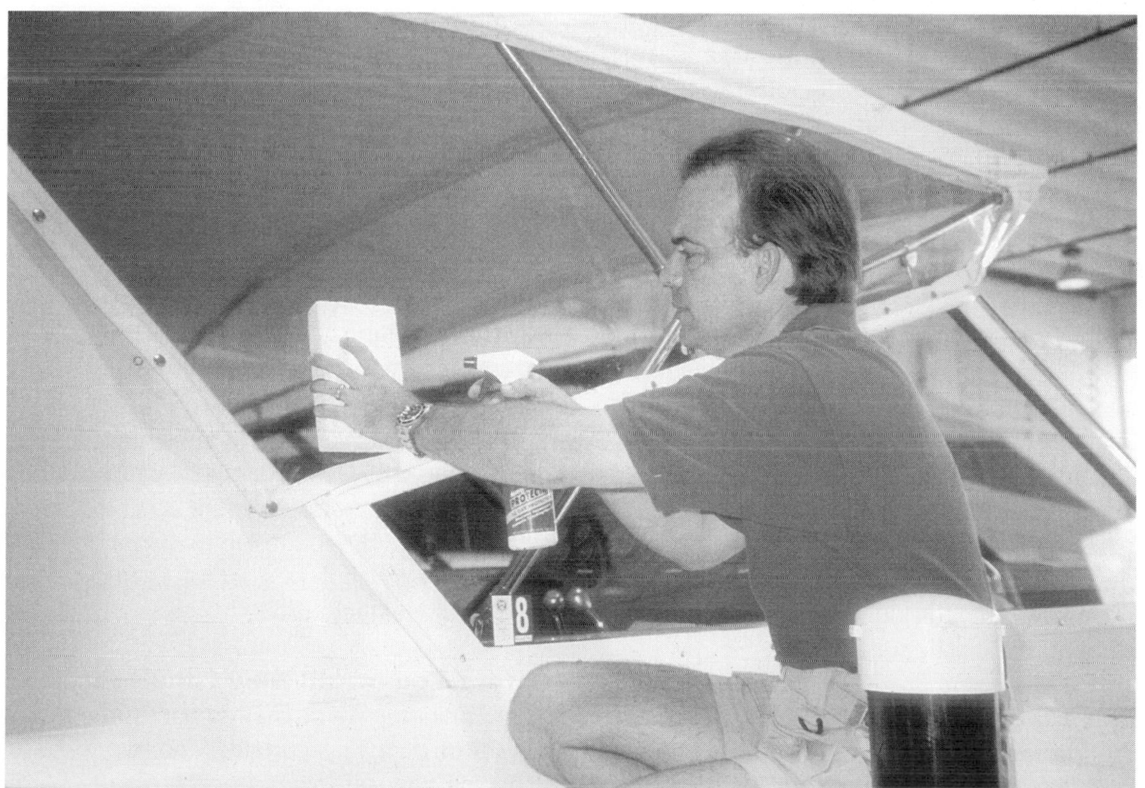

To protect the isinglass fully from oxidation and scratches, apply a coat of plastic polish.

When the winter winds are expected to blow below the freezing mark, add 2 tablespoons rubbing alcohol to either of the previously mentioned window cleaners to help inhibit ice from forming on your windows.

Ice Removal for Glass Windshields and Windows

If your glass windows are already covered in ice, dip a rag in ammonia and wipe down the windows. Ammonia helps dissolve ice from windows.

An alternative frost remover is to wipe down windows with a rag saturated with a mixture of ½ cup white vinegar and 1 gallon warm water.

Wiper Blade Tricks

If your windshield wiper blades are streaking across the windows, but the blades themselves are not yet ready to be replaced, wash the blades with a solution of baking soda and water and thoroughly clean the window beneath with a mixture of half vinegar and half water.

Noisy windshield wiper blades can be repaired by first turning on the wipers and then stopping them midstroke. Next, take the blades off and check whether the wiper tip is parallel to the window glass. If it isn't, gently bend the arm until it's parallel to the glass and replace the rubber blade. This should solve the problem. If it doesn't, you may need new wiper arms.

Greasy Plexiglas Windscreen Relief

Got oil or grease on your Plexiglas windshield? Instead of reaching for glass cleaner, use a cleaner/degreaser such as Star brite's Super Green to cut through the residue without harming the plastic surface.

Beware of Ammonia on Plexiglas!

Wonder why your Plexiglas or Lexan windscreen looks so cloudy? Could be you've used Windex or another glass cleaner that contains ammonia. Ammonia and plastic don't get along, so instead, use plain soap and water or plastic polish on the windscreen.

Your Port Lights Won't Get Cavities, Either

If your acrylic port lights are scratched and fogged, try polishing with tartar-control toothpaste and a soft cotton rag. It takes some patience, but it works.

Can't See Through the Clear Panels in Your Boat Canvas?

If the clear panels in your convertible top are scratched, make a paste of 2 tablespoons each of glycerin, jeweler's rouge, and water. Dab the paste onto a clean rag and rub into the scratches; then rinse off with water. Deep scratches may need repeat applications. This works on scratches on Plexiglas and real glass, too. It's also good for a final polish on gelcoat touch-ups.

When the clear panels on your convertible tops and side curtains get hazy, give them a coat of Pledge furniture polish. It helps clear them and adds a protective coating against further hazing.

Merely cleaning the vinyl isinglass windows that complete your canvas enclosure isn't enough. If you're going to leave your canvas up as a boat cover, you have to fully protect the isinglass against lay-up damage, which ranges from oxidation from exposure to the sun to scratches from the rough winter wind. The easiest way is to apply a coat of plastic polish, monthly if weather permits.

Before You Install New Panels . . .

Your Bimini top frame marred and burned your old set of clear vinyl curtains, and you want to keep the new set looking good. Hit the hardware store and get some sections of foam pipe insulation. Cut them to length, slide them over the support stanchions, and hold in place with tie wraps. Your clear vinyl will thank you by staying clear longer.

Clean Before You Clean

Rinse down your boat thoroughly before washing it. Dirt and grit caught under your sponge or cleaning rag can scratch the fiberglass finish or, over time, dull it. Brittle, dry sponges can leave small pieces behind that cause a light surface abrasion. Throw them away.

A TEAK TUTORIAL

Homemade Rust Remover

Rust spots disfiguring your unvarnished teak? Wet down the stain with a mixture of 1 part oxalic acid in 2 parts water and allow it to set for 10 minutes or until you see the stain begin to loosen. Rinse thoroughly with clean water afterward. Repeat, if necessary.

Another quick way to remove rust stains from unvarnished teak is to use part one of any two-part teak cleaner—it is actually a weak acid—and let it set for 10 minutes, or until you see the stain begin to loosen. Then rinse thoroughly with clean water. Repeat, if necessary.

Docked Near Trees?

Leaf stains on an unvarnished teak deck can be removed with a mixture of equal parts household bleach and water. Soak average stains for 15 minutes, rinse thoroughly, and repeat, if necessary.

Tree or leaf sap stains should be scraped off your unvarnished teak deck as soon as you discover them. Use bronze wool or a putty knife, and then wipe down the spots with turpentine to remove any remaining residue. Turpentine is flammable, so use sparingly and with care. Do not smoke while using turpentine, and keep it away from high heat and sources of open flame or sparks.

After-the-Party Teak Repairs

Stains from beer and other alcoholic drinks dropped by guests on unvarnished teak can be removed with a rag dipped lightly in ammonia, or with an application of silver polish.

To remove wax droppings from citronella candles on an unvarnished teak deck, allow the wax to dry first, and then saturate a rag with mineral spirits and place it on the deck. The wet rag absorbs the wax. If the rag begins to dry out, replace it with a fresh wet rag, until all the wax is gone.

Did a guest leave a suntan lotion or baby oil stain on your perfect unvarnished teak deck? Dust the stain generously with baking soda. Let it sit until the stain is absorbed and the baking soda has yellowed. Brush off. Repeat until the stain is completely gone. For a particularly tough, oily stain, dab a few drops of paint thinner on the spot. Follow with a quick dusting of baking soda to keep the paint thinner from soaking into the teak and damaging it.

Greasy Stain Deterrent

To clean grease stains—whether from working on your engine or from a sloppy party guest —from an unvarnished teak deck, wait until the deck area is in the shade, and then use a water-rinsable automotive degreaser or carburetor cleaner or strong household detergent. Allow the chemicals to do their work, and then rinse down the deck as you normally would. ***NOTE:*** Engine cleaner and carburetor cleaner contain strong solvents. Always work outdoors and wear rubber gloves and protective clothing when using them.

Watermark Removal

Watermarks, residue from previous stains, and other splotches that remain after thoroughly stripping teak can be removed with liquid household bleach, and black water stains call for oxalic acid. ***NOTE:*** Using bleach may lift the wood grain, which may then need to be resanded to its normal level after the wood has completely dried.

You can remove water rings from sweating soda cans left on unvarnished teak surfaces and the hard water line on your wooden boat hull by rubbing a paste of half mayonnaise and half table salt on them. Allow the mixture to sit for 30 minutes, and then brush off any excess. The mayonnaise and salt combine to neutralize the ring or stain line and loosen it.

Unsightly water spots on unvarnished deck and cabin teak can also be washed with a clean, dry rag dipped in baking soda solution (1 box baking soda, 1 gallon water). Wipe down gently. Do not let the teak actually become wet.

To remove hard water spots from unvarnished deck teak, rub them with toothpaste on a damp cloth.

Salt, olive oil, and petroleum jelly also work to remove watermarks from unvarnished teak.

All-Purpose Teak Stain Remover

To clean general stains on unvarnished teak economically without removing any of the wood, use liquid dishwashing detergent with a stiff nylon brush or Scotch-Brite pad. Work in the open air or a well-ventilated space and wear

To make varnished areas last longer, rinse them down every time you visit the boat and dry with a chamois cloth.

rubber gloves, because these detergents contain chlorine.

Get More Out of Your Cleaner by Using Less

For unvarnished teak that gleams, use hot water to dilute the cleaning mixture, particularly when using a crystal or powdered cleaner.

Mother Nature's Teak Problems

Mold stains on an unvarnished teak deck or wooden hull can be somewhat difficult to remove, but you can control them—if not eradicate them completely—with a mixture of 4 parts bleach to 1 part water. Mold stains often return because the mold has taken root in the wood.

When your unvarnished teak has taken on the fishy smells of the water she sails upon, sprinkle some baking soda on a damp sponge and rub it into the teak to deodorize. This works equally well on other porous surfaces.

Don't Plan on Tanning While Cleaning Your Unvarnished Teak

Teak cleaners work better on overcast days because you can leave the mixture on the wood longer without it drying out.

Teak Cleaner and Aluminum Don't Mix

If you have to use a caustic teak cleaner, first wax any surrounding metal, especially anodized aluminum. Lay the wax on thick, and don't rub it off until you're finished with the teak cleaner to prevent pitting and scarring the aluminum.

CPR for Teak

Teak and other woods that have an oil finish can be given new life with a mixture of half turpentine and half boiled linseed oil. Shake the mixture well in a sealed container. Pour a small amount of this potion onto a rag, and rub back and forth in the direction of the wood grain. It appears oily at first but should be absorbed in an hour, leaving a fresh sheen behind. ***NOTE:*** Wear rubber gloves when using this volatile mixture.

Been Too Generous with Your Teak Oil?

After cleaning, staining, and allowing teak to dry thoroughly, sprinkle on some cornstarch to absorb excess stain and oil. Allow to sit for an hour, and then dust off. You'll find a high shine beneath.

The Right Brush Is Critical

A stiff nylon short-bristle brush (the rectangular kind with a wooden backing) is ideal for cleaning teak because you can apply full hand pressure and lean into your work. Longer-handle brushes with springy bristles can allow caustic teak cleaners to splatter into unwanted areas.

On older teak, use a soft-bristle brush at a right angle to the planking to keep from opening up the teak's grain, which provides more space for dirt and mildew to collect and hastens

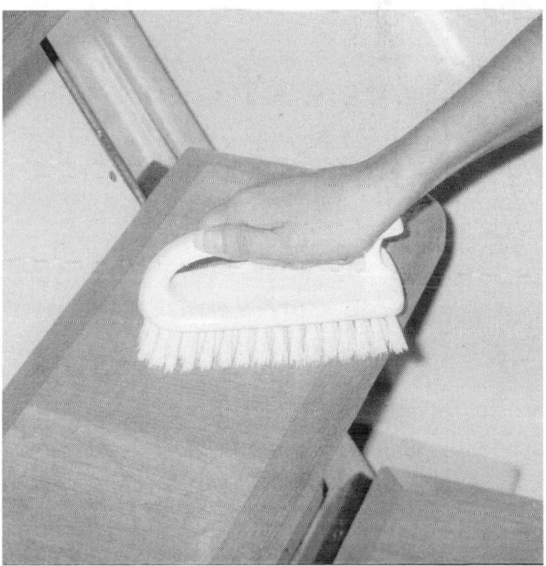

To make varnished areas last longer, rinse them down every time you visit the boat and dry with a chamois cloth.

the dreaded day when you have to sand your decks smooth again.

Sometimes No Brush at All Is Best

Clean dirt and dust from tight teak corners and intricate designs by pumping an empty squeeze bottle like a blower, or use a can of compressed air, available at office supply and photography supply stores, which is designed to clean computer keyboards.

I'm Gonna Wash That Dirt Right Off of My Teak

When hosing off teak cleaners, use a soft shower spray with a brush to get grime out of the grain. A sharp blast with a hose may work faster, but it poses the risk of a less-thorough rinse and may scatter still-potent teak-cleaning acids.

A Cup of Tea, Sir?

Varnished teak can be quickly cleaned with leftover plain (no sugar, no milk) tea poured on a clean rag.

Sun Isn't Bad for Only Your Skin

Always apply sealants to a teak deck in the early morning or evening hours. Direct sunlight is the enemy of teak finishes. Double-coat exposed ends, such as teak railings, because moisture is more likely to penetrate there first.

Tried-and-True Worn Varnish Treatment

When touching up worn varnish, lightly sand the bad spot, and then use teak brightener on the wood before varnishing. Dab varnish on the wood to build up the film before sanding and the final recoating.

Protective Maintenance Before Your Teak Discolors

Want to prevent those ugly black spots from forming in the wood beneath your varnish when it chips or scratches? Grab the nearest bottle of clear nail polish. When you spot a crack, scrape off any loose flakes of varnish. Next, clean the surrounding area with the corner of an alcohol-moistened rag. When the alcohol evaporates, dab on a generous coat of nail polish. Be neat, overlapping the surrounding varnish just slightly and using no more than two coats. This stopgap measure prevents water from entering the wood beneath the varnish and then damp-staining the wood.

A Simple Way to Make Your Varnish Last Longer

To help teak varnish last as long as possible, each time you visit your boat, be sure to rinse off the morning dew, which contains dirt particles and acid. The dirt and acid in dew, combined with midday sun, spell serious trouble for your varnish.

Sanding Tips and Tricks

When sanding teak in preparation for oiling or varnishing, the last sandpaper you should use is a 220-grit, which leaves a slight "tooth" to the wood so that the varnish can grip but doesn't dig in so deeply that it's visible through the finish coat. For an even finer finish, you can use a 320-grit after the 220 but before applying varnish or oiling.

To sand corners, wrap sandpaper around a putty knife and use the edge to get in close without marring the adjacent finish.

When doing a lot of hand sanding, wrap masking tape around your fingertips to save your skin.

Sandpaper works better than green mesh sanding pads when refinishing teak for a variety of reasons. Because sandpaper isn't as susceptible to finger pressure as a green pad is, it gives a more even finish. Also, wood dust builds up in Scotch-Brite pads more quickly and isn't as easy to shake out.

To get the longest life out of sandpaper, store it in an airtight plastic bag. Dampness can quickly ruin even high-quality sandpaper.

Leave the Steel Wool in Your Sink at Home

Never use regular steel wool when refinishing teak; it leaves microscopic fibers behind that eventually rust and stain the teak. Using bronze or stainless steel wool eliminates this problem.

The Scotch-Brite Alternative

Before laying on your finish coat, don't sand the existing varnish or oil finish, but use a Scotch-Brite pad to scuff it. Pads are less expensive than sandpaper, and they take off just a small amount of varnish or oil—which is important when you need buildup.

If you're going to use an imitation Scotch-Brite pad, make sure it's white. Some of the cheaper brands leach color under the pressure of the scrubbing motion.

Picture-Perfect Oil or Varnish

Nothing ruins a good oil or varnishing job like gnats, dust, and hair getting stuck in your work. Sometimes you can brush them out, but then they're stuck in your brush—and at some point they will end up back in the oil or varnish. Cleanse them out of the brush by submerging the bristles in a tall, thin can of paint thinner, twirling the handle between your hands. For a 1½-inch bristle brush, a small tomato juice can works perfectly.

Store Your Varnish Like They Do Down Under

If your partially used can of varnish develops a skin on top while stored, using the remaining contents becomes difficult—but not if you clean the rim of the can before resealing, tap the lid securely into place, and store the can upside-down. When you want to use the remaining varnish, any skin that forms will be on the bottom. To avoid skin problems altogether, buy varnish in smaller containers.

Your Teenage Daughter's Nail Polish Fixation Isn't All Bad

Put a little varnish or teak oil in an empty nail polish bottle for small touch-up jobs. This saves opening cans and cleaning brushes.

You Can Do the Twist on Deck, But . . .

Never shake varnish—it can cause bubbles that will give you a less-than-perfect finish.

A Nutty Solution

To hide scratches in bare teak decking or elsewhere, rub the meat of a walnut or pecan over the scratch but against the direction of the teak grain. For interior teak, liquid shoe polish of the appropriate color applied carefully with a cotton swab can also make a quick repair.

Quickie Scratch Concealment

To conceal nicks and scratches in stained teak, use a Bondex Wood Stain Pen. It works just like a felt-tip marker. Simply stroke it in the direction of the scrape and wipe off any excess with a clean rag. The pens are available in standard light and dark teak stain colors. Call Bondex at 314-225-5001 for more information.

To camouflage scratches in "antiqued" teak, dip a damp cloth in a mixture of half boiled linseed oil and half turpentine and rub on gently until the scratch disappears.

You Don't Have to Live with Dinked Teak

Fix dents in teak (where the wood fibers are crushed and/or compressed) by lifting them back up. Place a damp rag over the dent and hold a medium-hot iron over it. The resulting moisture should raise the dent, but be sure not to burn the surface.

Smokers on Board

Minor cigarette burns in teak can be removed by gently rubbing very fine sandpaper or fine bronze wool against the grain. You may need to retreat the area (oiling, staining, varnishing, etc.) to make the newly repaired spot match the rest.

Shhhhhh!

For a quick fix to silence a squeaky teak deck, sprinkle talcum powder on the squeaking joints. Sweep about until all the cracks are filled. This works great in the salon and cabin, but if the area is constantly exposed to rain and the elements, a more lasting solution will soon be needed.

Protect Fiberglass During Teak Work

For protection when sanding wood trim that's adjacent to fiberglass, run a strip of masking tape next to the trim; then any sanding beyond the trim—either by hand or power sander—won't damage the gelcoat.

Got a Screw Loose?

To set a loose wood screw back in its hole, insert a long sliver of wood, and break the wood off flush with the edge of the screw hole, set the screw at the tip of the hole next to the wood sliver which makes the hole smaller and the fit tighter, and turn the screw home. Or cut a ¼-inch strip of wet or dry sandpaper (80-grit to 120-grit works well). Run the abrasive strip over the edge of a work table, or other sharply angled edge, paper side down. The sandpaper coils around the wood screw making it slightly larger. Put the enlarged screw back into the hole, and tighten it up well.

The Swollen Thumb Club Report

To avoid injury to your thumb when hammering nails on a shifting deck, slip the nail between the teeth of a comb and use the comb to hold it in place while hammering. Instead of a comb, you can also use a paper clip.

A Spare Pair of Hands That Won't Offer Unwanted Advice

If you never seem to have enough hands when working on teak, take a paper or plastic cup and cut two vertical slits the size of your belt, approximately 1 inch apart. Now slip your belt through the two slits, and you have an instant holder for nails, screws, bungs, and other small parts that goes where you go.

Splinter-Free Teak

When sawing through teak, place a piece of wood underneath the section to be cut to lessen both splintering and the strain on the teak.

When Splinters Happen Anyway

When trying to remove a teak deck splinter from a bare foot, dab a bit of iodine on the splinter so that you can see it better. If you have rubber cement on board, coat the splinter area with it lightly, and allow to dry. The splinter should come out when you pull off the glue.

Outdoor Storage Can Lead to Snow Removal

If you need to remove snow or ice from a teak deck during the winter, your best bet is halite salt because shoveling can scratch the teak surface and dink the coating, leaving the now-exposed wood vulnerable to moisture damage. The salt should just brush right off—if not, treat it as a "saltwater spot" (see water spot tips).

VINYL

Soft, Fresh Vinyl

To keep boat vinyl fresh and new looking, wash regularly with mild dish detergent, and then coat very lightly with petroleum jelly; use spar-

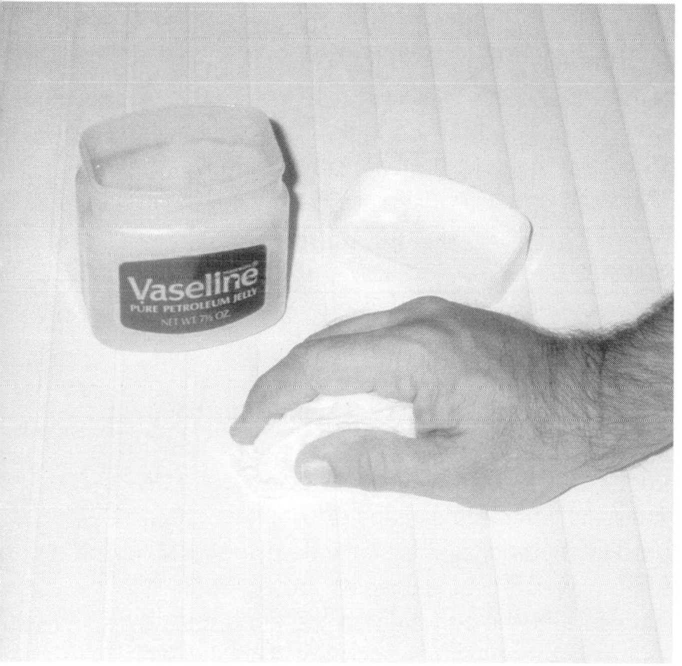

To keep vinyl new looking, wash it regularly with a mild dish detergent, and then coat it very lightly with petroleum jelly.

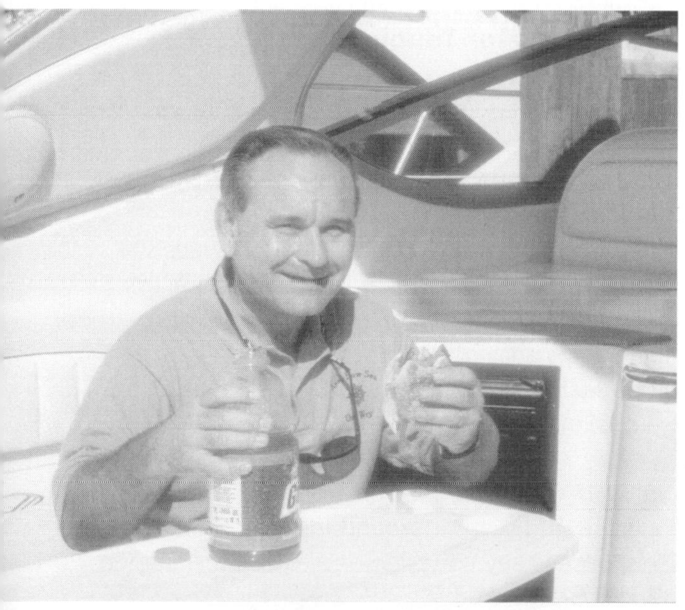

Don't get mad at your boat guests: Soda and mustard drips on vinyl come off easily with a paste of baking soda and water.

ingly to avoid making the surface slippery or attracting dirt or dust.

Sweat and body oils from legs in shorts and bodies in bathing suits can harden vinyl, so even if you do nothing else, be sure to thoroughly rinse vinyl cushions with freshwater after each voyage.

Stain Removal

Soda spills, mustard drips, and even pen marks and other annoying stains on your vinyl seats can be removed by wiping down with a paste of baking soda and water. Baking soda won't dry out vinyl like oil-based cleaners can.

Spray deodorant works just as well as hairspray to remove pen marks from vinyl, boat canvas, cabin upholstery, and so on.

Suturing Vinyl

Got a slit in your cockpit cushion? Head for the first-aid kit. Put a few butterfly bandages across the tear—as many as you need to fix the cut. These bandages are waterproof and flexible, and they generally hold until more intensive care can be administered.

Get Out the Turkey Knife

To cut foam rubber to size when replacing vinyl deck cushions that have become flattened from years of use, use an electric carving knife for the fastest, smoothest, and most accurate cut.

Do-It-Yourself Seat Repair

The plywood bottoms of your helm or other weather-exposed cockpit seats have rotted, but you don't want to spend the money to have new seats made. Your best bet? If the upholstery is in good condition, it's relatively easy to untack or unstaple from the plywood bottom. When you remove the upholstery, take out the foam cushion underneath, too. Use the old piece of wood as a pattern for the new one, and then reinstall the foam and

DON'T SCRUB IT IF YOU CAN UNSCREW IT

We know a boater who takes keeping his boat clean to such an extreme that his fellow dockmates think he's been out in the sun too long. Because he is intent on spending more time cruising and less time cleaning, this guy—we'll call him Joe—made some unusual requests when his boat was being built. Instead of the standard cabin wall carpeting, Joe specified a gelcoat finish, which won't mildew and can be rinsed clean. There are no bolsters on deck to attract dirt, fray, or fade, and there is no teak anywhere on board, not even the steering wheel center disk.

Each time Joe comes in from a day on the water, he makes several trips to his sport utility vehicle, stuffing it with the helm seats he's taken off their pedestals and the cushions and just about every other boat part he can unbolt, until his truck looks as if he made a real killing at a marine flea market. Next, he quickly rinses down the bare deck, which only takes him about 15 minutes because he has a raw water washdown on board that he uses throughout the trip.

Joe's boat cover is designed for a similar, but larger boat. Although the cover does look silly hanging down almost to the waterline, it protects his boat, including the boat name, from fading and dirt. And when he pulls off the cover, he's got a pristine deck that's ready to go just as soon as he reinstalls his immaculate, garage-stored, vinyl seats.

Joe estimates he's cut his boat maintenance time in half. He is currently using a significant part of this time savings designing a high-pressure boat wash for his slip.

upholstery on the new piece using weatherproof staples, copper tacks, or small stainless screws with finishing washers. You'll be surprised how good the job looks. To avoid having to repeat this repair, when you remove the foam and upholstery, replace the plywood with a ½-inch plastic sheet. Cut drain-ventilation holes in the sheet to allow the foam to shed accumulated water.

Cruising the Knobless Way

Seats that fold down into sun lounges are handy, but after a few years it's common for the turning knobs to shear off the bolts. To loosen or tighten the seats, put electrical tape or shrink-wrap tape around the end of the bolt where the turning knob was and heat it until it's secure. You'll still have to turn the bolt without the knob, but the shrink-wrap is much easier to get a grip on with your hand than bare metal.

BOAT CANVAS

Treatments for Tough Snaps and Zippers

Are your canvas snaps hard to snap? Are your zippers hard to zip? A little dab of lip balm such as Chap Stick on the offending snap or zipper puts the snap and zip back into their life.

Petroleum jelly also lubricates tough snaps so that they go on and off with ease. The extra dollop, when applied regularly, temporarily protects snaps against further corrosion.

Vegetable spray also works as an excellent snap lubricant.

If the Lift-A-DOT snaps for your boat cover are stiff, insert a screwdriver blade into the opening and work it around inside the spring. This loosens any corrosion and allows the snap to lock on the stud.

If snap buttons don't connect, clean the male surface with bronze wool. Wipe on a coat of

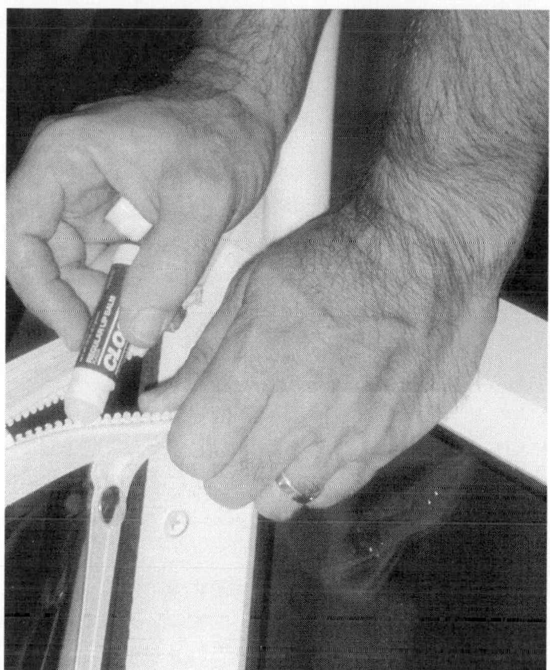

Lubricate new life into your snaps and zippers with lip balm.

wax, and buff. It's less messy than wiping with petroleum jelly.

Lubricate stuck zippers with a graphite pencil or wax candle. WD-40 works equally well, but be careful not to get any on the canvas because it can stain.

Loose Zippers Irritate Skippers

Old zippers that won't stay closed should be sprayed with lacquer hair spray. Allow to dry, and you'll find that the zippers work almost as well as when they were new.

Shrunk Enclosure Zippers Don't Mean You Have to Get Wet

If the stitching on enclosure zippers has shrunk, you can get better leverage on the zipper puller by looping a short piece of nylon cord through the opening.

Dirty, Moldy Boat Canvas

When washing dirty or moldy boat canvas in your washing machine, hose it down first so you won't be washing the grime into the machine.

Keep Colors Bright and Whites White

To keep colored boat canvas from fading as you wash it in your washing machine, add ½ cup salt to the rinse cycle.

Worried about the color in your boat canvas bleeding in the wash? Try setting the color by soaking the article in a mixture of 1 part white vinegar to 20 parts water. Soak for about 20 minutes. You should now be able to wash as usual.

A Bait Net Full of Rust-Removal Tricks

Cement cleaner gets rust stains out of boat canvas. It also works on delicate cabin fabrics. But before using, test it by rubbing it on an inconspicuous area. Cement cleaner is available at most home maintenance superstores.

A more natural way to remove rust from boat canvas is to soak the stain in a small amount of lemon juice and salt in 1 pint warm water.

Another excellent rust remover for canvas is 3 tablespoons oxalic acid in 1 pint water. ***NOTE:*** Use extreme caution when working with oxalic acid, making sure not to ingest it or splash it in your eyes. Rinse it off skin quickly if spilled.

The Grass Isn't Always Greener

A squirt of shampoo for oily hair gets grass stains out of that Sunbrella cover that you thoughtlessly left on your lawn while you went boating. Scrub in the shampoo, and then put the Sunbrella cover in a washing machine for a thorough cleaning.

Phew! Mildew Removal

Add ½ cup vinegar to the washing machine during the rinse cycle to remove mildew smells

from just about everything—from your boat canvas to your fragile boat linens.

Another effective mildew treatment is to pour on a sufficient amount of laundry detergent to pretreat the spot. Then wash the canvas in your washing machine if it is small enough (or by hand if it's not). If any stain residue remains, sponge it down with a mixture of lemon juice and salt. Dry the canvas in sun, and then wash out the lemon juice and salt, using hot water, detergent, and color-safe bleach. ***NOTE:*** Mildew must be treated as soon as possible in order for the treatment to work.

Cures for the Accident Prone

Blood on your boat canvas from an accident-prone party guest can be cleaned out immediately (or as soon as possible) by soaking the canvas in cold water for 30 minutes. If a blood stain remnant remains, soak the canvas in 3 tablespoons ammonia and 1 gallon lukewarm water for an additional 30 minutes; then rinse thoroughly. If a stain outline still remains, work in detergent, and wash in a washing machine if the piece is small enough, or by hand if it's not, using color-safe bleach.

Another quickie blood remover is to apply a small amount of hydrogen peroxide directly to the stain. Let soak for approximately a half hour. The stain should be history!

Caffeine and Canvas Don't Mix

Coffee spills from those early-morning fishing outings can be cleaned out of boat canvas by sponging or soaking the affected area with cold water as soon as possible. Then wash in a washing machine if the piece is small enough (or by hand if it's not) using detergent and color-safe bleach.

Greasy Canvas Stains

Been working on your engine and then touched your boat canvas with greasy hands? Place a thick coating of talcum powder, cornstarch, or chalk on the grease stain to absorb as much grease as possible. Pretreat with laundry detergent or liquid shampoo, and then wash the canvas in a washing machine in the hottest water available. Be sure to use plenty of additional detergent in the wash water, but not so much that you turn your washing machine into a sudsy monster.

The Painter's Potential Problem

To get water-based boat paint spots out of your boat canvas, scrape off the paint spots with the edge of a very dull knife, and then wash the canvas in your washing machine with regular laundry detergent in very hot water.

Hot Weather Canvas Stains

To get perspiration from a sweaty sailor out of your boat canvas, wipe down the stain while it's still fresh with ammonia; if it's an old stain, use vinegar. Soak the canvas in your washing machine's presoak cycle, and then rinse. Next, wash in hot water. If fabric has discolored, use bleach (color-safe bleach, if applicable). If the stain still remains, dampen it and sprinkle on meat tenderizer (the same stuff you should have on board to take the sting out of jellyfish stings). Let it work for an hour, and then brush the residue. If there's a lingering odor, dampen the canvas with color-free mouthwash.

Getting Food Out of Canvas

To remove a soda spill from boat canvas, wet the stain immediately with equal parts cold water and 70 percent isopropyl alcohol.

Chocolate stains on your boat canvas from kids' dirty hands? Simply cover the chocolate or candy stain with a cloth soaked in lukewarm water. Blot until stain is saturated, and wipe up until removed. Repeat if necessary. (This may take a while, so be patient.) Allow to dry.

At the Washing Machine

Don't wash boat canvas in warm or hot water unless the stains really warrant it (remember, bleach works best in hot water). Cold water not only stops shrinking but reduces wrinkling, which makes your canvas easier to stretch back into shape.

If you've used too much detergent in a previous boat canvas wash, and the canvas is attracting new dirt at a rapid rate, use Wisk Power Scoop Concentrate to remove not only the new dirt but the excess soap as well.

Bleach Techniques

When in doubt about bleaching, start with 3 percent hydrogen peroxide on the stain (this is probably already in your first-aid kit). ***NOTE:*** Hydrogen peroxide loses its efficacy after about 12 months.

Didn't your science teacher ever tell you? Never mix chlorine bleach and ammonia, or you'll form a toxic gas.

Sunbrella Advice

The best way to care for your boat's Bimini top is to clean it regularly before too much dirt accumulates and becomes embedded. Lightly brush off loose dirt and hose down the fabric, cleaning with a mild soap and lukewarm water, no hotter than 100°F, and then rinse thoroughly and sun dry. For stubborn spots, soak the fabric for 20 minutes in a solution of 4 ounces nonchlorine bleach and 2 ounces natural soap per gallon of lukewarm water. Rinse thoroughly with cold water.

The Grommet Shortage

Boat covers never seem to have enough grommets. You could go to the store and buy a grommet kit. Or you could ball up an old sock and press it against the inside of the cover so it makes a bulge on the outside, and then tie your line around the base of the bulge.

Larger Covers Are Better

The canvas cover you made for a hatch or window doesn't fit quite right anymore. What happened? Canvas shrinks when it gets wet, so even though you were careful to make the cover the perfect size, you'll have to start from scratch. Next time, make it about 2 percent larger than necessary to allow for shrinkage.

A Rip-Roarin' Solution

Need a quick fix for a rip in your Bimini top or canvas cover? Shrink-wrap tape does the trick, and it comes in various colors that may match the canvas. Just peel off the backing and place a section on both sides of the tear. It's available where boating supplies are sold.

Be Kind to Your Boat Vinyl

Clear vinyl curtains can wear out fast, but how you treat them plays a big role in how long they last. If you launch your boat early in the year or use it through the winter, leave the curtains at home. The vinyl shrinks in the cold, so it can rip or stretch out of shape when you try to zipper it in place.

DECK CARPET

General Deck Carpet Stain Remover

To clean general boat carpet stains, mix a gallon hot water, a generous amount of liquid dish detergent, and 1 cup white vinegar. You'll need a hard-bristle brush to work the mixture thoroughly into the carpet fibers. Let sit for 30 minutes, and then blot until dry with clean towels or thick, absorbent rags.

No-Rinse Deck Carpet Cleaner

Want a no-rinse deck carpet cleaner? Mix ¼ cup liquid Wisk laundry detergent and ¼ cup white vinegar in 1 quart hot water. Dip a sponge into the solution, apply to the stain, rub in a circular motion, and blot dry. Be generous with the solution. This works on most general stains.

Seasickness, Spills, Etc.

Seasickness stains on deck and even cabin carpet should be diluted and neutralized (vomit is acidic) by saturating the spots with club soda or a mixture of baking soda and water.

Beer and other alcohol spills on your boat's carpeting should be immediately diluted with cold water so that they don't permanently change the carpet color.

Never use soap and water on a coffee, fruit juice, ice cream, or milk stain on your deck carpeting because this sets the stain. Instead, wipe the spot with a cloth soaked in cold water. If necessary, rub with household clothing stain remover.

A Common Fisherman's Stain

Blood stains on carpet, whether from injured guests or recently caught fish, should be immediately covered with a paste made of dry laundry starch and cold water. (Do not use hot water because it sets the stain.) Allow to dry, and then brush or vacuum the residue away.

For the Saltwater Boater

Sea salt that's tracked into cabin carpet can be removed by applying a mixture of half vinegar and half water with a sponge. Be sure not to drown the carpet. Vacuum up when completely dry.

Fido's Embarrassment

Dog urine a problem on your deck carpet? Sponge the stain with lukewarm mild soapy water and rinse with a clean cloth soaked in cold water. Then soak a second cloth in a solution of one part ammonia to five parts water. Hold it on the stain for 1 minute. Rinse with clean, cool water.

A Window Cleaner's Advice

For extremely difficult deck and cabin carpet stains, use a glass cleaner (yes, a glass cleaner!). Soak the area, allow to sit for 5 minutes, and blot it up. Glass cleaner works on all types of carpet without leaving the soapy residue of most traditional carpet cleaners, which actually attracts more dirt after use. For the toughest spots, use a scrap piece of carpet as a scrubber. The textures mesh, to lift out even the darkest stains. Once your carpet is cleaned, it's time to use fabric protectant spray to limit future staining.

Don't Recarpet, Restore!

To brighten a fading carpet, first vacuum, and then use a sponge mop to lightly apply a mixture of ½ cup clear ammonia and 1 pint water. Test this mixture on a discreet area of carpet first.

Before your boat's deck and cabin carpets begin to show excessive wear and tear, vacuum them just as you would your carpet at home. This lifts the fibers back upright and counteracts the long-term ill effects of the dirt and sand that's been pounded into it. If the situation is really bad, you might consider a steam-cleaning machine. If you do, be sure to bring up all the water when you're done, because walking on a wet carpet damages the fibers further.

If you're tired of cleaning the boat carpets and seeing them immediately get filthy again, place a mat or rug remnant on your dock at the point where you normally board, and another one just inside at the hatchway to your cabin for your guests to wipe their feet.

DOCK AND ANCHOR LINES . . . AND FENDERS

Anchor Lines Don't Have to Harden with Time

Stiff anchor lines difficult to coil? Add ½ cup fabric softener to 2 gallons water and soak your lines in it overnight. Allow them to dry away from the sun, and your lines are as flexible as new.

Are your docklines dirty and extremely stiff due to age and overexposure to the sun? Machine wash them on a delicate cycle using a very mild detergent. Rinse well. Be sure to first tie a stopper knot in each end of the line to keep it from fraying in the wash.

Another tip for aged and stiff anchor line: Reverse it. Most boaters don't use more than half of their anchor line when anchoring, so by using the fresh section, you can double the life of the line.

Tie Wrap Your Anchor Shackle Pin

Seizing wire is generally used to secure the pin in your anchor shackle. A common tie wrap, placed through both the eye of the pin and the bight of the shackle after tightening securely, is easier, is cheaper, and works just as well.

Make sure lines are stored neatly with sufficient air space between them to help prevent that boater's nemesis: mildew.

A Knotty Predicament

To loosen overly tight knots, generously spray the knotted section of line with silicone spray. Wait until it soaks in thoroughly before trying to unknot it. It should be much easier now.

Too Kinky for You?

You just bought 200 feet of anchor line that's kinkier than an X-rated video, and coiling won't get rid of the twists. Try trailing the line behind the boat while under way at slow speeds until the kinks work themselves out. Be careful not to run over it with the prop!

Lines Need to Be Ventilated, Too

Few boaters dry lines before stowing them. If damp lines stowed in your cockpit lockers or deck boxes have become mildewed and smelly, increase the locker ventilation by adding off-the-shelf louvered vents and/or louvered doors. When away from the boat, wedge a tennis ball under hatches to let air circulate. A little ventilation goes a long way.

Tangle Prevention

Coiled anchor line and docklines that get tangled in your lockers can be tough to sort out. Use vinyl electrical tape or ½-inch medical adhesive tape to wrap lines. It's easy to apply and tears quickly for easy removal when the stowed line is needed.

Chafe Prevention

To prevent line chafe on concrete docks, connect a section of chain to the dock cleat, place a thimble on the loose end, splice a rope dock line through the thimble, tie the opposite end to the boat's cleat, so that the chain touches the concrete and the rope dock line touches the boat. Never connect a chain directly to the boat or serious damage can occur.

Chafing gear is cheap insurance, but don't make the mistake of wrapping tape around your lines to protect them. The tape wears through and deposits adhesive all over your boat. Instead, use old garden hose held in place by a tie wrap or seizing wire at just one end. If you seize both ends tightly, the stretching of the line under tension breaks one end loose.

Dip lines into Star brite Liquid Electrical Tape to keep them from fraying.

Unraveling the Problem

Dip fraying lines into shellac or Star brite Liquid Electrical Tape to keep them from unraveling further. ***NOTE:*** For the best results, snip off the frayed section first, and then dip the base of the intact section of line into the shellac or Star brite Liquid Electrical Tape.

Waxed dental floss is perfect for whipping the ends of docklines that are starting to fray, and you don't have to learn any fancy marlinspike seamanship to use it. Just cut a length of floss about 30 times as long as the line diameter, double it, and lay the line in the middle of the loop. Tie an overhand knot in the floss, and pull it tight. Now tie another overhand knot in the floss on the other side of the line. Keep doing this until the whipping is about 10 times as long as the line is thick, and then finish with a square knot on each side.

Cover a Cleat That's Not in Use

Tired of catching your lines on an extra cleat? Cut a foam block slightly larger than the cleat, and then cut a slit in the middle of the block. Slide it over the cleat and—presto!—no more tangled lines.

chapter 2

HULL WORK

FIBERGLASS HULL CLEANING AND MAINTENANCE

Two Buckets Are Better than One

This may sound simplistic, but when washing down your hull, use two water containers—one for soapy washing water and the other for rinse water. Otherwise, you're putting dirt back onto the boat each time you dip your sponge, rag, or brush for more water.

Natural Additives That Make for Easier Cleaning

Add a few tablespoons of vinegar to cleaning water to cut through sea slime and other greasy substances and leave your hull sparkling.

For a shinier hull, add a handful of baking soda to your rinse water bucket.

To remove greasy stains from the hull, such as from fuel and oil floating on top of the water, add 2 to 3 handfuls of baking soda to your regular hull wash.

No More Ring-Around-the-Hull

A baking soda paste (baking soda with just enough water to make it into a paste) can be used to rub off a thick ring-around-the-hull line without scratching.

Many Cleaners Leave a Residue

The easiest way to remove the residue left by your all-purpose boat cleaner is to rinse down the deck and hull with vinegar. The wax you apply afterward adheres much better to the residue-free fiberglass.

Temporary Light Oxidation Removal

To remove a light layer of fiberglass hull oxidation (which looks like white dust) add 3 tablespoons vinegar to 1 gallon water and sponge down. As soon as you can, though, you should begin proper restoration.

Scientific Cleaning

Greasy stains a problem? Let's get scientific. Grease is acidic, so you'll need to use an alkaline cleaner, such as ammonia, to thoroughly cut through the greasy residue. On the opposite end

Specialty applicators, such as a reggae mitt, make cleaning go faster and easier.

of the pH spectrum, light calcium or lime deposits (alkaline) that come from hard water can be removed with full-strength lemon juice or vinegar (acids). Although lemon juice and vinegar are more pleasant to work with, they are not nearly as effective as oxalic acid mineral removers.

Tar Treatments

To remove waterborne tar from a fiberglass hull, spray with oven cleaner, and then sit back and watch it eat into the tar for 5 to 30 minutes, depending on the thickness of the tar. Rinse off, and repeat if necessary.

To remove a thin layer of tar from a painted hull, rub with a moist rag dipped in baking soda. Let the paste sit for 5 minutes or longer, and then rinse clean. This also works with tar and bugs on some metals.

Bugless Trailering

Trailer boaters can clean road tar and bugs off their boat and tow vehicle with a mixture of equal parts apple cider vinegar and water.

Rust and Water Stains on the Hull

To remove rust and water stains from your boat's fiberglass hull, use Star brite Rust Stain Remover. Be sure to avoid runoff onto painted areas and thoroughly rinse the surrounding fiberglass.

100 Percent Cotton Is Best

If it seems to take forever to hand-dry your boat, check your rags. Many of today's fabrics are treated to deflect water rather than soak it up. Old cotton towels or old cloth diapers make the best rags.

Keep the Cleaner Clean

Wrap a washcloth around your wrist and secure it in place with a rubber band when you clean high surfaces (such as the hull of your boat when it's out of the water) to keep the wash water from running down your arm and onto your clothing.

Oven Mitts and Rags

To make polishing a hull easier, use an oven mitt, a potholder, or a cotton work glove as an applicator.

Want to keep your new boat looking as shiny as it did in the showroom? Don't shine it up with regular rags; they'll pick up dirt, which can leave tiny scratches in your perfect gelcoat. Instead, use cloth diapers—nothing's softer and more absorbent.

Keep Your Stripes Looking Sharp

To neatly repair a nick in vinyl hull striping, use a razor to cut diagonal lines across the stripe on either side of the nick. Heat with a blow dryer to warm the glue, and then remove the nicked section. Use acetone to remove any remaining glue. Cut a new tape section slightly larger than the old to allow for shrinkage, and apply, overlapping the tapes.

BAKING SODA ON BOARD

Baking soda is probably the most versatile boat cleaning and maintenance product around. It can be used as everything from a rust remover for metal and an oil spill cleaner to a deck paint additive to provide a light nonskid tread. And if you forget to bring your toothpaste along on a cruise, just use some of the baking soda that's deodorizing your cabin fridge to scrub your teeth. How many of the following uses for baking soda have you tried?

TIP	PAGE
Nonabrasive stainless steel polish	1
Brass discoloration remover and lacquered brass restorer	3
Deck metal rust remover and tow vehicle bumper cleaner	4
All-purpose boat cleaner	6
Black streak remover	8–9
Paint texturizer (nonskid)	13
Windshield wiper blade cleaner	16
Suntan oil and water spot remover for teak decks	18–19
Teak deodorizer	19
Nondrying vinyl stain cleaner	23
Seasickness stain remover for deck carpet	28
General hull cleaner, greasy stain neutralizer, and ring-around-the-hull remover	31
Easy tar remover	32
Paintbrush cleaner and renewer	34
Cabin freshener	37
Mildew stain remover for the head	39
Musty linen freshener and mildew spot remover	39
Wet cabin carpet restorer	40
Cabin deodorizer	40
Toilet cleaner	40–41
Head deodorizer/protectant and wall stain remover	41
Soap scum remover	43

TIP	PAGE
Environmentally friendly head unclogger	44
Foul-odor killer	44
Galley drain deodorizer and line cleaner	45
Natural scouring powder	45
Rusty appliance pick-me-up and hard water stain remover	46
Appliance whitener	48
Microwave explosion cleaner and deodorizer	48–49
Stove burner unclogger	50
Fire extinguisher	51
Cutting board revitalizer	52
Upholstery deodorizer	54
Carpet steam cleaner	56–57
Cat litter freshener and cat shedding preventer	60
Itchy cat ear cure	61
Flame arrestor soak and heat exchange unclogger	64
Gas and oil spill cleaner	78
Hand cleaner	78
Battery terminal corrosion remover and protectant	79–80
Battery acid neutralizer	80
Fishing lure pick-me-up	99
Water ski cleaner	100
Bilge winterizer	114
Mosquito and bee sting itch reducer	133
Sunburn first aid	136

BOTTOM PAINTING TIPS AND TRICKS

Stretch Your Bottom Paint Dollars

To keep your expensive bottom paint from accumulating in the can rim and running down the sides—which not only wastes paint but means that you won't be able to close the can properly when you're done—punch or drill small holes in the rim groove to allow the accumulating paint to drain back into the can. While you've got the drill out, drill small holes in your paint stirrer to make mixing easier and more thorough. You may also want to tape a paper plate to the can bottom to create a drip catcher and further reduce the mess.

Get the Paint on the Boat, Not on the Boater

To keep bottom paint from dripping back on you, cut a hole in a small dessert-size paper plate wide enough to put a paint brush handle through, and push it toward the middle of the brush just beneath where the metal band holds the bristles. This forms a cheap, replaceable drip catcher. Hold the brush against the underside of the plate to hold the catcher in place as you work.

Bottom Paint Paintbrush Strainer

Lay down your paint can handle after opening the can, and then straighten a metal hanger and attach it to one side of the paint can handle where it attaches to the can. Run it straight across the top of the paint can, and secure to the other side, where the wire handle meets the can. Now you've got a brush cleaner that runs directly over the top of the can and puts all the drips back inside the can. This keeps the edge clean, making the can easier to close securely, and thereby extends the life of your unused bottom paint.

Don't Nick as You Go

When painting, wrap the metal band that holds the brush bristles in place with plastic wrap to prevent it from nicking the paint as you go. The plastic wrap can also smudge the paint, but the damage won't be as bad, and if caught right away, it can usually be smoothed out.

Brush Prep

When you're ready for a lunch break, wrap your brushes loosely (loose enough not to mash the bristles, but tight enough to keep air from circulating around them) in aluminum foil, plastic wrap, or grocery store plastic bags. This keeps your brushes fresh and ready for use later.

After cleaning your bottom paint paintbrushes with paint thinner, clean the thinner residue off in a solution of 1 part baking soda and 4 parts warm water.

Revitalize hardened bottom paint paintbrushes by soaking them in a solution of ½ gallon boiling water, ¼ cup vinegar, and 1 cup baking soda.

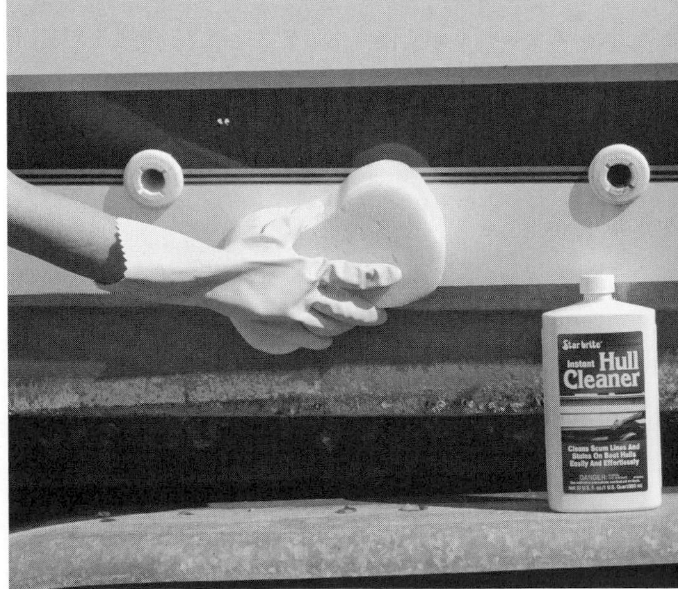

Naturally occurring oxalic acid is a powerful yet safe hull cleaner.

The Seamless Roller

Trim the fuzzy edge off both sides of your bottom paint roller to eliminate the roller lines that often appear after the paint has dried and it's too late to do anything about them.

Potpourri Away the Paint Headaches

If you're using an oil-based paint and the fumes give you a headache, add a teaspoon of vanilla extract to each gallon to lessen odors. To further lessen the odor of all types of paint, set a dish or two of ammonia or vinegar nearby. This is especially important when painting your boat or dinghy inside a work area with minimal cross-ventilation. Open doors and windows and use a fan to increase ventilation if you cannot work outside.

Paint Pick-Ups

To remove accidental paint drops and spills from fiberglass or wood hulls, wrap a clean rag around a putty knife and gently scrape up the paint. Then wash with warm, soapy water. On a wooden hull you can also use a damp sponge with scouring powder such as Comet. Rub gently so as not to hurt the wood, and dry thoroughly.

Avoiding Masking Tape Tragedies

When masking tape starts to pull off paint, use your hair dryer to warm up the adhesive so that the tape lifts off cleanly.

Make Your Stripper More Efficient

To make your paint stripper lift more paint from a wooden hull, brush it heavily on the wood, and then cover it with sheets of plastic wrap. This prevents the active solvent in the stripper from evaporating easily into the surrounding atmosphere. By slowing the solvent's evaporation rate, more solvent stays against the surface of the coating, allowing the stripper to cut the paint film better. Hours later, or even the next morning, peel off the plastic a section at a time and remove the softened paint film.

Soft Sanding

Try wrapping your sandpaper around a sponge instead of a hard sanding block when sanding a contoured surface before painting or varnishing. The soft sponge allows the sandpaper to conform to the surface better.

Not Too Late for Touch-Up

Long after you've put away your painting equipment, when you find spots that you've missed (and you know you will find them), don't roll your eyes and begin hauling out all your equipment again. Instead, quickly touch up the area with a cotton swab.

Touching up with old paint that has curdles in it? Strain the paint through the leg of a pair of panty hose, and you'll have like-new paint to work with.

Stand in the Corner on Your Head

To save excess bottom paint for next year, first make sure you put the lid on *tightly*, and then store the paint can upside down to stop a skin from forming. Test the lid first before storing upside down.

How Much Bottom Paint Is Enough?

The general formula for figuring out how many gallons of bottom paint you need for one coat is your boat's LOA × beam × 0.85 ÷ square feet covered per gallon as listed on the paint can.

Longer-Lasting Bottom Paint

Want to lengthen the life of your bottom paint? Don't use metal putty knives to scrape off marine deposits. Instead, use a scrub brush or plastic scrubbing pad—they're much gentler on your bottom paint.

THRU HULL TIPS AND MORE

The Dry Blister Test

You've sanded open the blisters on your boat's hull, a week has passed, and you'd like to start spreading on the epoxy. But first, you need to know for sure if the blister has completely dried out. The day before you intend to start sealing the blister, tape a piece of plastic wrap over it. Be sure to completely seal the edges of the wrap to the boat. When you return the next day, check for moisture inside the plastic wrap. If there is none, go to work. If it's dewy in there, the blister needs more time to dry.

Pro Hardware Installation

Pro boat builders use this trick for preventing leaks when installing hardware on fiberglass that will be beneath the waterline: Mark, center punch, and drill your fastener holes. Using either a larger-diameter drill bit or a countersink bit, slightly countersink the hole in the fiberglass beneath the spot where the hardware will rest. Before installing the screws or bolts, run a ring of polyurethane caulking neatly around the perimeter of each hole. When you install the hardware, the rubber caulk squeezes into the chamber, creating a waterproof rubber washer beneath the fitting, no matter how tight the fasteners are.

Protecting Hardware While Painting

Protect underwater hardware, such as a transducer or thru hull fitting, with petroleum jelly before painting. Then if you accidentally get a paint spot on any of them, you'll be able to easily wipe it off. For best performance, don't forget to clean off any remaining petroleum jelly when you're done painting.

Try wrapping your sandpaper around a sponge for easier sanding of contoured surfaces.

chapter 3

CABIN CONCERNS

THE COMPLETE CABIN

Static and Dirt

Static created by opening and closing your cabin hatchway causes dust to be attracted to the interior door frame. Wipe down the door frame regularly with a clean rag, especially if you have allergies. Turning on your cabin television has the same effect, so dust it regularly, too.

Mildew-Away

To keep mildew from forming on your cabin's vinyl fabric liner, regularly spray with a disinfectant such as Lysol. Alcohol is a main ingredient in disinfectants and is safer on fabrics than bleach, which can drip on upholstery and ruin it.

Bulkhead Drilling

Need to drill a hole into a padded bulkhead? To prevent the material from winding up on your drill, go slowly in reverse. When the drill hits firm material, switch to forward. Continue cautiously to prevent the material from being grabbed by the bit.

Keep Your Clothes on Their Hangers

To stop clothing from falling off hangers in high seas, apply silicone rubber adhesive to the hangers and allow it to dry into a nonskid surface.

MILDEW PREVENTION AND MAINTENANCE AND ODOR CONTROL

Odor Versus Odor

Place a bowl of vinegar in the middle of the cabin to absorb dank odors. But don't forget to remove the bowl before taking the boat out, or you may find yourself with a strong vinegar odor that is almost as offensive as the mustiness. Extremely strong, foul mold/mildew odors will require the use of a chlorine dioxide odor eliminator.

If after cleaning off mildew, your cabin still smells bad from the combination of mildew and vinegar, mix 1 cup baking soda and ¼ cup ammonia in an empty 1-gallon milk jug. Add 16 cups warm water and 1 tablespoon vanilla extract. Pour a small portion into a pump bottle for air freshener that kills even the most offensive odors.

How Thomas Edison Fought Mildew

Another way to combat cabin mildew, if you've got the necessary shore power, is to hang a bare lightbulb in the cabin when not in use. The dry heat from the bulb will combat mildew. To make the process work even better, leave a small fan on to circulate the air.

Gentle Air Freshener

To remove musty cabin smells, place a dryer softener sheet by the return register of the air conditioner.

Filter Out Foul Odors

To help eliminate cabin closet odors when your boat's not being used, fill a small bowl with charcoal (available for potted plants at most home improvement stores) and place it on a shelf. It will absorb odors rapidly.

Vanilla Sachets

A little vanilla poured on a piece of cotton and placed on a shelf will also help eliminate musty odors.

Homespun Mildew Preventer

To keep mildew from growing in the cabin, fill a spray bottle with 40 percent bleach, 40 percent water, and 10 percent liquid fabric softener; leave the remaining 10 percent of the bottle empty. Don't spray directly on fabric, or the bleach could discolor it. Instead, lightly coat nearby wood and metal surfaces.

Easy Carpet Deodorizer

To deodorize mildewed carpet, first clean and allow to dry thoroughly. Then generously sprinkle borax on the carpet. Let it sit undisturbed for an hour before vacuuming up the Borax, along with the unpleasant smells.

Oven cleaner is the answer to mildew in the head.

What Do the Head and an Oven Have in Common?

Oven cleaner is the answer to a head overrun by mildew. Make sure you've got proper ventilation, and then generously spray oven cleaner on the head. Give the oven cleaner 5 minutes to attack the grunge before wiping the head clean with a pad of damp paper towels. A sponge paintbrush works great for cleaning out tight places such as shower door tracks.

The Mildew-Stained Head

If mildew has stained your fiberglass head, use liquid detergent or a mixture of baking soda and just enough water to make it into a paste. Apply liberally, let it work for 30 minutes, and then wash off.

The De-Mildewed Galley Fridge

Clean the cabin refrigerator with white vinegar to remove mildew odors. For continued deodorizing, don't rinse afterward. When not using the boat, empty the refrigerator and fasten the door open to prevent a musty stench from forming. For additional deodorizing, place some fresh (unused) coffee grounds in a cloth pouch and toss it on the center shelf of the refrigerator.

Clothing and Linens Left on Board

To safeguard stored clothing, sheets, towels, and so on left on board, put fabric softener sheets in between them to absorb odors and leave a fresh scent.

If clothing and linens left on board are musty, lay them out, sprinkle with baking soda, and refold them. After an hour or two, shake off the baking soda and toss in a dryer that's set to cool.

If the odors are too embedded for the baking soda tip to remove them completely, machine wash the musty items thoroughly. Then soak them in a mixture of 4 tablespoons baking soda in 1 quart water. After a couple hours, wring out the items and let them dry. The smells should be gone.

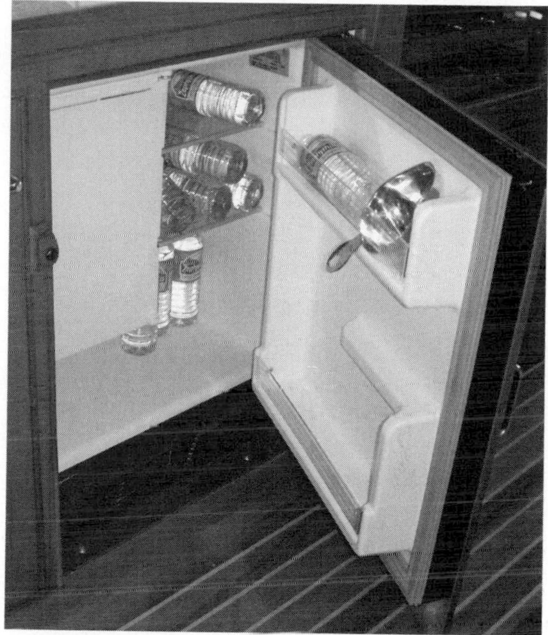

To remove mildew and grime, wipe down the fridge interior with white vinegar. You don't have to rinse it off afterward.

To remove dark mildew spots from clothing, towels, and linens left on board, mix 5 tablespoons baking soda to ¼ cup water and use as a pretreatment before laundering.

Fresh Air Is the Nemesis of Mold and Mildew

Vacuum cushions thoroughly, and then prop them at odd angles to the cabin furniture so that air can flow around them. Do the same for PFDs left on board. Sufficient ventilation is the nemesis of mold and mildew.

When Mildew Is Your New Wall Covering

Vinyl wall covering can be easily cleaned by mixing ½ cup vinegar and 1 quart water and applying the solution with a sponge. Be careful not to get the vinyl too wet or allow water in the seams, or the vinyl may come away from the walls. To make a vinyl wall covering cleaning mousse, add ½ cup liquid dishwashing soap to 1 cup warm water, and mix the solution with an egg beater until it becomes a stiff foam. Work it into the vinyl covering gently with a sponge, one section at a time. Rinse off the cleaner and dirt with a slightly damp, clean sponge.

Proper Ventilation for the Stored Boat

When covering a boat with a tarp, first toss the fenders overboard, and then tie the cover or tarp over them. This holds the tarp slightly away from the hull and ensures the necessary ventilation to retard mildew without leaving the cover dangerously loose. If possible, leave some hatches and maybe a window slightly open, but only if doing so won't allow in rain. Prop open all interior doors—from the head door to the storage and galley lockers—and leave drawers slightly ajar for increased ventilation.

Curtain ℞

You left your cabin windows open too much (horrors!) and now your curtains are soaked with water stains—a potential playground for mold and mildew. Take two damp rags (yes, damp!). Hold one underneath the water stain, while you work the spot from the middle outward with the other rag. If your curtains are simply dusty, vacuum them. And don't forget to close your cabin curtains when you leave the boat; they protect the cabin furnishings and fittings from the fading effects of the sun's ultraviolet rays.

Damp Cabin Carpet

An open cabin window can also lead to a wet carpet and all the mildew nightmares that brings. To restore wet mildewed carpet, blot up as much water as possible, sprinkle on baking soda, and let sit. Vacuum after the carpet has thoroughly air dried.

A Bookworm's Advice

Most books stored in the cabin eventually get musty. Corn starch deodorizes the pages.

Baking Soda Eats Musty Odors for Lunch

If you carry a humidifier on board, add two tablespoons baking soda to eliminate musty odors.

QUICKIE HEAD CLEANING

Don't Throw That Flat Cola Away

When cola goes flat on board, don't throw it away. Instead, pour it into your head. Let it stand, undisturbed, for an hour, and then scrub and flush with water. This is an excellent nontoxic toilet bowl cleaner.

Lessen Your Toilet Cleaning Chores

Put 2 cups vinegar in the toilet tank and bowl, and let it soak overnight. In the morning, brush to a sparkling clean. The vinegar even removes lime and calcium scales.

Before scrubbing your toilet, drop two Alka Seltzer tablets in the bowl. After they fizz, brush the bowl as usual for a sparkling new shine.

Periodically flush the head with 1 gallon warm water to which you've added 1 cup baking soda to deodorize and clean. Then flush with 1 gallon warm water. Baking soda works well with the waste digester–deodorant found in most holding tanks.

To get rid of light "ring-around-the-toilet" stains, pour a mixture of half vinegar and half water into the toilet. Let sit for 15 minutes, and then flush clean. For tougher rings, fill the toilet with 1 part muriatic acid to 3 parts water. Do not leave this dangerous mixture on for more than 15 minutes, and remember to wear protective gloves and goggles. Always add acid to water; never vice versa or the acid may splash back on you.

Full-Strength Toilet Cleaning

It's a good idea not to clean a head while there's water in the bowl because water dilutes your cleaner so that it acts at only one tenth its intended strength. Instead, push a bowl brush into the neck of the bowl and move it like a plunger to remove water from the bowl. Now your cleaner can clean the bowl at its intended strength.

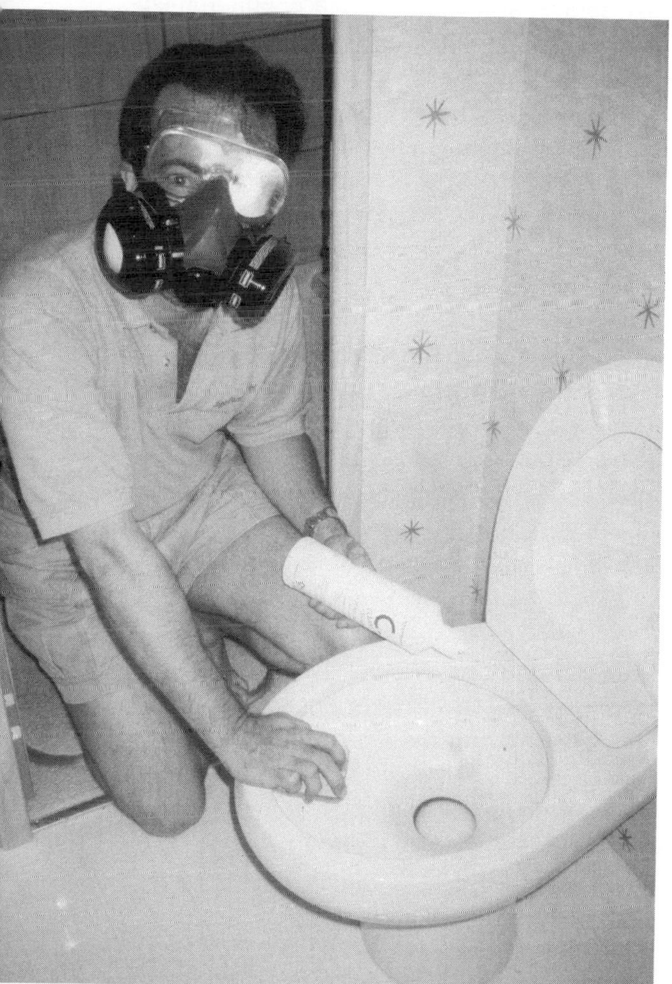

Head cleaning doesn't have to be unpleasant.

There's No Need for a Fishy Smell When There Aren't Fish on Board

Just because your raw-water head uses seawater doesn't mean you have to live with a fishy smell. Simply pour full-strength vinegar down the head and flush it thoroughly through the system. Be sure to thoroughly scrub out the channel under the rim that rinses the bowl. Seawater trapped here is the main source of that raw-water system stink.

If You're Not Going to Use It, Seal It Up

If your head isn't going to be used for a few days, put some Saran Wrap over the toilet bowl opening to prevent the formation of an unsightly ring and lessen water evaporation.

Proper Head Cleaning and Disinfecting

Clean and deodorize fiberglass head walls, toilet exterior, and floor with a solution of 3 tablespoons baking soda to one quart warm water. Do not rinse with water—just wipe dry.

If you're going to disinfect your head, clean it first. Dirt can play havoc with disinfectants, even to the point of stopping some from working altogether.

Head Whitening

To remove yellow water marks on the walls and floor of your fiberglass head, use a paste made of half cream of tartar and half peroxide. This mixture will both loosen and lighten the spots.

The walls of your fiberglass head are lightly stained, you say? Try a liquid detergent or a mixture of baking soda and just enough water to make it into a paste. Apply liberally, let it

To keep your head's mirror from steaming up, wipe it down with ½ cup white vinegar in 1 gallon warm water.

work for 30 minutes, and then wash off. Soft Scrub and other nonabrasive cleansers work equally well.

Mirror, Mirror, on the Wall

To keep your head's mirror from steaming up, wipe it with ½ cup white vinegar in 1 gallon warm water.

A neglected head mirror can be brought back to life with a mixture of ⅓ cup clear ammonia and 1 gallon water. Spray on and then buff off with a clean, lint-free rag or paper towel. If you don't like working with ammonia, you can use vinegar in the same proportions.

Another quick mirror trick is to clean it with a piece of newspaper dipped in straight white vinegar. Wipe all around the mirror, and then when the mirror is nearly dry, buff to a shine with a second piece of newspaper. Instead of grabbing a section or two from the top of the newspaper pile, dig deep for the oldest paper you've got. Paper several months old cleans better because the newsprint ink is drier.

Got a vain first mate on board? When your head or stateroom mirror becomes dull from too much hairspray, wipe it with rubbing alcohol to loosen the buildup and restore the shine. To remove caked-on hairspray from the door or wall behind where you stand when preparing your coif, use fabric softener mixed with water and applied with a sponge. It dissolves the crust.

A third witch's brew for mirrors is concocted from 2 cups isopropyl rubbing alcohol (70 percent solution), 2 tablespoons liquid dishwashing soap, and 2 cups water. Mix thoroughly and then spray onto the grimy surface. Buff immediately with a clean cloth or paper towel.

Use Your "Assistants" Properly

Pump bottle spray nozzles are your best friend. Don't forget to adjust them to the proper spray width to avoid overspray of your cleaners. Insufficient spray pattern is almost as bad because it causes you more work.

Keep the Toilet Paper on the Roll

To keep toilet paper and paper towel rolls from unraveling with the motions of a choppy sea, squeeze the roll slightly and bend the inner tube. Make the bend slight enough so that you can still install the roll in its holder, but great enough to stop the smooth "roll off" that can be caused by the boat's motion.

Maximize Your Water Pressure

If your shower head gets clogged, remove the head and take out the rubber washer. Soak the head in 1 cup vinegar and 1 cup water for about an hour. Scrub out any loosened goop with an old toothbrush.

Cleaning More Often Actually Makes for Less Work

This may sound simple, but wipe down the sink and shower stall immediately after each use, and you'll save yourself a lot of cleaning effort. This handy habit removes the dirt, soap scum, and mineral deposits from hard water before they've had a chance to set and are much harder to remove.

Another time saver is to put a squeegee in the head to clean the shower door after each shower. This is the easiest time to remove body oil, soap residue, and hard water spots.

Soap Film Be Gone

To both cut soap film and add shine to head walls and/or shower doors, wipe them down with a scrub sponge—the kind that's encased in a mesh bag and found at most grocery stores in the cleaning aisle—dipped in white vinegar.

If cabin mildew and soap scum have combined to make your shower door gruesome, fill a pump bottle with straight vinegar and spray on generously. Let sit for 10 minutes, and then scrub with a damp sponge, dusted generously with baking soda. Squeegee or paper towel dry.

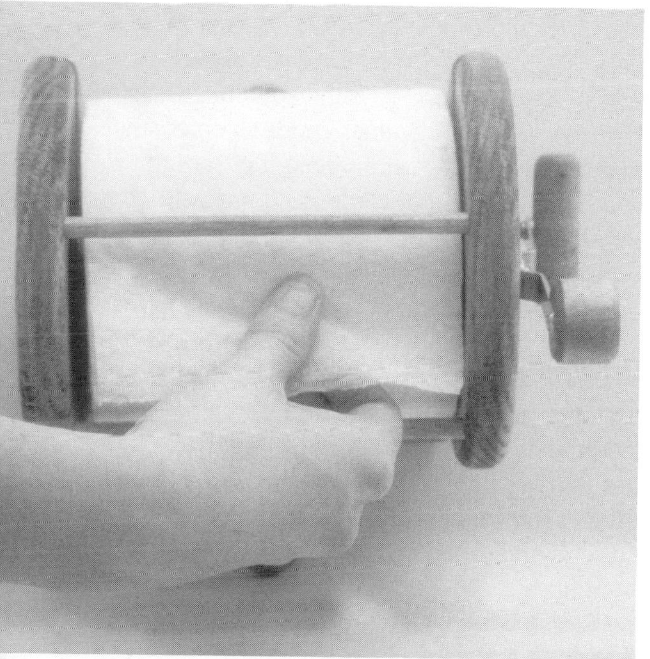

To keep toilet paper from unraveling in high seas, squeeze the roll slightly to bend the inner tube.

Maintaining a Porous Shower Door

If your shower door refuses to let go of dirt and hard water accumulation, it's probably gotten porous over the years from cleaning with traditional strong head cleaners. Apply a coating of polymer boat polish to the shower door to restore its slick, dirt-resistant shine.

The Hard Water Solution

Hard water deposits in a fiberglass shower enclosure can be removed with a mixture of equal parts white vinegar and water. Sponge on, let sit for a few minutes, and then scrub off with more of the vinegar-and-water mix.

To remove water spots from metal, rub it down with a sponge dipped in lemon oil. This not only works on the metal in the head, especially the shower enclosure, but on deck as well.

The Shower Curtain Soak and Snip

If you're an old-fashioned boater with a shower curtain, you can soak it in salt water to prevent it from mildewing. Repeat yearly during spring commissioning and winter layup.

Rather than go through all the trouble of replacing a moldy shower curtain with shower doors (another buddy of mold and mildew) in the middle of winter, simply clean the curtain, and then snip off the bottom of it with pinking shears. The uneven cut retards mildew.

To clean determined mold and mildew from a shower curtain, remove the curtain from the boat and lay it out on a flat surface. To prevent damage to the thin curtain from a cement or wood deck, lay the curtain out on towels, canvas, or your boat tarp. Now you're ready to scrub away with a mild detergent. Either air or towel dry. Then apply vinyl polish to help ward off future mildew. Buff to a pleasant shine.

Polish Your Chores Away

You polish your fiberglass hull, so why not polish your fiberglass head? The polish will not only repel soap scum and make the head easier to clean, but it will protect the sheen of the fiberglass beneath and make it look newer longer. For safety's sake, don't apply polish to any walking surfaces.

The Fluffiest Isn't Always the Best

You say your guests keep clogging up your toilet with Charmin? Perhaps it's not your guests but your toilet paper that's at fault. Only single-ply toilet tissue or specially designed marine toilet tissue, which is not made from wood fibers as most standard land-use brands are, should be used in a head, whose pipes are normally half the size of those of a standard land toilet. Remember that preventive maintenance is the best kind of maintenance.

Hose and Discharge Advice

Salt and calcium are building up in your hoses until the usable diameter diminishes significantly and they no longer function properly? Rather than replace your hoses yearly, run vinegar or muriatic acid through the system periodically as needed to remove the accumulated buildup. Closing the intake seacock and flushing a few buckets of freshwater through the system will also help loosen very small accumulations of salt, weeds, and so on.

When your head discharge begins to slow or, worse yet, backs up, put on your rubber gloves and mix 1 part muriatic acid to 10 parts water. ***WARNING:*** Always add acid to water, never vice versa. After closing the discharge seacock, disconnect the discharge hose at the toilet and pour the mixture into it. Pour slowly to avoid dangerous spillage. Allow the potion to work its magic for 10 minutes, and then carefully reconnect the system and flush, flush, flush.

Has your head discharge become clogged? Flush drain cleaner through the lines, and you'll be putting some nasty chemicals into the water. Instead, pour in baking soda, followed by boiling water. It works most of the time.

Ahoy! Foul Odors Below!

I've heard it before: Your head smells so bad you hesitate to go below except when absolutely necessary. Baking soda not only deodorizes your onboard refrigerator, but when poured down the shower drain or sink drain or dropped liberally into the head, it should do the trick. Let it sit undisturbed for 48 hours if possible. Washing the shower stall with baking soda further freshens the room. Again, do not rinse for 48 hours for the full deodorizing effect.

Part Smart

Replace the gaskets, seals, belts, impellers, flapper valve, and rubber joker valve once a year for peak performance. Or carry this list of parts with you at all times, along with the appropriate tools.

When O-rings, leather pistons, and other moving parts are either drying out or seizing up, you can lubricate new life into them with that old standby, petroleum jelly.

If the rubber and leather parts on your head are constantly in need of replacement, what you're flushing down the toilet may be the cause. Pine-Sol and other similar deodorant cleaners contain kerosene and other corrosive solvents, which eventually eat through the rubber and leather parts. To get rid of stains and odors safely, use liquid bleach instead of these corrosive solvents, let sit for a half hour, and then flush thoroughly with water.

Seacock Solutions

The seacock's tapered plug has become stuck from accumulated dirt? Use a wrench to wrest the stuck plug free, and then soak it in undiluted vinegar until the dirt loosens. Rub off the dirt with a mildly abrasive cloth. For scratches, use a fine abrasive cloth and then a grinding compound, if necessary, until the plug moves smoothly. Grease the plug before reassembling.

A not-uncommon problem for boaters out at sea is for the head waste released into the water through the discharge seacock to be pumped back in through the intake seacock. Usually the problem is that the discharge and intake seacocks are on the same side of the hull. Ideally, the intake and discharge seacock should be separated by the keel. If the problem becomes severe and your seacocks are on the same side of the hull, you may have to rerun your lines and relocate one seacock. If complete relocation is impossible, move either the intake or discharge seacock so that the discharge is above and aft of the intake.

When the toilet smells like rotting sweat socks from the grasses that get sucked into the intake seacock, cut a small piece of standard fiberglass screening and seal it into place over the intake seacock with a polyurethane adhesive. An internal strainer, like those used on engines, cut into the line, provides additional protection.

Just like when you find that your computer won't work, if your head won't flush properly, you should first check the electrical connection to make sure it's plugged in. The same holds true for the head's intake and discharge seacocks. Did you remember to open them before leaving the dock? This is one of the most common causes of head malfunction.

IN THE GALLEY

Environmentally Safe Drain Cleaners

Mix ½ cup baking soda with ½ cup salt and pour down the drain. Let sit overnight and flush in the morning with hot water. This environmentally safe mixture won't hurt pipes and can be used as needed.

Another option for free-running drains is to periodically pour 1 cup baking soda down the drain, and then immediately add 1 cup vinegar. After the mixture foams, add 1 pint boiling water. This solution is natural and won't harm the pipes in any way.

Slow-Running Sink Suggestions

A wet-dry vac is excellent for suctioning out clogged sink drains.

Before you take apart the drain system to your slow-running head sink, check the stopper. It's the cause more often than you'd think. Clean thoroughly and replace.

Scour Naturally

For an environmentally friendly multipurpose galley scouring powder that won't harm the sea life beneath you, mix 1 cup baking soda, 1 cup borax, and 1 cup salt.

Straight baking soda is an excellent substitute for scouring powder. Use as you would the conventional powder. It works almost as well as the baking soda, borax, and salt mixture.

Keep That Galley Shining

The cabin stainless (stovetop, sink and head fittings, and so on) has lost its shine. One of the best nontraditional stainless cleaners is window cleaner; simply spray it on and wipe it off. For additional protection, apply a thin film of cooking oil, and then buff with a clean rag to a high-gloss shine.

If water spots are making your stainless steel sink look less than clean, rub it down with vinegar, and then rinse with water. Towel dry, and then apply a polymer boat polish as you would your on-deck stainless that is exposed to the elements.

When you get rust and dark mineral deposits in your stainless steel galley sink from filling your boat's water tank at strange docks, fill the sink with boiling water and add 2 tablespoons baking soda and 1 tablespoon lemon juice. Repeat if necessary. Clean as you normally would afterward.

A second alternative for rust stains in your stainless steel sink is to scrub them off easily with lighter fluid. Make sure there are no open flames and the area is sufficiently ventilated when working, and be sure to wash both the sink and your hands thoroughly afterward.

Apply the same polish you use on the boat's hull to your stainless steel sink and fixtures. It will work wonders at keeping the stainless from becoming discolored or rusty, although even a waxed sink can rust if you leave utensils in it for a long time.

Rusty Enamel Sinks

For rust spots in an enamel sink, scrub with hydrogen peroxide and a scrub sponge. For tougher spots, mix salt and lemon juice into a paste and scrub thoroughly.

Don't Be the Cause of More Rust

Scouring pads rust quickly on board. Substitute nylon net, available in most fabric shops. It's cheaper, doesn't leave those annoying tiny wire bits in your fingers, and doesn't scratch delicate surfaces. Simply dampen the net and use with mild abrasive.

Appliances Pick-Me-Up

You accidentally left a window open over the winter, and the accumulated cabin moisture has caused rust streaks inside your refrigerator (which you dutifully left open to ensure proper ventilation). Wipe down with a baking soda paste on a damp sponge. Use a little elbow grease on the tough stains, and they should come clean. Most discoloration should disappear with minimal fuss. For tough spots, leave the paste on overnight, and stains should be gone by morning.

Scrub away hard water stains in the galley sink and in or on appliances with a mixture of white toothpaste and baking soda. A toothbrush or your finger wrapped in a clean rag works best for tight spots such as around faucets.

An Older Galley Needs Special Care

Got an older galley that just isn't cleaning up like it used to? Mix 1 part ammonia with 3 parts water in a spray bottle for a great all-purpose cleaner with gusto. Wear rubber gloves to protect your hands, and watch out for overspray onto surrounding teak or wall coverings.

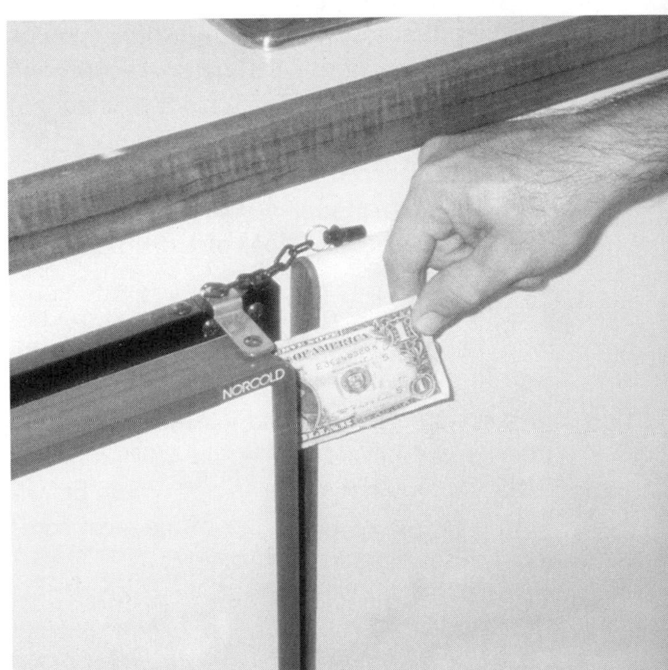

To check whether your fridge is leaking air, close the refrigerator door on a dollar bill, and then tug.

Hard Water Spot Removal

The water at your marina is so hard that it leaves a cloudy film on glass. Rub down dishes and glasses with warm vinegar to loosen the film buildup, and then wash with bottled or filtered water. This works equally well with windows that are getting buildup from dirty rainwater and rinsings with strange water in distant ports.

The High Seas–Ready Refrigerator

Line your refrigerator with aluminum foil. That way when a mess happens, all you have to do is remove the foil and toss. No more hours of scrubbing. This also works for lining stove top burner pans.

Clean Every Cranny

Dirt and grime are collecting beneath your cabin sole-mounted refrigerator. Slip an old pantyhose foot over a yardstick and slide back and forth to lift accumulating dirt. You should do this every few months to prevent buildup.

The Leaky Refrigerator Test

You think your cabin or on-deck refrigerator may be leaking cold air, but you aren't feeling certain enough to risk the expense of a repairperson on a false alarm call. Take out a crisp dollar bill and close the refrigerator door on it. Now tug. If you can pull the bill out easily, your door seal is not tight. Try this in all locations that are suspect.

The Malodorous Fridge

You've thoroughly cleaned out the cabin and galley yet still have a foul odor, you say? Check behind the rubber gasket strip on your cabin refrigerator. It's a nice moist home for mildew, not to mention spills and other gunk that may have piled up there over time.

If the refrigerator door won't close properly, you'll also want to check behind the inner door gasket for food and dirt buildup beneath. This is more common than you think. Your spouse's (old) toothbrush and a few drops of liquid dishwashing soap in warm water will do the rest.

To remove mildew and grime from a refrigerator, wipe down the interior with white vinegar. The best part is that you don't have to rinse it off afterward.

To remove a noxious odor that has taken residence in your fridge, put away your checkbook—you don't need a new refrigerator. Mix 1 part bleach with 5 parts water and scrub the fridge thoroughly. Repeat if necessary. After the fridge interior dries, rinse thoroughly with plain water.

The Temperature's the Thing

If your milk is cold, but not so cold that it has ice crystals, and the ice cream in the freezer is solid but not so rock solid that you can't dig it out with a spoon, then your refrigerator temperature is set correctly.

The average boat refrigerator can chill only 2 to 3 pounds of food per cubic foot of space at a time. Fill the refrigerator a small amount at a time for best results.

All's Quiet in the Galley

Rub a soft pencil across the hinge of a squeaky cabin or on-deck refrigerator door. Pencils are made of graphite, which lubricates and eliminates squeaks.

Ice Advice

To free an ice tray that's become stuck to the freezer, cover the ice tray with a towel soaked in hot water for a few seconds. The resulting steam should loosen the tray sufficiently to pull it loose without damage.

If your ice maker is making cubes with black specks in them, check the coating on the ice molding tray, and you'll probably find that it's deteriorating. Call the manufacturer for replacement information.

Wall Grease Isn't as Bad as You Think

To remove greasy cooking spots from galley walls, dip a cotton ball or powder puff in talcum powder and rub lightly over the grease spot. Dust off excess powder and repeat until the grease is completely absorbed.

For more stubborn cooking grease and/or mildew spots on cabin walls, whether painted or wallpapered, use a mixture of cornstarch and just enough water to turn it into a paste. Paint the mixture over the stain and let it sit for an hour. Brush off, and repeat if necessary, until the stain is gone.

Looking Brand New

To get rid of the yellow aging that often occurs to white cabin appliances during winter lay-up, mix ½ cup bleach, ¼ cup baking soda, and 4 cups warm water, sponge on, and let sit for 10 minutes. Rinse and dry thoroughly. Rubbing alcohol can be used to shine the appliances afterward.

If a bout of cabin mildew is causing your galley appliances to discolor, you can restore white appliances to their original color by rinsing them with ¼ cup baking soda and 4 cups warm water. Let sit 15 minutes before rinsing with clean water. Dry thoroughly.

Elsewhere in the Galley

When it comes to stained laminated countertops, leave the abrasive cleaners behind. Pour fresh lemon juice over the spots and let sit for 30 to 45 minutes, depending on the severity of the stain. Next, pour baking soda into the mixture and scrub up lightly. For a general wash, pour some club soda onto a sponge and wipe away.

To prevent coffee and other non-stainless steel canisters from leaving rust marks on the galley counter, cut small pieces of felt out for the canister bottoms and glue on. Spare hose washers also make excellent canister "legs."

Micro-Cleaning

Food explosion in the microwave? If it's a one-time accident, heat a cup of water for 1 minute. The moisture created should loosen the over-splash enough to allow it to be wiped up easily. If it's an accumulated disaster, add 2 tablespoons lemon juice or baking soda to a half-filled bowl of water and heat for 5 minutes. This steam treatment should loosen even the toughest goop.

If you're fed up with cleaning up food explosions inside your microwave, purchase a large plastic microwavable food storage unit (the largest that fits inside the dimensions of your microwave). Turn the lower section upside-down to cover the cooking food and any explosions. When a food explosion occurs, simply remove the container and toss it into the sink for a rinse. This is much easier than scouring the microwave walls and corners. The upside-down container also gives the cooking process a terrarium effect and adds moisture to the food.

To remove minor odors from a cool microwave, mix 4 tablespoons baking soda in 1 quart warm water and use it to wipe down the interior.

Keep Your Microwave Immobile

You've added an after-market microwave to your boat, and in high seas it shifts around on the counter. Screw a small wood or plastic wedge in front of, on both sides of, and on top of the microwave for a snug fit. ***NOTE:*** Make sure that your construction doesn't obstruct the microwave door. The same construction scenario works for other loose appliances as well.

Fire in the Microwave

Fire in the microwave!!! Immediately unplug the unit and grab the nearest fire extinguisher you have at hand. *Don't open the microwave door!* Most microwave fires burn themselves out because of lack of air.

This Caffeine Will Wake You Up

If the coffee maker is brewing a blend so vile that it not only wakes you up in the morning but keeps your abused stomach on full alert for the rest of the day, run a full pot of vinegar through the system to deodorize and clean. (Some systems require a second treatment followed by a pot of plain water, check your owner's manual if you still have it.) Each pot of vinegar should work for two to three deodorizations. Afterward, pour it down the drain to freshen there also.

Blend It Clean

You've been making piña coladas all summer and convinced yourself you could get away with simply rinsing the blender clean. Now your onboard blender smells vile. Fill the blender halfway with water, and then add 2 drops liquid dishwashing soap. Plug in and blend your way clean. Rinse thoroughly afterward.

Let Kool-Aid Do Your Cleaning

Got a dishwasher on board *Mom's Mink*? Put powdered orange or lemon drink mix (such as unsweetened Kool-Aid) in the detergent cup instead of your normal dishwashing detergent and run an empty load. The citric acid in the powder will remove accumulated stains and thoroughly clean the dishwasher.

Keep Your Galley Stores Where You Put Them

Do your drawers (galley drawers, that is) slide open when cruising, spilling their contents on the cabin sole? Try using self adhesive Velcro on the drawer lip and frame to hold the drawers closed.

When the food cabinets aren't full (wedged in box-to-box), the boxes and cartons shift and spill. To prevent this, take a pair of book ends of the standard inverted "T" design (available at most office supply stores) and glue them to the shelving at regular intervals with 3M's 5200. You can fill only those slots needed, and the boxes will be held securely in place.

If possible, store only nonfood products in the cabinets above the stove because even dry foods such as rice can go bad from repeated exposure to the rising heat from the stove. If you must store food products there, make sure you use them as soon as possible.

To prevent items from slip-sliding around in the refrigerator, fill the empty spaces with empty soda and milk bottles to achieve a tight fit. While you're at it, fill the bottles with water and allow it to chill so you can always have a cool, refreshing drink.

One of the first rules of boat cleaning is preventing the mess in the first place. Dishwashing soap bottles often spill, and soap bars never stay in one place for long. Try installing a shower-style push-type inlaid soap dispenser (found in most home superstores) next to your sink for a no-drip, no-slip solution. Or insert a magnet into your bar of soap and attach it to a stainless steel sink.

Condiment jars, coffee creamers, and sugar bowls can be problematic when set on a table or counter during a meal served in rough seas. Buy ketchup, mustard, and margarine in squeeze bottles. Use the empty squeeze bottles as no-mess coffee creamer, sugar, honey, pancake syrup, and cooking oil dispensers.

To increase storage space for galley utensils, take a tip from anglers, who cut PVC pipe into 8-inch lengths to mount vertically on deck as rod holders. To modify this for galley use, glue a round plastic bottom to a 4-inch to 8-inch tube. Your local hardware store can help you cut the bottoms to size. Mount the completed containers on galley walls to store cooking utensils, cutlery, and more.

The Enlarged Galley

To increase cooking space in the galley, fabricate wooden covers for the stove burners to make a large cutting area/workspace. You can make a similar cover for your sink.

Rough Seas Suggestions

It's hard to fill cups on a sea that's even slightly rough. Attach a pair of fiberglass or acrylic cup holders, such as those made for on-deck use, in the galley. Place the empty glasses inside the holder, and pour with ease.

In rough seas, dirty glasses and dishes often get bounced around and broken from banging into the sink. If the weather begins to darken before you have a chance to clean up after the latest meal, place a dish towel or two on the bottom of the sink before loading to absorb impact and store dishes flat.

Adapt your standard land-use potholders for sea-going duty by sewing two of them together and lining the area between them where your hand would be inserted with heavy-duty plastic to prevent your hands from becoming burned from hot liquid spills in choppy seas. The same holds true for cooking aprons: A plastic or rubber-coated apron is better for cooking on the often turbulent seas than a thin cotton one.

Wipe stove spills up while they're warm (note that we *did not* say hot) before they have time to harden, using a warm soapy sponge.

When rough seas and a few too many spills have left you with clogged stove burners, remove the offending burners and boil them in a large pot containing ⅛ of a 1-pound box baking soda to each quart of water. Dry thoroughly and replace the burners.

The easiest way to clean baked-on food from chrome drip pans is to drop them in a plastic bag filled with enough ammonia to cover them, close the bag tightly, and leave for 6 to 8 hours. Avoid inhaling ammonia as you open the bag. Rinse the pans thoroughly with water before replacing.

Fuel Frustration

Your two-burner stove probably runs out of fuel regularly because you can't properly gauge the fuel level before starting. Make your own dipstick out of a plastic dowel or thin metal rod. ***NOTE:*** After use, clean thoroughly and be sure not to leave the dipstick lying out near open flame.

If you think the bottled gas for your stove may be leaking, coat the seals with a mixture of soap and water, and then watch for bubbling, which indicates escaping gas.

Two-Burner Carbon Buildup

If your two-burner stove gives off malodorous smoke when turned off, give it a thorough cleaning. Make sure to remove the carbon buildup, which can prevent the needle valve from closing fully. If you still have the smoky odor after cleaning, check for a valve-packing leak and if necessary replace it.

If your alcohol stove is producing a yellow flaring flame that does not get hot enough to cook on, check the burner to see if carbon buildup has occurred. If it has, scour the burner holes with a fine-wire brush or pipe cleaner. Next, check the nipple to see if either it or the cleaning needle is dirty. Clean the nipple with a straight pin, not a toothpick, which can sheer off inside and cause further problems.

Stove Cooler than Usual?

For an alcohol stove that is preheating at a lower temperature than usual, first check the preheater cup. It's probably filled with spilled food or used match ends, which are using the available alcohol to catch fire in the preheater cup, thereby lowering the overall temperature. ***WARNING:*** A preheater cup full of food is very dangerous because it can lead to an onboard fire that is hard to put out as it has a steady fuel source from the stove.

Two-Burner Fire Procedure

If you have a galley fire caused by a two-burner stove, immediately turn off the fuel source. Then, if necessary, toss handfuls of baking soda at the base of the fire until it is extinguished. ***NOTE:*** Never take any chances when dealing with fire; if a commercial fire extinguisher is nearby, use it.

Rice: A Boater's Wonder Food

You're looking for food that will go with many things yet will stay fresh throughout a long boating vacation. Rice is your answer. Stored in a cool, well-ventilated place, rice will keep for months. Wash old rice before cooking to remove starch buildup.

Low-Water Cooking Tips

If your boat has a small water tank, there might not always be enough freshwater on board for a thorough dishwashing after dinner. If this is the case, don't cook foods with tomato paste or frying oil, and stay away from recipes that call for searing or burning; residue from these types of dishes requires a lot of water for cleanup.

If your freshwater supply is low, but your stomach is rumbling, unpeeled potatoes can be cooked in salt water without any adverse health effects. Cooking pasta and rice in salt water will cause them to be more tacky than usual. A mixture of half freshwater and half salt water can be used to cook pasta, rice, or vegetables.

The Voyager's Milk

If you don't plan on seeing any ports during your floating vacation, fresh milk won't last for your entire voyage, so nonfat dry milk is your answer. Before you turn your nose up at this unpalatable solution, add a pinch of sugar, a spoonful of powdered creamer, or a drop of vanilla to make this reconstituted milk more tasty. Make only what you will use in the next 12 hours, or it too may spoil.

Fruity Advice

Make sure all the fruit and vegetables you buy are in A-1 health because bruised items go bad more quickly. Purchase only what you can eat in a few days. The exceptions are bananas and tomatoes, which you can purchase slightly green and allow to ripen on board. Sweet potatoes, squash, and cabbage have long shelf lives; they have been known to last a month at sea.

Egg Recommendations

To make eggs last longer, purchase the freshest eggs possible, then paint them with varnish, store them in a wooded box, with the eggs covered lightly with salt, or set the egg carton out until the eggs are room temperature, and grease them with shortening or petroleum jelly.

Another trick for making eggs last longer is to store them large end up.

Scurvy Is a Thing of the Past

Lemons last for months if wrapped in aluminum foil or paper and placed in an airy basket in a cool location on board. Do not pile the lemons too deep as the weight accelerates spoilage. They supply you with a healthy dose of vitamin C.

Don't Let Dampness Ruin Dinner

To revitalize soggy bread and crackers, set the items on a clean plate or tray on deck and let them sun dry. This usually takes about an hour.

Basic Meat Maintenance

To preserve beef, pork, or lamb for a long voyage, cut it into small squares or strips and try until well cooked. Drain off the accumulated fat and let cool until it forms into lard. Place the meat in an airtight plastic container, covering with lard so that the remaining meat doesn't touch the air as the container is opened and small portions are removed.

Cutting meats in heavy seas can quickly scar your countertop. Clean scratches and cuts with a paste of baking soda and water. The marks appear to fade away. Repeat regularly, or as often as needed.

To lessen the amount of garbage produced in the galley, purchase boneless meats. Also, if possible, cook only what you will eat, thereby eliminating often quick-spoiling leftovers. Finally, although it will save time and effort, using paper plates and plastic utensils during a long voyage will soon cause the garbage can to overflow.

Additional Fridge Storage

You've filled the galley fridge and freezer and now you're looking for some other form of food storage. Put a slab of dry ice in a Styrofoam ice chest (1 part) along with 9 parts water ice for a deep freeze that will last a full week. Persons who suffer from seasickness may not want to use this method as the carbon dioxide gas from the dry ice may worsen the queasiness.

Replacement Utensils

You may be a galley gourmet, but not without your sieve, if you left it at home. The solution? Use a clean screwdriver to punch holes in a paper or plastic cup. For a larger sieve, use a plastic-bottle bottom.

If a frozen can opener is separating you from your dinner, wash it in warm water, scrub off the accumulated muck with a wire brush or equally thorough cleaning tool, and lubricate the wheel with vegetable oil. Work loose by hand . . . and get on with dinner!

Wrap a length of fishing line around each palm and hold taut between your hands for a makeshift cheese slicer.

Blister First Aid

Before blisters form on a burn you got in your galley, coat the burn with egg white, or a thin

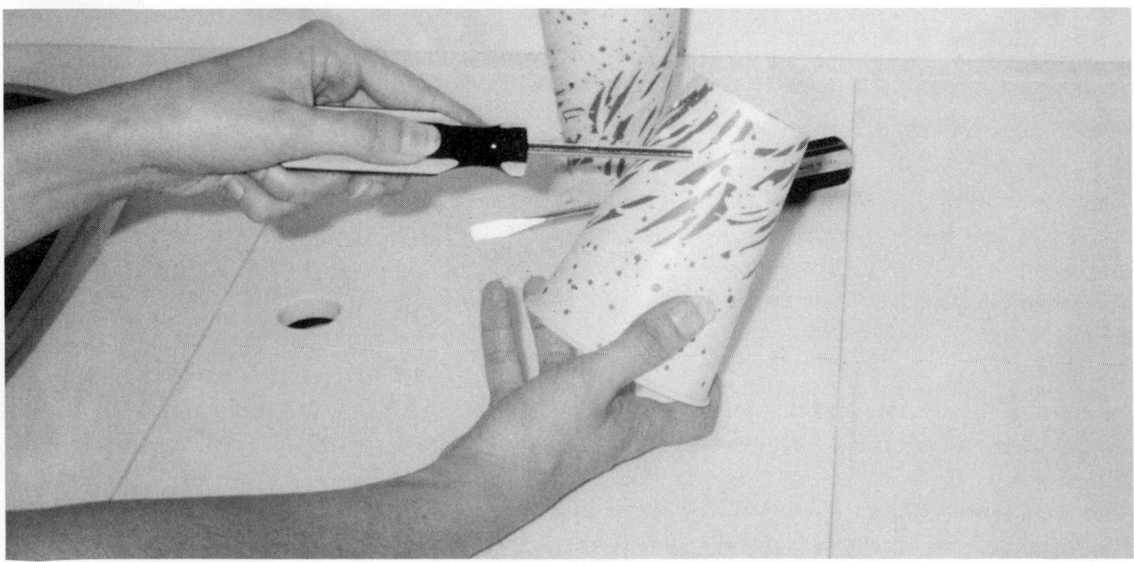

Punch holes in a paper cup to fashion a substitute sieve.

paste made from plain white soap shavings and water, or a paste made of freshwater and salt. For burns in your mouth from tasting hot foods, drink liquid coffee creamer or half-and-half. Honey is an excellent treatment for both minor skin and mouth burns.

Bring an aloe plant along on an extended voyage to keep in the galley as a quick, effective treatment for minor steam or other burns.

Lessen Grill Cleaning

Grilling on deck can cause as much cleanup as cooking in the galley. Next time you grill, wipe down the rack with a wire brush dipped in a solution made of baking soda and water, allow to dry, and coat with vegetable oil to keep food from sticking. Rinse again with the same baking soda solution afterward.

CABIN FURNITURE

The Cool Way to Clean

Set your cabin air conditioner to 62 degrees for the proper air temperature to counteract the sweat you would otherwise work up doing hard cleaning in tight quarters.

Steam-Free Upholstery Cleaning

You don't need a steam cleaner to clean dirty cabin upholstery. Instead, mix ¼ cup liquid dishwashing soap in 1 cup warm water, and whip the solution with an egg beater until it's a foam. Apply the foam with a soft-bristle brush. Rinse as you go, one section at a time, with a moist clean rag. Be sure to keep rinsing the rag as it dirties.

Got a greasy stain on your cabin upholstery? Never fear. Sprinkle the spot with talcum powder. Rub well and let sit until the grease appears to be absorbed. Brush off, and then wipe off any excess with a damp cloth. Repeat, if necessary.

WATERPROOF FILM CANISTERS

Empty film canisters are one of the greatest things invented for organizing the galley. These waterproof containers can be used to hold and organize

- Matches
- Salt and pepper
- Spices
- Birthday cake candles (great for impromptu festivities and better than nothing in an emergency)
- Baking soda for deodorizing

They also work as

- Toothpick holders
- Makeshift shot glasses
- Accurate 1 fluid ounce measures

Empty film canisters make great galley organizers.

A Dry-Cleaning Directive

Thoroughly air out cabin linens and upholstery that you've had dry cleaned before replacing them in the cabin. Unless the items are aired out properly, dry-cleaning solvents stay in the material, and in sufficient quantities in closed quarters, they can be toxic.

Quick Lint Pick-Up

Use a pair of old pantyhose to make picking up lint from cabin upholstery a snap. Their texture efficiently snags the lint in a way that a bare hand can't.

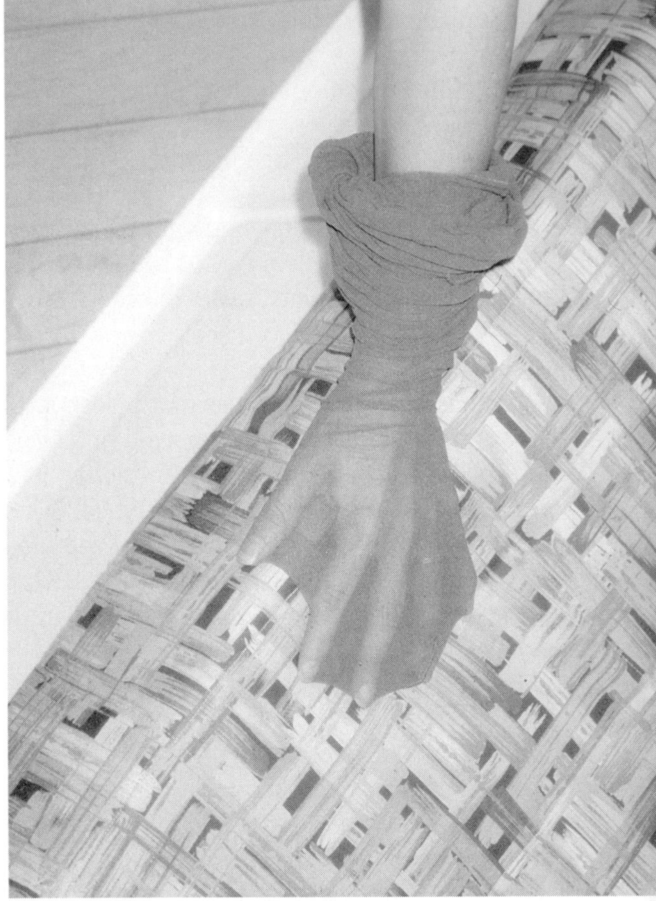

Old pantyhose make cabin lint pick-up a snap.

Stop Mildew Before It Starts

When you have your cabin cushions recovered, have the upholsterer sprinkle baking soda inside to help retard mildew.

Homemade Magic Duster

When dusting hard-to-reach places around your cabin furniture, such as around a bed's headboard, wrap a used fabric softener sheet around a yardstick and secure it with a rubber band. The dust clings to this sheet better than the magic dusters advertised on late-night TV.

Cabin Wood Wonders

Before varnishing cabin teak, turn off any cabin air-conditioning and heat units, which can circulate dust and dirt. But make sure you have sufficient ventilation before you begin work. The best ambient temperature for varnishing is 70–90°F.

To add shine to listless wood cabin furniture, rub it with a rag dipped lightly in vinegar before polishing. Allow the vinegar to dry thoroughly before applying the polish.

To remove wood cabin furniture polish buildup, blend ½ cup vinegar and ½ cup water. Dip a clean, soft cloth in the solution and rub in to loosen and dissolve the polish buildup. Dry immediately with a clean cloth.

Stuck Cabin Doors and Drawers

Warm weather and dampness cause wood to swell and stick. Sticking cabin doors and drawers open easily if you rub candle wax in the runners. Or aim a warm blowdryer at them for a few minutes to counteract the moisture and the swelling. A dehumidifier, which helps prevent cabin mildew, should help, too. If you still need to fix the problem, wait for a cool day, and then sand the drawer or door slowly with sandpaper just until it moves freely.

WINDOWS

Sparkling Windows

To make cabin windows and mirrors sparkle, dip a clean cloth in a mixture of half borax and half water or denatured alcohol, and then wipe down. Polish with a lint-free rag or paper towel. This works exceptionally well on windows that have salt spray buildup.

Neglected Windows

To clean windows that you've put off cleaning for so long that they're now absolutely filthy and completely daunting, add 3 tablespoons clear ammonia (not sudsy ammonia, which will leave streaks) or 3 tablespoons vinegar to a small bucket of cool water. ***NOTE:*** Do not use both ammonia and vinegar as they will neutralize each other.

Particular Problems

For particularly hard spots, use full-strength rubbing alcohol or mineral spirits, a clean rag, and some elbow grease.

Smoking boaters can use a mixture of half ammonia and half water to clean the smoke residue off the interior of cabin windows that are becoming opaque.

Clean with a Plan

To make cleaning small windows easier, cut a squeegee to the exact window size. First remove the rubber blade, and then use a saw to trim the metal blade holder. A pair of good scissors or garden snips should be all that's needed to cut the rubber blade to match. For a streak-free cleaning, run the squeegee across the top of the window pane, wipe the blade, and then run the squeegee in downward strokes, starting at the bottom of the horizontal line just squeegeed. Use overlapping strokes to eliminate water lines at the edges.

Methodical Is Best

To get the most out of your cabin window cleaning, wipe the outside with horizontal strokes and the inside with vertical strokes. This makes it easy to tell which side those last few streaks marring your perfect job are on, so that you can eliminate them instantly.

Adding Sweat to Your Cleaning

Another way to make window cleaning quicker and easier is to use an old all-cotton sweat sock on both hands. Wash with one hand, and dry with the other.

Brrrrr!

To keep frost from accumulating on cabin windows during winter storage, add 2 cups antifreeze or rubbing alcohol to each gallon of wash water.

Paint Removal

If your last bottom paint spraying left tiny paint flakes on your cabin windows, saturate the paint spots with a cloth dipped in vinegar to soften the dried paint. Scrape off with an ice scraper or, if necessary, a razor.

A traditional method for removing old bottom paint splatter on cabin windows is to use Murphy's Oil Soap and water. This cleans most bottom paint splatters off cabin windows and boat woodwork, often even weeks after the paint has dried.

Hard Water Cleanup

If hard water leaves a cloudy film on your glass, rub the glass with warm vinegar to loosen the film buildup, and then wash with bottled or filtered water. This works equally well with windows that have a buildup from dirty rainwater.

Protect Your Cabin from Sun Damage

Taping a reflective vinyl coating to the inside of cabin windows will protect the cabin furnishings and curtains from the harsh effects of the sun. It will also keep the cabin cooler and more pleasant to use.

Budget Privacy

To cover cabin or head windows from prying eyes at your dock, mix 4 tablespoon Epsom salts in ½ pint flat beer, and paint on with a brush to create temporarily opaque windows. To remove, wash with a mixture of half borax and half water.

Windows Are for Looking Out, Not Leaking

Leaks around cabin window seals can be tough to caulk, especially when the recess between the window and fiberglass is thin. Normal caulk guns spread too wide a bead to seal the leak without getting caulk on the fiberglass and window. Solve the problem by loading a small plastic syringe (sold in most boating stores for epoxy repair) with caulk. Cut the syringe opening to fix your window's recess.

Cabin Blind Tricks

To prevent dust from settling on cabin blinds, rub them with a fabric softener sheet.

Clean cabin blinds by soaking them in a bathtub with 2 cups white vinegar. The vinegar won't rot the strings but it will loosen the grime!

Window Screen Wisdom

Use a vacuum to periodically clean dirty window screens while they're still in place to save yourself the trouble of removing them for washing and replacing them.

To make metal window screens last longer, paint them yearly with a light coating of spar varnish.

To keep aluminum cabin window screens clean, remove them every few months and scrub down both sides with a rag dipped in kerosene. Wipe off the excess and allow to dry. The remaining kerosene will act as a rust inhibitor. ***WARNING:*** Work with kerosene only in a well-ventilated area away from open flame.

Do-It-Yourself Window Screen Repair

The quickest way to repair a small hole in a cabin window screen (whether metal or fiberglass) is to push the weave back together and seal with clear nail polish, to keep out small bugs.

To repair a larger hole in a fiberglass screen, remove the screen and lay it flat in a work area. Place a sheet of aluminum foil beneath the hole in the screen. Place a fiberglass patch over the hole, and put another piece of aluminum foil over the spot. Run a hot iron around the edges of the patch. The heat fuses the old fiberglass screen and the new. Remove the foil and reinstall the screen. Metal screens can be quickly mended with an inexpensive patch kit available at most home maintenance superstores.

CABIN CARPET

No-Steam Carpet Cleaning

For quick cleanup of moderate dirt on cabin carpet, wet a towel with carpet shampoo solution or carpet cleaner such as Resolve. Wring the towel out until it's nearly dry, and then rub it back and forth over the offending stain while it's still fresh to gently absorb the offending spots. By lessening the amount of cleaning fluid used on the carpet, you're lessening the drying time and, if you can't ventilate the cabin properly, the chance of the wet carpet leading to a mildew problem.

Enhance Your Steam Cleaning

When using a steam cleaner to clean your cabin carpets, use ½ cup baking soda to each gallon of warm water, instead of using the chemical cleaning solution suggested. Sprinkle extra baking soda on particularly heavy stains, and then steam clean as usual. Baking soda is biodegradable and better for the marine environment than chemical solution.

Save $$

To save $$ on your cabin cleaning supplies, buy them at a janitorial supply store (found in the Yellow Pages under "Janitorial Supply" or "Custodial Supply").

Static Reduction

To eliminate static in your cabin carpet, fill a spray bottle with water and add a teaspoon or 2 of fabric softener. Mist the carpet lightly. The fabric softener eliminates static and therefore future zaps.

When Moving Cabin Furniture

If semipermanent furnishings have left indentations in your carpet, place a damp towel over the spots and press lightly with an iron on a low setting. The indentation will rise as the towel dries.

Another method is to set the iron to steam and hold above the carpet. Carefully use your fingers to lift the fibers as they warm. Be careful not to hold the iron too close to the carpet because synthetic fibers can melt.

Finally, you can place ice cubes in the indentations. As the ice starts to melt, the water expands the carpet fiber and causes it to rise. Use your fingers to raise any ornery wet fibers to complete the job.

Make Your Carpet Do Double Duty

If you're thinking of recarpeting your cabin and want to lessen engine noise and deaden other outside sounds, consider a deep pile carpet with thick padding. Plush carpeting will both soundproof and hide cabin floors that are in bad shape.

The Most Dirt-Resistant Boat Carpet

Nylon carpet repels dirt better and cleans up more quickly and easily than carpet made from other fibers. Remember this when custom ordering your next boat.

Place ice cubes in carpet indentations left by cabin furniture. As the ice starts to melt, the carpet fibers start to rise.

Don't let concerns about pet maintenance keep your dogs off the boat.

PETS ON BOARD

What to Do When Fluffy Sheds on Board

To remove pet hair on cabin upholstery, use a facial sponge to wipe it off. The rough texture lifts hairs. If you don't have a facial sponge, run a damp household sponge over the cushions, and then vacuum up the loosened hairs.

To keep the cabin pet hair free, spray a static preventer to repel pet hairs, and vacuum often.

Sweep both deck and cabin carpet with a wet broom to pick up the majority of the hair, and then vacuum the loosened remainder.

To keep pet hair from clogging the shower drain, cover the shower drain with thin netting such as pantyhose when washing your pet. When you're done bathing the pet, scoop up the netting for quick hair disposal.

Not All Pets Have Good Sea Legs

If your pet gets seasick on the cabin carpet, use lukewarm water to clean up the mess as best you can. Then soak the area for 15 minutes in a mixture of 1 quart warm water, ½ teaspoon liquid dishwashing soap, and 1 tablespoon ammonia. Rinse well. For the seasick animal: once her stomach has calmed sufficiently to hold down liquids, give her a small amount of milk to settle it further.

General Pet Grime

To prevent your pet from tracking dirty footprints on your deck and cabin carpet, toss some old towels just inside the doorway so that the animal will wipe his feet just by virtue of crossing the towels.

If your pet dries off on your carpet and upholstery after a saltwater swim, first allow the spots to dry, and then brush off the excess salt that has accumulated on top of the carpet or fabric. Warm water dissolves most other salts remaining in the material. In some cases, vinegar can be used to successfully restore color. Test a spot in a discreet area first.

Keep Your Dog from Turning Green

If your dog suffers from seasickness at the start of a voyage, but he's fine from then on, don't feed him for 6 hours prior to setting out. If possible, don't give the dog water for 2 hours before leaving. Feed and water the dog as soon as he gets his sea legs. To give him a special treat, freeze a bowl of water in an empty butter tub with a lid; in warm weather, it will soon melt and be deliciously cool to drink.

If the stress of boating has a different effect and makes your dog constipated, add a teaspoon of vegetable oil to his food each day. The oil will also cause your dog's fur to shine. (And don't forget to walk him every time you dock!)

Breaking a Puppy's Bad Habits

To keep a boisterous puppy out of certain areas, mix 1 teaspoon black pepper and 1 tablespoon paprika with ¼ cup oil of cloves to make your own natural puppy-repeller. A stamp moistener bottle makes a convenient applicator. Seal the spongy tip with aluminum foil if you don't use the mixture all at once.

To keep a puppy whose new hobby is scratching on a certain piece of cabin furniture from causing permanent damage, use double-sided tape to securely attach a piece of sandpaper to the spot where she likes to scratch. This should prevent further damage to the area and give puppy a manicure at the same time.

To stop chewing and peeing puppies, scent the areas they're damaging with oil of clove. The odor isn't perceptible to humans but is offensive to dogs.

To keep a persistent dog off your cabin furniture, place aluminum foil over her favorite spot. The crackling noise and ensuing confusion your pet will encounter when jumping up on foil will usually be enough to make her seek a new nap spot.

Insomniac Boat Dogs

Puppies, and even some adult dogs, may not sleep well on a boat. If you find yourself with an insomniac pet, wrap a ticking clock in a towel and place it in his bed. It will comfort him just as his mother's heartbeat did when he was first born.

Pets, like children, need their own appropriately sized PFD.

Cool Weather Cruising Canines

When cruising in cool weather, your dog's skin may become dry, causing her to itch and scratch. To stop this painful process, add a teaspoon of vegetable oil to the dog's food each day (use less for small dogs). This should stop the itching and make her coat shiny. Discontinue immediately if diarrhea results.

Do the pads of your dog's feet become rough and cracked as you walk her at the marina in winter climates? Is there snow around? Salt and other chemicals used to melt snow can hurt a dog's feet. If you must walk her in this environment, get her booties. You can also use petroleum jelly to soothe and moisturize dry, cracked paw pads.

If You Can't Bring Fido along on Your Cruise . . .

Replace his regular ID tag, the one with your contact info on it, with a tag that has his sitter's name and phone number to avoid having your pet's rescuer calling in his whereabouts to an empty house.

Is the Cat's Litter Box Odor Taking over Your Cabin?

A smelly litter box can ruin your entire boating excursion. To keep your cat's litter box odors inoffensive, mix a full box of fresh cat litter with 16 ounces baking soda and 4 teaspoons dried mint (or any other natural scent of your choice). Of course, you will still have to scoop out all solid matter daily, but this deodorizing should keep you from getting to the point where you're ready to sell either your boat or the cat.

To eradicate cat litter box odors in the head (where most people keep litter boxes), wipe down the box and the surrounding area with a cloth lightly dipped in ammonia.

Cleaning a litter box in the cramped quarters of a small boat often means making a mess. To keep things neat and tidy, slide the litter box into a large, sturdy garbage bag before dumping it directly into that same bag. This will eliminate mess and the dust cloud that chokes you as you shift the litter around.

Cat Litter Alternative

If you run out of cat litter while on the water, put shredded newspaper in her litter box (which she's already used to using). It will not be as absorbent, but it will work.

Cat Litter Psychology

Some cats on their first boat trip have been known to choose an area other than their litter box as a bathroom. If this happens with your cat, move the litter box to that spot, and then slowly shift the litter box back toward its original spot, effectively guiding the cat with it.

Hairballs on Deck

To keep Kitty from barfing up hairballs all over your boat, give him a small amount of mineral oil or petroleum jelly once a month to settle things down in his tummy and make hair exit the natural way. ***NOTE:*** It's best to start this practice well before you start your boat trip.

Keep Kitty's Fur on Her

To keep your cat from shedding on board, wipe her down daily with a sponge dipped in water and baking soda solution to remove loose hairs.

Keep Kitty's Claws Away from Your Cabin Furniture

To keep kitty from scratching up your furnishings when you don't have room in your cabin to install a full-size scratching post, Velcro a carpet remnant to the appropriate available surface and sprinkle catnip on it. When the cat finally uses the carpet as a scratching spot, don't forget to reinforce her good behavior with petting and praise.

If Kitty continues scratching your wooden furniture, despite having a makeshift scratching post, wipe down the wood with chili sauce and blot dry. The odor isn't perceptible to humans but is offensive to cats.

The Cat Belongs on the Floor with His Food Bowl

Some cats like to jump up on the galley counters. To stop this behavior, put disposable aluminum pans or aluminum foil on the counter. The cat won't like the feeling of landing on them and the resulting noise. He'll soon find a new way to amuse himself.

Bathing on a Rocking Boat

Before you bathe your cat on a rocking boat, put a drop of mineral oil in each of the cat's eyes to prevent soap irritation.

Pets Yes, Fleas No

If Fido and Fluffy have brought additional guests—fleas—on board, lightly cover your deck and cabin carpet with borax, allow it to sit for a few hours, and then vacuum it up. Reapply the borax generously, this time letting it sit for a few days until the flea eggs hatch, and then vacuum it up completely. You can use this treatment as often as necessary. Plus you'll get the bonus of cleaner carpet. Don't forget to use the vacuum nozzle on all corners and crevices, where eggs may have been laid. Toss a couple of mothballs into the vacuum bag to kill any fleas that might have been taken alive.

If fleas have invaded your cabin cushions and bedding, place some cedar shavings or pine needles underneath your mattress if you're going to be sleeping on it, or both below and on top of the mattress if you won't be using the boat for a few days. The smell will make the fleas move to more comfortable surroundings, hopefully to your borax-treated carpet, where they will die.

If fleas are in a dog or cat's foam bed, wash the bed with a briny mixture of salt and water. Salt repels fleas.

Fleas on You

When the summer flea problem is so bad that they've gotten on you also, don't turn around and head for home (unless of course you're allergic to flea bites and are therefore in medical danger). Instead, take a daily bath with a soap that contains green dye, such as Irish Spring. The green dye and its accompanying scent are unappetizing to hungry fleas.

Fleas on Pets

Never combine use of a flea collar with flea powder, no matter how buggy the area you're traveling in. It could result in a toxic overdose.

Mosquito Alert

If your pet is being attacked by mosquitoes, you can use Avon's Skin-So-Soft on dogs and cats to repel the needle-nose biters. Do a tiny "patch test" first to make sure the product doesn't irritate your pet's skin.

Can You Hear Me?

If your pet gets an itchy ear, perhaps from swimming in buggy water, wash the inside and exterior of the ear with a solution of 4 parts warm water and 1 part baking soda.

Tick Treatment

If your pet picks up a tick in the bushes near a questionable dock, rub the embedded tick with a cotton ball saturated in alcohol, and then grab as much of the tick as possible with your fingers or tweezers and pull it straight out. Try not to twist the tick when removing, or part may break off beneath the skin. Be careful not

SIGNS OF A TICK YOU CAN'T FIND

Signs that a dog may have a tick in his ear, where you may not be able to see it, are

- Fever
- Excessive shaking of the head, often while keeping the affected side held down
- An unexplained circling to or tipping over to the affected side
- Lack of interest in food and water, or an inability to eat and drink

If you suspect an embedded tick, transport your pet to the nearest vet immediately.

Lyme Disease and Other Pet Concerns

Other pet owner worries, depending on the area where you're traveling, are Lyme disease (signs of which are lameness, swollen and painful joints, fever, and a hesitancy to move), and Rocky Mountain Spotted Fever (signs of which include general weakness, fever of 105°F or higher, stomach tenderness, and water retention in the legs). If you suspect either disease rush your pet to the nearest medical care, and be sure to keep the tick after you remove it so the vet can examine it and make the most accurate diagnosis.

to crush the tick, or infectious fluids will be released. Do not handle a tick with bare hands; use gloves or a paper towel. Use rubbing alcohol to rinse the area from which you removed the tick to prevent infection.

Shock

If your dog's gums are a pale white, he may be either in shock or having an anemic reaction to fleas, ticks, or worms. Give him a spoonful of honey, and take him to the nearest vet.

STOW-AWAYS (BUGS AND VERMIN)

Environmentally Friendly Wasp Removal

To rid your boat of wasps, make a small hole in a sealed plastic container containing a solution of sugar and water and hang it in the engine compartment, cabin, or wherever the wasps have chosen to nest. The wasps will go in to get the sugar water, but they can't get out.

Many-Legged Guests Eating in the Galley

If bugs are constantly getting into your galley and food, place unwrapped spearmint gum sticks on the shelves. This keeps most many-legged varmints away, as does sprinkling black pepper, which works especially well with

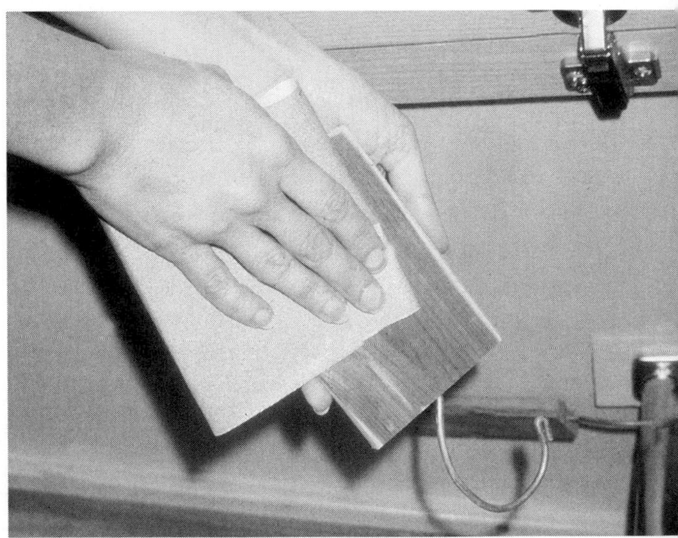

Cedar hangings help keep bugs out of your boat; sand them regularly to reactivate their effectiveness.

roaches. Also, you can put a few dried bay leaves in your containers to repel tiny intruders. Sealed glass jars are best for keeping unwanted pests out of boat food.

If bugs have taken up residence beneath the galley sink, liberally sprinkle boric acid under the sink, in cracks, and around drains and other openings. Bugs will track the boric acid back to their nests and die. ***NOTE:*** Keep children and pets away from areas containing boric acid to avoid accidental contact or ingestion.

Roach Balls

To keep roaches away, place homemade roach balls in the corners and backs of cabinets. Mix 1 cup borax, 1/4 cup sugar, 1/4 cup chopped onion, 1 tablespoon cornstarch, and 1 tablespoon water, make into a paste, and form nickel-sized balls. These roach balls will effectively combat roaches without having a noxious bug poison scent.

Water Bugs

To evict water bugs, get the rubbing alcohol out of your comprehensive first aid kit and put some into a pump bottle. Spray any and all water bugs that you see.

Flies Don't Use Hair Spray

Spray flying insects with hair spray when you run out of pesticide spray. Hair spray will clog their pores and breathing passages, while inhibiting movement as it dries.

A Mouse in the House

To rid your boat of mice, soak cardboard squares in peppermint extract and place where you suspect the mice are getting on board. It will not only act as a Do Not Enter sign to the mice but will freshen and deodorize wherever it has been placed.

The Bug That Signals More Bugs

The centipede's diet consists of eating other bugs. So if you see centipedes, you may have a real problem on your hands. Check further. Fumigating the boat may be in order.

Ants as Clues to the Condition of Your Boat

Carpenter ants like a moist environment. So if you have carpenter ants on board, you might also have leaks. After the leaks are discovered and repaired, if the ant situation is severe, call a professional exterminator; otherwise, treat with home-use pesticides designed for carpenter ant problems.

Boats Can Get Termites, Too

Termites are finicky eaters and devour only the soft part of your boat's wood. A sure sign of termites is gutted soft wood with hard grains and rings that are left completely intact. Call an exterminator immediately.

The Fragrant Bug Repellant

Cedar closet hangings help keep moths and bugs out of a stored boat. Sand the cedar every few months to reactivate their effectiveness.

Stop Bugs on the Dock

Prevent ants from coming on board by spraying docklines, shore power cords, and so on with ant repellent where they touch the dock.

Using Science to Knock out Flying Pests

If your cabin becomes inundated with flies from a shore breeze and your boat is air-conditioned, you're in luck. Shut all the doors and hatches and crank up the air. The chill will make the pests lethargic and easy to swat.

chapter 4

THE ENGINE

INBOARD TIPS

Start as You Plan to Go

Never start up an inboard engine that has been out of the water without first priming the pump. Remove the hose closest to the inlet side or a zinc plug, and pour in at least a quart of water to prevent the impeller from running dry on the first few revolutions as the engine turns over.

Irritable Starting

If your older inboard refuses to start right away in wet weather, check the distributor cap. Chances are it's cracked and allowing moisture into the ignition system. Spray with a moisture-displacer such as WD-40 or Corrosion Block on the distributor cap and the ignition system.

Protect Before You Clean

On older engines, before you spray engine cleaner, cover the distributor, coil, and carburetor with plastic wrap to avoid damaging these sensitive areas. Take off the carburetor's rainhat first so you can wrap the carburetor more easily. Protect any oxygen sensors and other electronic controls because some can be damaged through contact with water.

Environmentally Friendly Wire Flame Arrestor Cleaning

Clean wire flame arrestors by soaking them in a pan of hot water and baking soda. The oily residue wafts off and floats to the top of the pan. Dry thoroughly before running the engine.

Keep Your Inboard's Temperature Down

To unclog a heat exchanger that is not attached to an aluminum block engine, drain the old liquids and replace them with 1 pound of baking soda dissolved in a gallon of water. Start the boat and let it run for several minutes. Drain the heat exchanger once again, and refill it this time with antifreeze.

Water Belongs Under Your Hull, Not in Your Fuel

If you suspect there's water in your fuel, remove your fuel filter/water separator cartridge and dump its contents into a clean mayonnaise jar. Keep the jar still for several minutes. If water is present, it will settle to the bottom of the jar, and the gas will float on top. If you think you have water in your lube oil, heat a few tablespoons in a frying pan; if it boils, there's water present.

Cold Starts

Although it's never a good idea to rev a cold engine, especially a diesel, before it reaches operating temperature, running up your turbocharged diesel just before shutting it down could be the kiss of death. Why? Because the turborotor will keep spinning even after shutdown, and it won't be getting lube oil. That means wear and tear.

Get More for Your Money

Want more mileage for your money? For diesels, the best cruising speed for extended running is approximately 400 rpm below wide-open throttle (depending on sea conditions).

The Pro's Diesel Test

Afraid a boatyard has been selling dirty diesel? This happens most often in foreign ports, but it happens stateside too. Bad fuel shuts down a diesel engine quickly and can lead to expensive repairs. Keep a close eye on the fuel entering your boat by inserting a cone-shaped coffee filter in a funnel. Pump the first few gallons slowly through the funnel, and then pull out the filter and check it for contaminants.

Black Diesel Smoke

Black smoke coming out of your diesel engine could mean an improper air-to-fuel ratio. Check your air filter; it may look fine, but some of the cheaper paper filters don't allow enough airflow to move through. Also, look for collapsed hoses or a plugged exhaust. Injection pump problems can also cause black smoke. If you suspect this is the problem, call your mechanic.

White Diesel Smoke

White diesel smoke accompanied by a strong fuel smell usually indicates that the engine temperature is too low to burn the fuel properly. This problem is common in cold weather, when it takes your engine a while to heat up. Faulty plugs or a low engine cranking speed can also be at fault. If the engine continues to emit white smoke after reaching full operating temperature, your engine's timing might be off. Adjust accordingly. Air in the fuel lines can also be the culprit. Make sure that all hose connections are tight. Low engine compression and faulty injectors are two other potential problems that need to be checked out by a professional.

Don't Let Your Engine Run Away with the Situation

Your diesel engine is "running away"—running uncontrollably—and you need to stop it fast! The quickest and least dangerous way to stop it is to discharge a carbon dioxide fire extinguisher into the air intake. Remember to vacate the engine room immediately so you're not breathing carbon dioxide. Vent the engine room thoroughly before reentering.

Packing Gland Advice

You continually tighten the boat's packing gland or glands, but they still leak. The solution? Keep in mind that the packing glands should drip occasionally to keep the shaft cool. But if the water's pouring through the gland, it's time to retighten or repack. Replace the flax packing with industrial-grade Teflon-impregnated square gland packing. Smear the packing with Teflon grease when installing.

Don't Forget the Propshaft Seals

Yes, it's been turning regularly, but don't bypass removing the propeller and thrust washer to examine the propshaft seals for signs of fishing line or other waterborne trash. Clean the shaft splines and grease the shaft. On inboard boats, clear away any fishing line caught in the cutlass bearing, or it can literally saw through your shaft.

Small Parts Need Not Be a Big Hassle

Prevent losing small screws and parts by stretching a towel or rag under your working area. With luck, it'll catch any small bits and pieces you drop.

When you drop a brass washer or stainless steel screw into a crevice smaller than your fingers, use a screwdriver tipped with grease to recover it. The same grease-tipped screwdriver can be used to start tiny machine screws into their holes.

OUTBOARD TIPS

Proper Priming of a Cold Engine

To start a cold engine, squeeze the primer bulb until it is firm, and then slightly advance the throttle and operate the choke while cranking until the engine fires. If the engine fires but chokes out after a few seconds or minutes, repeat without using the choke. If it still dies, try bumping the choke a little until it stabilizes.

Flywheel Won't Engage?

Your outboard starter won't engage the flywheel? Try putting a drop of oil on the starter shaft at the pinion gear. This might do the trick, but if it doesn't, don't go crazy with the oil. Too much, and the hub could slip when the engine's engaged.

To clean flooded spark plugs, wash them in gasoline and allow them to air dry.

When the Plugs Are Too Wet to Spark

To clean a spark plug that has been flooded and is too wet to start, remove the plug and wash it with gasoline (not a gasoline/oil mixture) and allow to air dry. For faster results, carefully burn off the excess gas. Turn the motor over to blow out the lines before replacing the plug.

Lessening Speeds

In cases where the engine runs fine but boat speed is less than usual, the conditions of the prop, the boat's bottom, or boat load, and/or an increase in relative humidity and temperature could be to blame. First check the prop and make sure it's not damaged. Nothing can bring down speed more quickly than a dinged prop. If you keep your boat moored in a slip, peak performance can be maintained only if the hull is kept clean. As you add gear (and thus weight), boat speed decreases. Remove extra gear that you really don't need. High heat and humidity also rob your engine of horsepower, but there's no cure for that but to avoid boating on hot, humid days.

A Quick Compression Primer

Compression values vary from one outboard manufacturer to another, but values between cylinders should not exceed 10 to 15 percent. Generally, an OMC engine needs new rings when it falls below 85#, whereas a Mercury commonly needs them replaced when pressure readings are in the 160# range. This gives you an idea of the wide variety of compression ratings, but you need to check in your outboard manual for your exact rating. ***NOTE:*** A tune-up will never improve an engine with poor compression.

Quick Cleanups

To clean a dirty nondisposable fuel filter element quickly, wash it down with gasoline.

Furniture polish is good for a quick cleanup of the crud that seems to appear inevitably on the cowling of your outboard.

Covering a Cowling Is Easier than Restoring

If the cowling on the motor of your boat is getting faded, turn a large tote bag upside down to make a small engine cover. Secure the carry straps together so that the bag doesn't blow away.

Get That Impeller Installed

The impeller fits in the pump housing but is still reluctant to go all the way in? No problem. Just take a block of wood, place it over the impeller, and tap it in with a small mallet. If access is limited, try levering it in with a small piece of wood from each side. Coat the inside of the pump housing and shaft with waterproof grease to make life easier.

Cooling System Cleanout

Does your outboard's cooling water tell-tale seem to be spitting less water than usual? Clean the outflow tube with a piece of heavy monofilament fishing line. Just slide it up the tube and work it back and forth. Then start the engine and check out the flow. It if hasn't improved and you're sure the intake isn't clogged, the water pump may need to be replaced.

Need to get dried mud out of your outboard's water intake holes, but you're afraid of knocking some dirt back into the intake? Bend a paperclip into a fishhook shape, insert it in the closest clear intake hole, and knock out the dirt from the inside.

Oil ℞

If the oil reservoir from your outboard is down in a compartment where it's hard to reach, try pouring oil through a long-stemmed funnel first. If that doesn't help, buy an inexpensive wood-pulp-based oil-absorbent mat. Cut it into strips and line the compartment so they catch spills. When they fill with oil, remove and replace with new strips.

Need to check your outboard oil injection reservoir for water, oil, and debris without emptying the tank? The best tool for the job is a turkey baster. Remove the fill cap, and use the baster to pull a sample from the lowest point. If you can't reach the bottom of the reservoir, extend the baster with a hose.

Clean the Plugs Without Opening the Cowling

If you've been idling for a while, chances are you've gotten a bit of carbon buildup on the spark plugs. Give the engine a short burst of high revs, if possible, to burn off the excess carbon.

Spark Plug Checkup

Examine spark plug wires and terminals at least twice a year. Look for nicks, cuts, or other dam-

ETHANOL ISSUES

Know Your Fuel

After it was determined in the early 2000s that MTBE caused health and environmental concerns, ethanol was chosen to replace it as an oxygenate in fuel to create a 10 percent ethanol, 90 percent gasoline mix called E10. While ethanol is a fuel that can be used to power engines all on its own, some issues need to be considered when it is added to gasoline. Ethanol does not produce as much energy as gasoline; thus, engines running on E10 fuel cannot reach the same wide-open throttle speeds as those fueled by 100 percent gasoline, and they will experience reduced fuel efficiency as seen in a reduced overall cruising range. Because ethanol does not chemically bond to gasoline, E10 (or E15, E20, etc.) fuel begins to degrade in as short a period as a month after the two are mixed. As the ethanol-blended fuel ages, the "light ends" begin to evaporate, leaving behind gums and other solids that can clog fuel injectors, carburetors, and fuel filters. As a result, engines are more difficult to start and will often run poorly.

Additionally, because ethanol is an alcohol, it attracts and chemically bonds with moisture that can further degrade the overall fuel quality. If there is more than .5 percent moisture in the fuel, the ethanol/water mix literally falls out of the gasoline, settling to the bottom of the fuel tank to form a distinct layer. This is *phase separation*. Yet another ethanol issue is the fact that it can degrade plastic and rubber, leading to fuel line or primer bulb failure, as well as damage to fuel-delivery components.

Despite its many issues, E10 can be used as a marine fuel, but it needs to be treated in order to mitigate most of the problems. However, no fuel treatment can "remove" ethanol or prevent it from damaging plastic or rubber, so alcohol-resistant fuel lines and other parts need to be used. And no treatments can remove water or make it burn—these are chemically impossible tasks. Traditional fuel stabilizers that are great for use in 100 percent gas simply cannot solve ethanol problems, including the loss of power, water absorption, and gum formation. Just stabilizing is not sufficient. One fuel treatment that has proved to be effective at resolving ethanol issues is the unique Star Tron. Originally developed for industrial use by power companies, commer-

Ethanol fuel requires its own class of fuel treatments such as enzyme-based Star Tron.

cial fishing vessels, and municipal bus fleets, it uses a blend of enzymes that allows fuel hydrocarbons to burn more completely, disperses moisture throughout the fuel so that it can be eliminated as the engine runs, disperses gums and other debris so that they can be burned off in the combustion phase, and stabilizes fuel for up to 2 years, making it ideal for boats that are in long-term storage. When treating ethanol-blended fuels, take care not to use those containing alcohol or its derivatives. Some additives actually contain ethylene glycol—automotive antifreeze—or chemicals more often used to dry clean clothing. Additional amounts of alcohol will only exacerbate the negative aspects of E10. ***NOTE:*** E85 is a mixture of 85 percent alcohol and 15 percent gas. While your car or truck may run on E85, chances are your boat will not, since this fuel requires specific fuel-delivery-system upgrades not often found in marine applications.

age. Spark plug wires can get caught on the motor cover when you're installing it, causing the wires to become damaged. Similar conditions can happen on other outboards as well.

Vibrating Outboard Diagnostics

When your outboard begins to vibrate excessively, chances are it's either a damaged prop or a bent prop shaft. First check your prop's blades. If there's no damage and the prop is securely attached to the shaft, try running your engine using your spare prop and see if it makes a difference. If it still vibrates, the culprit is most likely a bent prop shaft. By removing the prop and shifting your engine into neutral, you can easily rotate the prop shaft by hand. While turning the shaft, watch its end for wobble. If it wobbles, it's definitely bent and needs to be replaced.

Inconsistent Idling

An engine that runs fine at higher speeds but idles erratically can be caused by many things, but most of those causes would also affect how the engine performs at higher speeds. When only idling is affected, you most likely have a problem with the electrical or fuel system. Start by installing a fresh set of spark plugs. Heat range of spark plugs used with 2-cycle engines is critical. When buying the spark plugs, follow the outboard manufacturer's recommendations. Incorrect spark plugs could lead to engine failure. On older outboard engines, if new plugs don't solve the problem, try resetting the carburetor idle mixture screws according to the maintenance manual that came with your motor. While adjusting the carburetors, also check for fuel "spit-back" coming out of the venturi of the carburetors. Fuel coming out of the carburetors at idle indicates that your engine has cracked or broken reed valves. This type of failure is usually caused by overrevving the engine, and repairs are best left to the experts.

Air Vent Hole Leak

Is your older Johnson or Evinrude outboard suddenly squirting water out the air vent hole in the thermostat housing? If the bypass valve doesn't seat perfectly, it will allow water to pump right past it and out the vent hole. Take off the cover and clean all the salt and sand out of the thermostat and bypass valve housing. Use a new gasket when you reinstall the housing cover.

When Your Outboard Acts Sluggish Under Load

Your outboard idles fine but bogs down under load? A common cause is a cracked or displaced O-ring at either the tank or engine. The O-ring can be pushed out of place by someone trying to hook up the fuel connector backward. Have someone squeeze the primer bulb as you try to throttle up. If the engine suddenly regains power, you've found the problem. Replace the O-rings.

Exhaust Smoke

There's thick smoke coming out of your post-1987 Yamaha's exhaust. Bad news and big bucks? It could be if you don't know a simple secret. The on-engine oil reservoir has a screen that, if not properly aligned, can hold down the oil level float; it's telling the pump to send more oil. The oil reservoir overflows, and oil leaks through a vent line into the carburetor's air silencer. Once sucked into the engine, the oil-rich mixture produces a nasty white cloud. It's no big problem if you know where to look.

Slow-Cranking Warm Outboard

Your engine's warm so you don't bother priming it, but getting it started takes a lot of cranking. There seems to be fuel flowing, so it must be the ignition. Not always. It could also be a tiny air leak in your fuel line or in an in-line fuel filter or the water/fuel separator filter that's not big enough to seep gas but just large enough to allow air rather than a healthy shot of fuel to be drawn into the combustion chamber, which makes starting a lot harder, if not impossible. This isn't a problem with a cold start because the engine is primed and the bowl filled. Check and tighten all hose clamps and fittings.

Four-Cycle Complaints

Your older, carbureted four-cycle is not running smoothly like normal. It sounds like a cylinder isn't firing, so you go right to the ignition system. But a better place to start is the carburetor's jets. Four-cycle engines have small jets that are easy to clog. Remove each one and clean with a thin strand of unraveled household wire. Don't blast them with an air hose while they're still on the carburetor because this will only push the clog farther in. Drain the bowls if you're letting the engine sit for more than a month. Honda engines have valves on their carburetors that take a ³⁄₈-inch hose for draining.

Correct Gasket Installation

You pop the bowl on your under-40 hp Evinrude and wipe it with a lint-free rag (not a paper towel, whose fibers can clog the carburetor). You even reassemble it with a new bowl gasket. But now the engine won't start. It's hard to believe you did anything wrong, so you look elsewhere for the problem. Check the gasket: You might simply have put it in upside down and covered a tiny hole for the low-speed jet. It happens all the time.

Corrosion Inspection

Sounds like an ignition problem, but the plugs and wires look fine, and you're loath to dig into one of those high-tech black boxes. But it's not a dead end, for the answer is often very low-tech. For instance, on pre-1990 Hondas the ignition coil is grounded through its base. If there's corrosion between it and the engine block, you lose juice. Just look for any buildup of white crud. Removal and a wire brushing may be all it takes.

Don't Forget to Check the Fuel Pump Diaphragm

You're using way too much gas and leaving a thick cloud of foul blue smoke. Looks like it's time to rebuild the carburetor, clean the fuel injectors, or replace the piston rings, which means it's time for that second mortgage. Then again, it could cost only $4 because your fuel pump's diaphragm has blown out. If you keep pumping the priming bulb, but it never gets hard, it means the fuel is just dribbling down into the crankcase and not being held in the pump.

Keep Your Spare Parts out of the Water

You need to work on your outboard while waves are tossing the boat around? Sounds like a great way to drop tools or engine parts overboard. To keep everything inside the boat, after tilting the motor up, drape a towel under it and secure two corners to the skeg or prop with tape, one corner to each side. Then secure the other corners to the transom on either side of the motor. The towel will catch flying parts and tools when your fingers fumble.

Throttle Cable Repairs at Sea

The connecting rod between your small outboard's throttle cable and throttle vibrates loose and falls overboard while you're at sea. Now what? If you're with a crew, have someone sit safely in the stern and operate it manually, but if you're cruising solo, try this quick fix: Push the end of the throttle cable into the eraser of a pencil until it's solid, and then break off the pencil to the appropriate length and tape the end to the throttle. Use it as little as possible, preferably once to get up to speed and once to slow down. If the cable pulls out of the eraser when you try to slow down, use your kill switch.

Stuck Prop

Your prop is stuck to the shaft? You should have greased it better before putting the prop on. For now, you'll have to take alternative action: First, loosen the retaining nut and lower the drive unit into the water. Then start the motor and keep it at idle speed. Shift in and out of forward and reverse briefly. The change in direction should break the prop free.

Shear Pin Surgery

Broken shear pins can be temporarily repaired by moving the part that was in the middle of the shear pin to one end and reassembling the prop unit. You will now have drive on only one side of the boss (grooved shaft end), so keep your speed low and you should be able to limp a few miles.

RPM Protection

You're trimmed up for all-out speed and the tach is at the redline. Suddenly the buzzer goes off, the engine quits, and your heart stops. Blown engine? More likely the problem is only the rev-limiter that's kicked in. Put the engine in neutral and start again, making sure the engine isn't overheated.

STERN DRIVE TIPS

Cooling System Tests

Having a cooling problem with your OMC, Volvo Penta, or other drive where the water pump is mounted on the engine? First, check to see if the intake is clogged. If it's okay, temporarily insert a section of clear plastic hose ahead of the pump's suction side. If you see bubbles, there is a leak somewhere in the system. If the hose collapses, the problem is a clog between the pump and the intake.

Beware of High Pressure

High-pressure washdowns can generate up to 3,000 pounds of pressure. This is enough to cut into the rubber bellows or blow past a seal. Keep the spray away from the prop, exhaust, universal joint bellows, and trim cylinders.

10 CLUES THAT YOU'VE GONE OVERBOARD ON BOAT MAINTENANCE

1. You spend more time at do-it-yourself boater seminars than actually cruising on the water.
2. You slouch to one side from the weight of all the multitools on your belt.
3. You single-handedly caused a Scotchgard shortage in your county when prepping your new boat's cabin.
4. You replaced the drawers under the master stateroom bed with a Craftsman tool chest.
5. You've been known to bring along your corrosion-resistant tool kit when cruising on friends' boats in the hope that they'll need some emergency work done.
6. Your ultimate boat guest would be Al Borland.
7. You've built a drive-through boat wash on the side of your house.
8. You were once kicked out of a boat club because of a heated argument about why 320-grit is better than 220-grit when sanding teak prior to varnishing.
9. You own more than 20 "wonder tools" purchased at boat shows.
10. West Marine and Star brite send you Christmas cards, thanking you for helping them have yet another record sales year.

Top-Speed Slipping?

If your top speed has dropped while revolutions per minute have risen, something is slipping. A likely suspect is the rubber sleeve on the inside of the prop's hub that acts as a shock absorber to save the blades. Draw a line on the rear of the hub and across the rubber. After running the boat, check to see if the one on the rubber still matches the one on the hub. If not, the rubber sleeve is slipping.

Listen to What Your Oil Tells You

Petroleum-based oils let you know when water has gotten into your lower unit by turning a milky brown. But synthetic oils, which do not emulsify in water, do not do this. They stay separate from water and sit above it. Your only clue that water is present is if the oil level rises (being pushed up by the water) or if there are small beads of moisture on the dipstick. To check, drain the lower unit. If there is water, it will come out before the oil.

I'm Gonna Hammer That Outdrive Right Off of My Boat

When removing a stuck gearcase or outdrive, use a rawhide hammer, rubber mallet, or inertial hammer and strike the case in the beefy areas rather than the fins or skegs. The skeg and fins are thin aluminum and are more likely to break on impact.

U-Joint and Gimbal Bearings Exam

Concerned about the condition of your stern drive's U-joint or gimbal bearings? With the engine running in neutral, turn the steering wheel hard to port and to starboard. If you hear a whining noise or there is chattering at either extreme, it is likely that the joint is in bad shape and should be inspected.

Hard Shifting

If it's getting hard to change gears, disconnect the shift cable where it meets the linkage on the stern drive. Have a helper put some tension on the end and try moving the control lever. The motion should feel silky, with no binding and only negligible friction. If it doesn't, replace the cable. If it's okay, then the problem is in the drive.

The Fastidious Oil Change

Tired of messy gear-oil changes on your outboard or inboard/outboard? Try this: Put a piece of masking tape about 4 inches long on the skeg, letting an inch or so hang off. Now when you remove the drain plug, the oil will flow down the side of the gearcase until it gets to the tape. Then it will follow the edge of the tape directly into your drain pan.

O-Ring Education

You remove two plugs to drain your stern drive's oil. On one plug the O-ring comes out with it, but the O-ring on the other stays in the housing. You go about your business and mistakenly reverse the plugs. Now one has two O-rings, and the other none. The oil leaks out, water leaks in, and problems result. Mistakes happen, but this one shouldn't. Each time you take out a plug, replace the old gasket or O-ring with a new one.

Prevent an Oil Gusher

On MerCruisers there is a reservoir for the power trim pump oil that can be opened at any time (best checked when the drive is down and the engine cool). But on OMC and Volvo Penta drives there is a sealed container. Open it while the drive is down, and you'll have an oily geyser in your engine room. The drive must be all the way up and the engine off.

Let the Sealed Out Stay Sealed Out

Don't undermine the engine manufacturer's efforts to seal out moisture from the wiring harness. When using a volt/ohmmeter to troubleshoot a system, avoid puncturing the wire insulation or connection covers with the sharp point of the probe. Capillary action will draw in dampness through even the smallest pinhole. Disconnect the wires and take a reading off their ends or at the terminals.

Shallow Runnings

If you run your stern drive rig in shallow water, chances are you'll wear the paint off the skeg when you occasionally hit sand. Aluminum needs an acid wash prior to painting to ensure good adhesion. Although commercial formulas are available, common household vinegar works, too. After sanding it to bare metal, bathe the skeg in vinegar and wipe dry. Apply primer and paint as desired.

Maintain Proper Transmission Fluid Levels

Having trouble shifting your stern drive in and out of gear? First, check the transmission fluid level; if it's overfilled, shifting will be tough. If the fluid looks good, try pulling the drain plug and look for grit or metal filings. If there's enough to roll between your fingertips, have your mechanic give the transmission a look-see.

Permanent Engine Mounting

Without a little preventive maintenance, the bolts that hold on your inboard/outboard or outboard motor's lower gearcase can corrode in place forever. Before they do, back them out, wire brush the threads, and paint on some non-hardening gasket sealer. Then torque them back into place. The sealer prevents water from getting onto the threads, knocking out corrosion before it starts.

GENERAL ENGINE TIPS

The Dry Gas Dilemma

Resist the temptation to put dry gas potions sold in auto part stores in your boat's fuel tank. These are methanol-based products and simply act as an antifreeze to prevent accumulated water in automotive fuel lines from freezing and blocking them in winter. As stated previously, you don't want to add more methanol to your boat's fuel system. If you have a large amount of water in your tank, it must be pumped out.

Zen and the Effect of Unleaded Fuels

Unleaded fuels have not been the problem many mariners originally thought. Most marine engines built since the late 1970s have hardened valves, so unless you zoom around in your boat at 80 percent or more power for long periods of time, unleaded fuels shouldn't cause excessive valve seat wear. Be sure, though, that the octane level is sufficient to prevent detonation and the fuel contains as few unwanted additives as possible. Splurge and get at least 89 octane fuel for your marine engine. A lot of the fuel sold today is of borderline quality and loses even more octane sitting around in your tank between outings.

Check Out Your Used Oil

When changing the oil, stop and take a moment to examine the oil coming out of your outboard's lower unit. Clear amber oil is the best, but what you've probably got by now is malodorous and dark. That's normal. Gray or metallic oil is a sign of heavy wear or potentially significant damage, as are large chunks of metal. All indicate that a trip to the outboard doctor is in order. Water droplets or milky-looking oil are signs that water has entered the gearcase and should be checked out more thoroughly because they indicate a leaking seal and the need for professional attention.

The difference between dirty and clean fuel injectors can be a significant amount of performance.

Oil Filter Instruction

If your spin-on filter is on too tight, removal is challenging. Use a strap-type wrench to grab the filter at the very top or the bottom—these are the strongest points and are least likely to cause the filter to crush. (Collapsed filters are almost impossible to remove without access to the filter mounts.) If the wrench slips, wrap the band with duct tape for a better grip.

Cylindrical oil filters can be slippery. If your filter wrench is slipping, get a grip by putting some sandpaper between the wrench's strap and the filter. If the filter wrench just crushes the filter without unscrewing it, move the wrench closer to the filter seat.

Oil Estimation

For a 50:1 mix of oil to gas, use 1 pint oil for every 6 gallons gas. For a 100:1 mix, use ½ pint oil for every 6 gallons gas.

Release the Oil Filter Vacuum

You know how awkward it is to change an inverted spin-on oil filter without dripping dirty lube oil all over the place. Next time punch a hole in the filter near its highest point to release the vacuum. Use an old screwdriver for this if you don't have a proper punch, and push it through the filter shell with a hammer. Wait a few minutes for the oil to drain, and then

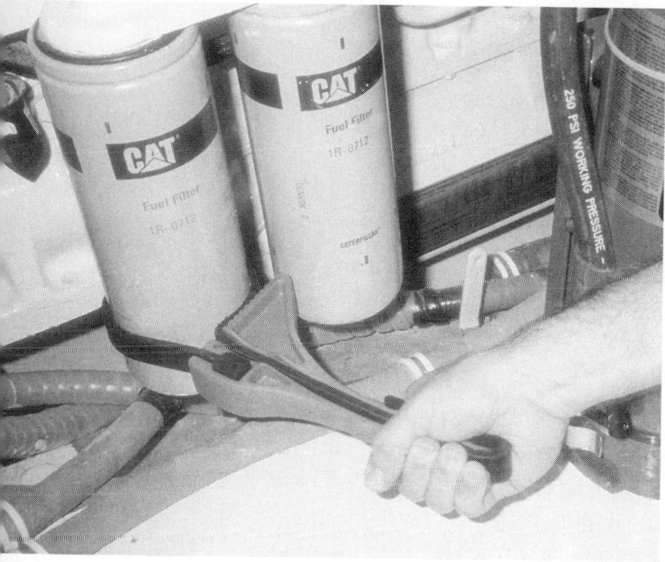

Remove a stuck spin-on oil filter with a strap-type wrench, grabbing the filter at the very top or bottom.

unscrew the filter. Position an absorbent rag to catch the residual drips.

Oil Changes Don't Have to Be Messy

Before spinning off any spin-on oil filter, slip a heavy-duty zipping plastic bag under the filter. Drop the filter into the bag, and zip the bag closed. Dispose of the old filter in an environmentally responsible manner, such as at the nearest auto parts store that accepts used oil.

Save your used disposable aluminum baking pans. When changing oil filters in tight, cramped spaces, slip a pan under the filter. You can mold the pan to fit the available space. Make sure you keep a good lip on the pan to retain any spilled oil.

Prop Helpful Hints

Increasing a propeller's pitch by 1 inch will generally reduce rpm by 150 to 200.

Your prop has some nicks and burrs, but not enough to warrant reconditioning? Use a file to smooth out the blades. While you're at it, smooth out the skeg.

Low-Impact Raw-Water Impeller Removal

No, it's not impossible to remove your raw-water impeller without destroying it. Just skip the screwdriver. Lever it out with the end of your toothbrush, working carefully from one end to the other. When you replace it, wrap a cable tie around the impeller vanes until they compress enough for the impeller to fit into the pump housing.

Carburetor ℞

Spray the carburetor and surrounding linkage with a protective lubricant such as WD-40 to make sure the linkage works freely. Performance can be significantly reduced and fuel consumption increased by a dirty flame arrestor. To prevent this, take the flame arrestor off and clean it thoroughly with carburetor cleaner spray. Be careful, though! This spray is very flammable and toxic. It should only be used outdoors, away from the boat. Also, wear rubber gloves to protect your skin. Allow the flame arrestor to dry and then reinstall it. The flame arrestor is a safety device that protects your boat from fire or explosion in case of an engine backfire. Never operate your boat unless your flame arrestor is properly installed and in good working condition. Never substitute an automotive-type air cleaner for the flame arrestor.

To check the carburetor for leaks properly, squeeze the primer bulb to pressurize the system while examining the carburetor area.

If It's Made for Land, Don't Use It on the Sea

Never substitute an automotive-type hose for any marine-rated hose. They just don't stand up well to the abuses of the marine environment and you don't want to have them fail at sea. While you're at it, check that your hose clamps and fittings are tight. Make sure all fuel filters are the proper marine-rated units for your engine. Change old elements and clean out system sediment. Replace any filter cans showing corrosion with the correct stainless marine units. Spin-on filters must be replaced once a year with the exact replacement because they can rust.

Never remove your boat's thermostat or substitute an automotive unit of a higher temperature. These thermostats regulate the engine running temperature—a higher-temperature filter will cause the engine to run too hot. Salt precipitation and corrosion increase considerably at high temperatures. Closed engine cooling systems should have a mixture of half permanent antifreeze and half water year-round to properly retard corrosion.

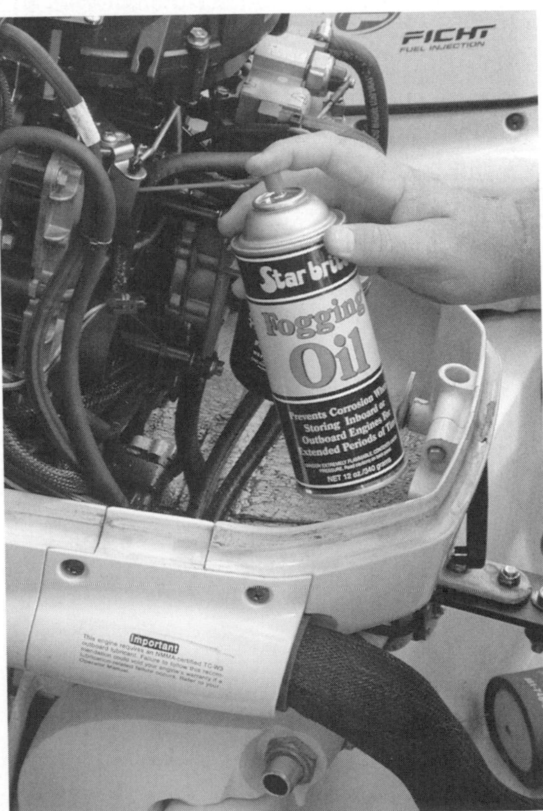

Engine fogging oil, used to winterize the inner workings of your boat's engine, also makes an excellent penetrating oil.

When Your Boat Acts Like a Magic Fingers Mattress

Think your vessel's got some new vibration, and you'd like to figure out why? Start at idle and slowly increase boat speed, paying close attention to the vibrations. If they increase with speed, suspect a bent running gear. If they seem to occur only at certain speeds, secondary equipment attached to the motor—such as a water pump or an alternator—could need tightening or adjustment. If the vibrations increase as load is applied (but not necessarily an increase in speed), look for worn or loosened couplings or motor mounts.

So you've checked out your engine thoroughly and it's in fine running order but still has an annoying vibration that worries you. Inspect the prop. A nicked prop can be filed smooth and in most cases is reusable. If the prop has a buckled blade, replace it or have it reconditioned.

Installing Bolts in High-Vibration Areas

Need to reinstall a bolt and nut in a vibration-prone area, but don't have a lock washer or proper thread sealant on hand to keep them from loosening? Put a tiny dab of silicone or polysulfide (not 3M 5200 or other polyurethane) sealant on the bolt threads before reassembly. This will lock the assembly against vibration but let you take it apart easily if you need to later.

Hydraulic Steering Fluid Substitutes

If you're ever cruising and lose your hydraulic steering oil, remember this: Any liquid will get you back to the dock. Drinking water, sea water, or even Snapple will work. Expect your steering to be sloppy, so be conservative with the power. Once you get to port, turn your system over to a marine mechanic for cleaning and reconditioning.

Penetrating Oil Substitutes

Engine fogging oil, used to winterize the inner workings of your boat's engine, also makes an excellent penetrating oil. When sprayed, this oil foams out the nozzle, coating surfaces that ordinarily are hard to reach. Once coated, this low-viscosity oil penetrates into the same cracks and crevices as standard penetrating oil.

Out of penetrating oil? Dig out the boat's first aid kit and use hydrogen peroxide. Lemon juice works equally well.

Alternator Belt Alternatives

For an alternate alternator belt, try untwisting a single strand from a section of your 3-strand nylon anchor rode. Tied in place with a small knot, it'll work just as well as nylon stockings.

Waterproofing Substitutes

Hair spray, which is relatively inexpensive, makes an effective waterproof coating for distributor caps, plug wires, and coil connections. The high lacquer content of this spray seals out moisture. Make sure the parts are clean, and then spray liberally.

The Paper Bag Gasket

You just blew a gasket and need a quick fix to get home? Cut sections of a brown paper bag will work for a few hours. Use the sharp inner edges of the casing to cut the proper size holes and layer sections of the bag to get the necessary thickness. As soon as you get home, pull the paper and get a new gasket.

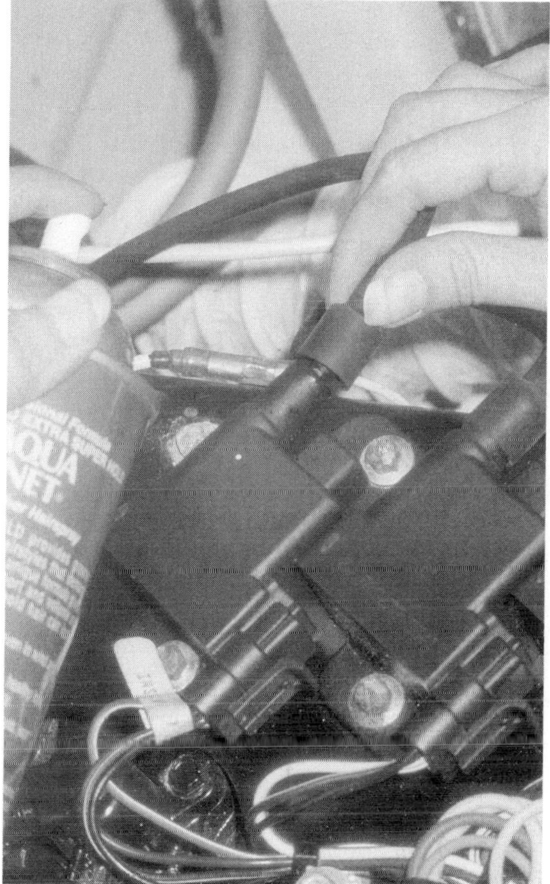

Hair spray makes an effective substitute waterproof coating for distributor caps, plug wires, and coil connections.

Slooooow Starting

Your starter motor seems to be cranking more and more slowly. You know the problem isn't with the battery, so what is it? You could have a voltage drop from dirty or corroded connections. To perform a quick test to find out if and where there's a bad connection, first disconnect the distributor and/or cut off the fuel supply so the motor doesn't catch, and crank it for about 15 seconds. Then feel the battery, solenoid, and starter motor terminals, as well as the ground to the motor block. If any one is warmer than the others, it indicates a connection in need of a thorough cleaning.

Use the Correct Wrench the First Time

Crankcase bolts can be tough to reach—and that may mean it's a battle just to figure out what size wrench you'll need to fit them. Solve this problem by dabbing motor oil on the bolt head. Then place a scrap of paper over it. Use the image on the paper to find the correct wrench size.

Spark Plugs 101

Spark plugs should be light to dark brown, with a slight wetness. A very dry plug indicates lean running or a possible overheating condition. An extremely clean or white porcelain area could mean that the cylinder is not firing or is overly rich. Rust means water is getting into the cylinder, and a grayish plug is showing aluminum deposits, indicating a serious problem that requires a mechanic. Replace plugs when the electrode is showing rounded or worn gap surfaces.

Never oil your spark plugs. Yes, this makes installation easier, but it makes taking the spark plugs out a nightmare after the oil has bonded them to the cylinder heads.

When gapping a spark plug, use a round-wire gap. It's much more accurate then a flat gauge.

Don't Let Oil Foul Your Fiberglass

Gas and oil spills on a fiberglass deck can be cleaned by pouring a tiny amount of paint thinner and covering it immediately with a generous amount of baking soda. Let it set for a couple hours. In many cases baking soda alone does the trick.

Warm sponges in the microwave before wiping up engine oil stains or spills. This will soften the sponge and enlarge its pores to make it more absorbent and able to get the spill quicker.

A Clean Engine Is the Best Engine

If your older, carbureted engine resembles the LaBrea Tar Pits more than the original 454 it was, spray it down with a degreasing engine cleaner. Before you spray, however, cover the distributor, coil, and carburetor with aluminum foil or plastic wrap to avoid damaging these fragile areas. You may also want to take off the carburetor rainhat to make cleaning more effective and to be able to wrap the carburetor more easily. Make sure you protect any oxygen sensors as some can be damaged by even minimal contact with water.

Use a plastic or wooden paint stirrer to remove thick coatings of engine grease without scraping the engine paint as a metal scraper would.

Get That Fuel Smell Off of Your Hands

After filling your tank at the dock, get that gas smell off your hands by taking half a handful of baking soda, rubbing your hands together, and then wiping them off on a moist rag or paper towel.

After a day spent mucking around with the engine, clean your greasy hands with a squirt of shaving cream in the right hand, and approximately a teaspoon of sugar in the other. Rub together, and then rinse. Next time, spray your hands with nonstick vegetable oil to make cleanup even easier.

One of the cheapest, easiest-to-find (it's in every supermarket), and perhaps gentlest hand cleaners to use after a day of mucking around in a greasy engine is Dawn liquid dishwashing soap.

Handy Tool Advice

To make working in the dark crannies of an inboard easier, or for when you don't have enough hands, make a suction cup flashlight holder by placing an appropriate-sized swivel clamp (available at most hardware stores) in a suction cup. Slip the flashlight into the swivel clamp, and attach the suction cup wherever you choose. You'll find the beam easy to manipulate to your exact specifications.

To avoid losing small screws and other parts while working on your engine, you can sort them in an old egg carton. There are plenty of compartments to keep different-sized components organized.

A mechanic's inspection mirror on a small handle (like the one dentists use to look in your mouth) has a variety of uses on board, from reading awkwardly placed model and serial numbers on engine parts to monitoring your work in hard-to-reach areas you can't see directly.

Line the bottom of your onboard toolbox with carpet remnants; it'll cushion your tools in rough seas.

To keep your tools from rusting prematurely, toss a few mothballs into your onboard toolbox.

To keep Allen wrenches neatly stowed in your boat's toolbox, use Super Glue or epoxy to affix a long magnetic bar inside the lid of the box. Let the tools cling to the strip.

To keep the entire toolbox from slip-slidin' away on deck, affix nonslip bathtub strips to the box's bottom.

Hammers are useful to drive a point home, but don't forget the other end. The handle has many uses. If the alternator belt is loose, wedge the edge of the hammer between the alternator and the engine block to act as a lever while you tighten the belt.

That same hammer handle can be used to reseat a Mercury/MerCruiser water impeller base. Lightly grease the outer edges of the base. Hold the hammer with the head at the top, handle end down toward the impeller base near the drive shaft. Lightly tap the base until it's seated.

If you get a hole in your boat, the hammer handle can also fill the hole as a last-ditch effort to save your pride and joy from sinking. Wrap fabric over the handle end to make a secure fit and plug the hole with the hammer.

Check the water level in wet-cell batteries every few weeks to be safe.

BATTERIES

Engines Get Cranky Without Enough Cranking Volts

The engine cranks, but nothing's happening. It can't be the battery . . . or could it? An outboard needs at least 13.8 to 14.2 volts to trigger the magneto. Go as low as 12 volts, and the engine spins without starting. Check your voltmeter. If it's marginal, try cleaning the battery posts and all other connections. Sometimes, that's all it takes.

Where the Kitchen and the Boat Battery Meet

To add water to your batteries without a mess, use a turkey baster.

To remove corrosion from battery terminals, mix 3 parts baking soda to 1 part water, and apply the paste to the terminals to allow the baking soda to neutralize the corrosion. ***NOTE:*** Always wear eye protection when working around battery acid, and handle this dangerous chemical carefully.

To prevent further corrosion to battery terminals, apply a thin coating of petroleum jelly, dielectric grease, or a paste of baking soda and water.

To neutralize spilled battery acid, have an emergency solution of ½ cup water and ½ cup baking soda on hand.

Direct Connections

Wires that power electronics connected directly to a battery must be fused at the battery. Other accessories can be either supplied from a fused power strip or in-line fuses installed at the source of power to prevent accidental electronics breakdown or an onboard fire.

Run the power cord for your fish finder directly to your boat's battery and add a fuse and rubber-covered, two-pole quick-disconnect plug. The separate wiring minimizes noise from gauges and electronic gear and makes it easy to remove and stow.

Emergency Connection Wire

Electrical problems are more often caused by wiring failure than by a dead battery, but if you can't get the juice out of the battery, what good is it? Always carry in your toolbox a length of #10 wire, some alligator clips, and a role of electrician's tape; crimp-on terminals are even better. Then, when the wiring fails, you can at least jury-rig power to the VHF or a 12-volt light.

Noncorrosive Solder

Soldering is an excellent way to make an emergency repair to your boat's electrical system at sea. However, solder is vulnerable to corrosion, so as soon as possible, you must insulate the connection with electrical tape, Star brite Liquid Electrical Tape, or a shrink-on insulation tubing.

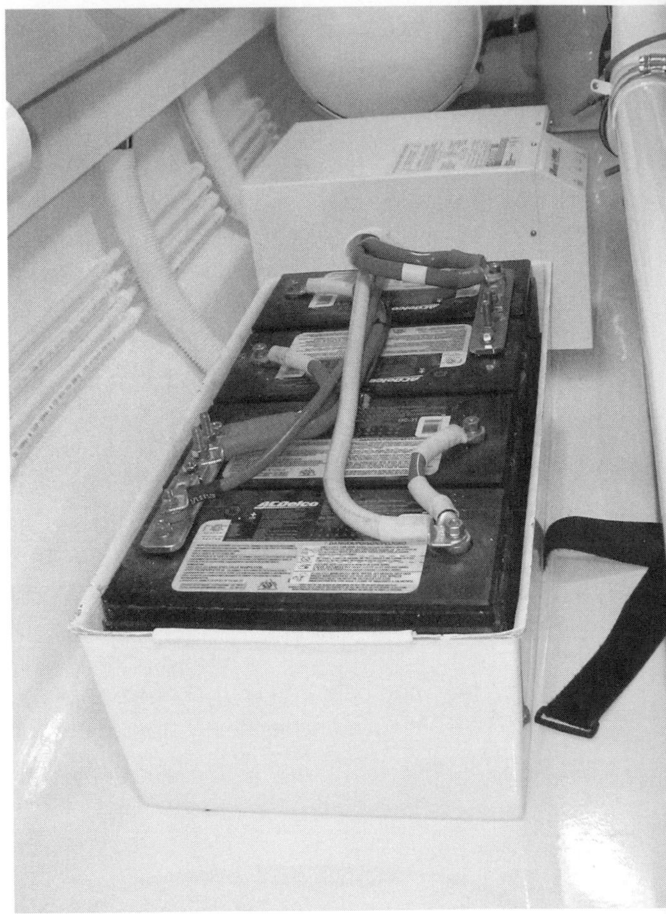

Battery boxes keep boat batteries and their connections safe and secure.

Dry Is Better than Wet

If you are tired of checking your wet-cell batteries every few weeks, consider swapping them for absorbed glass mat (AGM) batteries. Not only do they eliminate the need to ever check the water level, but they will outlast wet cells by many years, so they are also cost-effective.

These high-efficiency batteries are used by the military and race cars because they will not leak and can be used even upside-down. They have an extremely long shelf life, making them ideal for boats that remain idle for extended periods of time, and they also hold a charge much longer than the traditional wet-cell batteries. AGMs are truly no-maintenance batteries in that they never need water. (Wet-cell batteries need to have their water level maintained, and they must be secured to avoid spillage of the corrosive acid. If wet-cell batteries are allowed to drain down, they can fail due to a "bad cell" and need to be replaced.)

The best way to keep any battery—wet or AGM—healthy is to use a trickle charger during periods the boat will remain unused. These chargers range from solar-powered models to 110-volt units.

It's Best to Use Like to Like

When jump-starting boat batteries, it is best to work with a boat of the same general size and batteries of the same voltage. Read your owner's manual for the proper jump-starting technique.

AGM batteries have an extremely long shelf life.

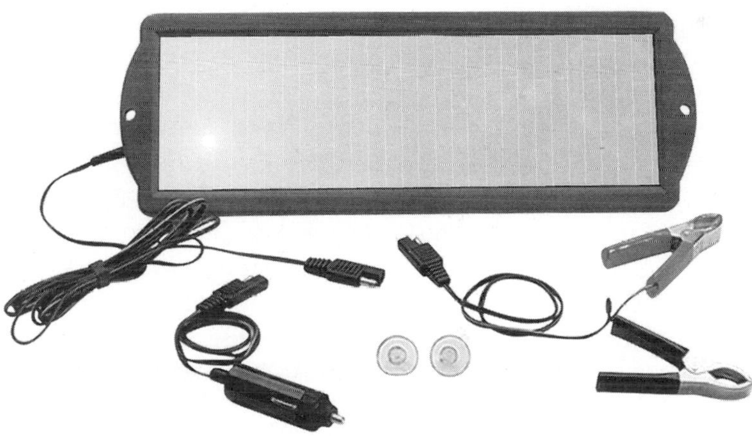

The best way to keep any battery alive is to use a trickle charger. Solar models are one easy option.

chapter 5

OTHER CRITICAL BOAT AREAS

THE ELECTRICAL SYSTEM

Innovative Wire-Running Techniques

A wire coat hanger can double as an electrician's snake when you're running electrical wiring to navigation lights and elsewhere on board.

When replacing old or damaged electrical wiring, solder or splice the new wire on to the end of the old. When you pull out the old wiring, the new will be pulled through the wiring bundles at the same time. When pulling new wiring through wiring bundles or rubber grommets, wipe down the wire with liquid soap to reduce friction. Wire will slide quickly and easily past tight spots.

If you don't have a snake handy when you need to run new wires on board, try using a metal tape measure as the chase.

Running wires, control cables, and hydraulic lines through the tight confines of a tuna tower or hardtop legs and stanchions can be difficult at best, and impossible at worst. A liberal application of baby powder makes the cables slippery and the job easier.

Awkward Area Corrosion

Corrosion in your fuse box connections? Cut a ¼-inch dowel long enough to accommodate your hand and the depth of the fuse connection, wrap a piece of sandpaper around the dowel, and then rotate the dowel around the fuse socket to sand off the corrosion.

Keep Your Feet (and Eyes) on the Grounds

When doing your biannual boat wiring check, pay special attention to ground connections, especially on power packs/switch boxes and electronic ignition components; loose connections in these areas can cause these components to fail quickly.

Dress Your Electrical Connections for the Weather

Coat all electrical connections with three coats of Star brite Liquid Electrical Tape. It is available in several colors, so you can even color-code your wires at the same time. Paint the bare metal and 1 inch of the insulation. This will prevent corrosion, keep screw connections from coming loose, and add tensile strength to the connection.

Erase Your Troubles Away

Twelve-volt bulbs and sockets can carbonize, leaving you in the dark. Before replacing the compass or navigation light sockets, insert a pencil eraser and rub the carbon off both the socket and bulb contacts. To dramatically cut down on ongoing maintenance, consider replacing burnt-out bulbs with LEDs. They provide just as much light but with minimal heat at a fraction of the voltage.

Do It Before, or Repair It After

Before installation, coat all bulbs with a moisture-displacing lubricant that has dielectric properties so that the current will flow freely; this will prevent the metal surfaces from surrendering to the elements. Do the same to your trailer tail and brake lights.

Shock-Proof Boating

If your boat takes a lot of pounding when you're running offshore, shock-mount your electronics. Put thick rubber washers under the mounting brackets to help lessen the damage to delicate internal components.

Battery Charger Facts and Figures

Trying to figure out what size battery charger to outfit your boat with? Here's a simple formula to remember: A 110-volt AC supply charger should give off 10 percent of your battery amp-hours. Does your charger also supply DC power to onboard lights, gauges, or other equipment? If so, double the percentage to 20.

Corrosion-Resistant Junction Boxes

Your electrical terminal strip is exposed to spray, and it just shorted out! Prevent future shorts by protecting it with a junction box made from a plastic leftovers container. Screw the bottom of the container to a bulkhead and reinstall the terminal strip inside the container. Lead the wires through a small hole in the side. Want a junction box with a door? Do the same thing with a child's plastic lunch box.

Quick Tips for Easier Wiring

Tired of trying to wiggle those little rubber wire connectors together? Hit 'em with a dose of isopropyl alcohol. It will lubricate the rubber and won't leave any residue behind.

If wire cutters, scissors, and so on get dull during a repair job, slice a sheet of sandpaper with them several times to resharpen them.

GPS Mounting Options

Your handheld global positioning system mount broke and the manufacturer no longer makes replacements? No problem. Cut open an old life jacket and remove a block of foam

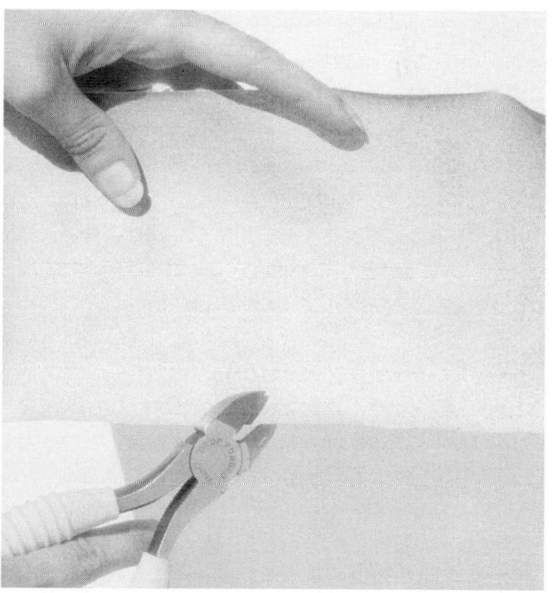

Slice sandpaper with dull scissors or wire cutters to resharpen.

that's larger than the global positioning system. Then fasten it to the dash with self-adhesive Velcro. Put more strips of Velcro on the back of the global positioning system and the front of the foam block, and stick the global positioning system to the foam. The foam will absorb vibrations and keep the global positioning system safe from damage.

A Recipe to Avoid Moisture Buildup in Electronics

To prevent a potentially dangerous moisture buildup in electronics stored on board, put some dry rice near them to absorb moisture. Heat the rice in a clean, dry frying pan until it browns. Place the brown rice in a cheesecloth bag to keep the grain from getting into the equipment and harming it. Check the bags frequently and replace as necessary when the rice becomes moist.

The Western Union Twist

For on-the-spot wiring repairs, use the "Western Union Twist": Strip 1 inch of insulation off each end of the wires you want to connect. Tie them in an overhand knot and then twist the ends together. This connection is strong and makes good contact. Cover with electrical tape and spray with Boeshield T-9, but go back and solder the connection as soon as you can. Cover the solder, which can corrode, with an insulating layer of Star brite Liquid Electrical Tape.

Fuse Recommendations

Check all your fuses to make sure they're the right size. A fuse too small in amperage can fail under normal operating conditions, and one too large won't protect the internal circuits in the event of an overload. Fuse size is listed on the back of the unit, on the power cord tag, or in the owner's manual. Most electronics require fuses below 10 amps.

Organize and support electrical wiring with tie wraps to eliminate chafing and minimize stress.

Speaking of fuses, a little dielectric grease works wonders at keeping corrosion out of your critical connections.

A Tie Wrap a Day Keeps Wire Problems Away

Support all your electrical wires, power and antenna, with wire looms or tie wraps about every foot. This eliminates chafing and minimizes internal stress on the conducting wire strands.

Engine Noise

Your electronics aren't functioning properly when the engine's running? Try special spark plugs that reduce radio frequency interference. Spark plugs and other ignition components can put out their own little radio signals that cause interference.

Protect Electrical Components at All Times

Keep a zipping plastic bag handy when onboard electronics require disassembly. If you are not able to reassemble the unit that day because you need to shop for spare parts, place it in the bag to keep dampness away from the vulnerable interior. If you have one, toss a silica gel packet, such as those that come with cameras and binoculars, into the bag for additional protection.

Fewer Holes Are Better

To avoid drilling lots of holes in your boat when installing a transducer, temperature gauge, livewell pump, or other device to your stern, first mount a high-density polyethylene pad at the

VINEGAR: THE BOATER'S WONDER CLEANER

Vinegar helps keep your boat good looking and fresh smelling from bow to stern. Vinegar and boating have long gone together, and not only as an effective, inexpensive cleaner. In fact, apple cider vinegar was used by boaters in the late 1800s; they added it to their drinking water to protect against illness from tainted water and potential food poisoning. How many of the vinegar uses listed here have you tried?

TIP	PAGE
Sticky stainless steel cleaner	2
Aluminum etcher for painting	3
Cheap brass cleaner	3
Baking soda tester	3
Gelcoat shiner	5–6
Homemade all-purpose boat cleaner	6
Hard water spot dissolver	7–8
Epoxy remover	12
Homemade glass cleaner	14
Glass scratch remover	15
Window ice preventer	15
Frost remover	16
Wiper blade cleaner	16
Boat canvas color setter	25
Mildew odor remover	25–26
Perspiration stain remover	26
General deck carpet and no-rinse carpet stain removers	27–28
Sea salt carpet stain remover	28
Hull cleaner enhancer	31
Fiberglass cleaner residue remover	31
Light hull oxidation remover	31
Hard water deposit remover	32
Road tar and bug remover for trailer boaters	32, 96
Hard bottom paint brush softener	34
Paint odor reducer	35
Cabin odor remover	37
Refrigerator cleaner and deodorizer	39
Vinyl wall covering cleaner	39–40
Toilet bowl soak and ring-around-the-toilet remover	40–41
Raw-water head deodorizer	41
Mirror defogger and neglected glass restorer	42
Shower head cleaner	42
Soap film cutters	43
Freshwater hose cleanout	44
Seacock fixer	44–45
Environmentally friendly drain unclogger	45
Stainless steel sink cleaner	45–46
Glass buildup remover	47
Mildewed refrigerator cleaner	47
Coffee maker revitalizer	49
Cabin furniture polish	54
Wood polish buildup remover	54
Paint spot remover	55
Cabin blinds cleaner	56
Carpet color restorer	58
Aluminum acid washer	73
Gentle inflatable cleaner	101
Mosquito bite treatment	133
Boat clothing rust stain remover	148

base of the transom. Bed it with a quality below-the-waterline caulking compound, and secure it with stainless steel bolts. Then install the transducer and speed-temperature sensor on top.

Refrigeration Protects

To keep spare flashlight or global positioning system batteries left on board from becoming corroded, store them in a zipping plastic bag placed in the cabin refrigerator.

BILGE

If It Works on Your Clothes . . .

Laundry detergents create too many suds to be used in the bilge, so use one of Star brite's bilge cleaners or other commercial cleaners. They are all biodegradable in order to not harm sea life, and the motion of the boat does all the scrubbing for you. They won't harm wiring. The pine and citrus formulas leave a pleasant scent.

Clean like a Janitorial Service

Put a generous dash of antibacterial liquid in the bilge to ensure sanitary conditions if water accumulates.

Raise Your Arm if You're Working Correctly

Make sure the electric bilge float arm is functioning properly. The bilge pump should go on when the arm is manually raised and the switch is set to automatic.

Keep Things Free-Flowing

Check that all weep holes, pipes, and hoses are free of obstruction. A plumber's snake will clear most blockages.

The Art of Antifreeze

For boats that remain in the water during winter storage, water and moisture buildup in the bilge can freeze in severe temperatures. Before storing, add antifreeze to the bilge water and the discharge hose and—don't forget—the pump itself. Salt in the bilge water also prevents freezing.

Unprotected Wires Will Corrode

No matter how careful you are, bilge-pump wires usually end up lying in standing water and often fall victim to corrosion. If you can't avoid making wire splices close to the pump, waterproof them with a generous coating of liquid electrical tape (available in marine supply stores), covered by a shrink-wrap sleeve.

Searching for the Loch Ness Monster (and Dropped Objects)

You can't locate those bolts you dropped into the bilge? Stop looking down from above. You'll never spot them. Instead, place a flashlight in the very bottom of the V so its beam shines parallel to the hull. Anything poking up (such as your bolts) will be much easier to spot.

HOLDING TANKS

Foul Odors Can Signal Imminent Danger

If there always seems to be a foul odor coming from the holding tank, this can be dangerous. Make sure that the holding tank vent isn't clogged. Not only does a clogged vent increase accumulated odors, but it can also cause a dangerous methane buildup, which can actually become explosive.

Good Versus Bad Bacteria

Aerobic (good) bacteria thrive in open air and are used in sewage treatment ponds that are relatively odor free. Anaerobic (bad) bacteria thrive in a closed environment such as a septic tank, which stays odor free as long as the contents of that tank do not move. This, of course, is impossible on a boat. To keep your tank smelling sweet, it must be well ventilated with as much fresh air as possible. Do this by increasing the vent line from the stock 5⁄8 inch to at least 3⁄4 inch. Keep the hose short (ideally under 5 feet) and as straight and horizontal as possible. The best setup is to have two vents, one on each side of the tank, to get cross-ventilation.

The Odor Isn't Always Coming from the Holding Tank

When you've cleaned out the holding tank but still have an odor, you most likely have malodorous debris in the lines. Flush the lines with muriatic acid. If that doesn't work, you may have to replace the hoses. If you're using ribbed hoses, replace them with standard hoses. The ribs provide convenient nooks for waste buildup.

All Marine Sanitation Hoses Are Not Created Equal

If your hoses smell, then you're using the wrong ones. To temporarily reduce the stench, wrap them completely in plastic wrap. And we're talking actual Saran Wrap, not the cheaper knock-offs, as it is the only product with enough electrostatic cling to make a good seal. When you are ready to replace the hoses, use a marine sanitation–grade hose that has a smooth interior, because corrugations can trap and hold waste, leading to foul odors.

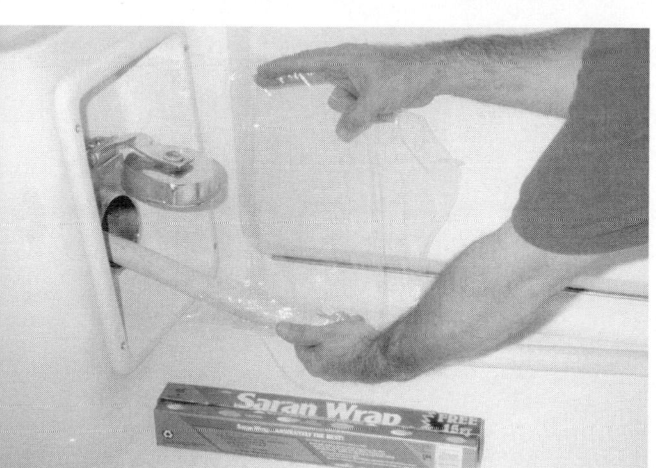

Wrap hoses in Saran Wrap to contain odors.

Lubricate Hoses to Make Installation Easier

When changing hoses, you may find that getting the old hose off is easy, but putting the new one on is an ordeal you wouldn't wish on your in-laws, unless they were threatening to visit again. Coat the connection with petroleum jelly as a lubricant. This will make most hoses slide on relatively easily. If you're working with an exceptionally tough one, drop the end of the hose in a bucket of hot water for 10 minutes. This will cause the opening to expand. If 10 minutes doesn't do the trick, try 20.

Flush Your Head, Flush Your Hoses

If the low spots in your hose are collecting sludge, this can be easily corrected. Simply flush enough water through the lines to push the sludge into the holding tank after each flush. It's false conservation to save water on board if it makes your boat unbearable to be on and perhaps eventually leads to larger repairs such as a complete waste system rehosing.

Other Potential Sources of Odor

Leaking connectors can be the source of odors just as often as the hoses. To check if the hose is the problem, wrap a warm, damp cloth around it. Allow the cloth to cool while on the hose, then take it off and sniff it. Stink free? Then the hose is okay. Make sure that all connectors are securely double-clamped.

Plastic Is Best

Plastic is the best material for holding tanks. If you have an aluminum or stainless steel tank, check it each season for corrosion. Urine is incredibly corrosive to these two materials. Be wary of epoxy or other internal coatings; they may crack, allowing sewage to seep behind and hasten corrosion. Stay away from fiberglass tanks because they are often porous.

A Short Backflow Guide

There are two possible solutions to the problem of backflow:

1. You may not be flushing long enough. Every 90-degree joint in your head's plumbing system is equal to another 18 feet of discharge hose. Pump at least 10 times after the last toilet tissue has disappeared down the drain, to make sure it's completely gone and not being left to solidify in the outlet hose.
2. Install a vented loop. This is a necessity if your head is going to be below the water line at any time, such as when turning sharply in rough waters. A vented loop works very simply; when the water and waste pass over the top of the loop, they cannot flow back into the toilet because the air allowed in by the vent stops the siphon effect that would otherwise bring it back.

A Gauge Is Better than a Guess

You probably never remember to empty the holding tank until it's too late. The solution is to install a holding tank level monitor. Not only will this remind you to empty the tank as needed (rather than finding it inconveniently full while out cruising), but it will save you from making unnecessary visits to the pumpout station only to discover that your tank was only one-third full.

THE FRESHWATER SYSTEM

Plastic Wrap to the Rescue

Do you have water hose leaks but you don't have a spare? Wrap the hose tightly with a piece of plastic wrap to seal the leak, and then wrap over it with electrical tape, duct tape, an Ace bandage, or even monofilament fishing line.

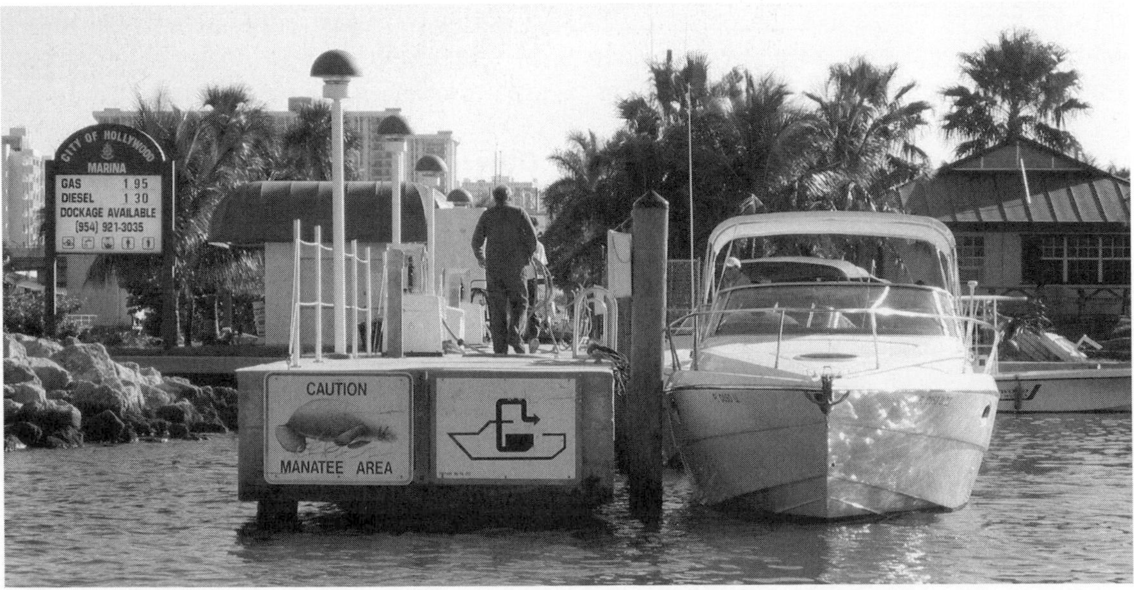

Adding a holding tank gauge will make trips to the pumpout station more efficient.

A Second Hose Repair

A leaking pipe can be temporarily repaired by placing a section of hose around the hole and securing it in place with hose clamps. For longer-lasting results, pack the hose with epoxy such as Marine Tex before wrapping it around the damaged area.

Wrong Size Hose? That's Okay

Installing a length of water hose on a barbed fitting, but the hose's diameter is too large? First wrap the barbed fitting with a piece of self-amalgamating plastic tape (or in a pinch, vinyl electrical tape), and then carefully install the hose and double-clamp it. The connection should be watertight.

Hose Clamps Tricks

If your hose clamp isn't large enough, screw two smaller hose clamps together to create one larger clamp.

The ends of the stainless steel hose clamps can cut like a scalpel. To prevent injuries to people and hoses, make rubber sleeves for their ends with heat-shrink tubing.

A short wire leader with a swivel eye crimped to one end and a snap on the other makes a good emergency hose clamp. Wind the leader around the hose and clip the two ends together. Insert a screwdriver into the slack wire and turn it as you would a tourniquet until it's tight enough to hold the hose in place. Don't overdo it, or the wire could cut through the hose.

Mother Nature's Hose Line Cleaner

Use the following recipe for keeping drains and vulnerable marine hoses clean without buildup: 1 cup table salt, 1 cup baking soda, and ¼ cup cream of tartar (all found in a supermarket). Use ¼ cup of this mixture at a time, pouring it down the drain and following with 2 cups boiling water. Let stand 5 minutes before using the drain.

Your Freshwater Pump Shouldn't Be Cycling

If your freshwater pump cycles—and many do after winter layup—it's because you're losing pressure at the compression fittings and hose clamp ends. Tighten all the clamps in your plumbing. Also, unscrew the compression fittings, coat the threads with petroleum jelly, and screw them back on. Not only will this help serve as a seal, but it will also make it easier for you to unscrew the fittings later on.

Morning Chores

To prevent sediment from building up in the water tanks, drain them periodically. This is best done in the morning, before any water is used, which stirs up the sludge at the bottom of the tank.

SPECIALTY BOATING

TRAILER BOATING

Longer-Lasting Brake Lights

To deter corrosion on trailer brake lights, remove the brake lights from their sockets and thoroughly clean out any existing corrosion with steel wool. Next, coat both the socket and the metal bulb base with dielectric grease. This makes the bulbs last longer, and it makes them easier to remove when they eventually need to be replaced.

To further maximize the life span of your trailer brake lights, even those that are reputedly waterproof, you must eliminate the thermal shock that occurs when lit trailer lights are backed into cool water. To do so, simply unplug the light harness from the tow vehicle before backing them into the water.

Warning: Potential Bearing Freeze

If you ever notice the smell of burning metal coming from your trailer, stop towing immediately and check the wheel bearings. If they're hot to the touch (be sure to touch them lightly so as not to burn yourself), it could be the sign of an impending bearing freeze. Allow them to cool, and then relubricate them and repack them generously.

Dr. Pepper to the Rescue

In a pinch, lost wheel bearing covers can be temporarily replaced by part of an aluminum can. Snip the bottom off a soda or beer can, making sure to leave a 1½-inch lip so that the can bottom fits relatively securely over the hub. Be sure to make more permanent arrangements as soon as you return home.

Brake Maintenance

To keep trailer brakes functioning their best, be sure to coat the rubber cups and actuating pins with white grease to ensure a moisture-resistant seal. This should be done at least 1 or 2 times per year. Otherwise, water might get in and corrode the cylinders, which will soon begin to leak and malfunction. Don't get any grease on or near the shoes or drums.

If your trailer brakes make a loud banging sound and begin to leak a dark fluid, you've burst a seal. In order to limp home, you're going to need a pair of locking pliers to cut off the brake line to the bad wheel, and then fill the reservoir with fresh brake fluid (which you should always carry in your trailer's emergency kit). Next, open the bleeder screws to the remaining wheels and bleed the lines until there is no more air in them. Close the bleeder screws and refill the reservoir. Drive home very carefully.

It isn't any great surprise to find that the brakes on a trailer that hasn't been used in a while have become frozen due to rust. If you're not in the mood for a home trailer brake repair and simply want to tow the empty trailer to the nearest garage, you can bleed the brake fluid lines until they're empty, thereby deactivating the brakes and freeing the wheels for this emergency tow. *Never* tow a boat on a trailer on which the brakes have been deactivated.

Be Prepared for the Road You're Towing On

Keep in mind that trailer jacks work best on hard concrete. If you're taking your boat out for some backwoods fishing, you'll want to bring along a plank of sturdy wood to place underneath the jack for use on soft dirt.

Tandem Trailer Temporary Flat Solutions

Flat tires are a trailer boater's nightmare. If you get a flat on a tandem trailer and don't have a spare:

1. If the flat is a front tire, remove the tire and then, using a piece of chain or aircraft cable, secure the axle spring to the trailer frame so that it is safely out of the way, and lock the chain into place with your trailer padlock. Drive slowly and carefully to the nearest garage for tire repair.
2. If the flat is a rear tire, after securely jacking up the trailer, remove the rear tire and then the front tire. Reinstall the front (good) tire in the rear slot and secure the front axle spring as previously directed so that you can limp to the nearest repair shop.

Fabricate Your Own Tandem Trailer Ramp Jack

You have a spare but forgot your trailer jack? If you have a tandem trailer you can fabricate a temporary ramp with a sturdy piece of 8-inch by 4-inch wood that is trimmed at one end to resemble a miniramp. You may find that you already have the exact piece of wood with you for use as a chock. Be sure to make certain that there is enough space on top of your ramp to support a tire. Slip your ramp just in front of the good tire, next to the flat, and drive the trailer onto it, being sure to keep the wheel centered on the ramp. Next, place chocks on both sides of the wheels on the opposite side of the trailer to prevent slippage. ***NOTE:*** This procedure is only to be used in an emergency, and you must be extremely careful as you remove and replace the flat. If your makeshift ramp seems shaky, stop immediately and wait for a more conventional method of repair.

Always keep the tow vehicle's back wheels and exhaust out of the water.

Bunk Slide Basics

Bunk-style trailers are easier to maintain than roller versions but can drive you to distraction at the ramp. To facilitate loading, apply a liberal amount of liquid soap to the bunks. Your boat will slide right on.

Rub some paraffin wax, found in the canning department of a hardware or grocery store, on the trailer bunks for a dramatically improved slide. This should significantly reduce boat hull wear and tear from on- and off-loading.

The Best Bed Cover

Sometimes wood trailer beds squeak, creak, and groan when you load your boat. You could cover the bed with outdoor carpet, but that will have a limited lifetime. Instead, try mounting ¼-inch-thick strips of polypropylene on the bed. It's slick, won't mar the boat, and lasts for decades.

Don't Put That Boat Polish Away Just Yet

Many boaters know to polish their boat's fiberglass and polished metal surfaces regularly to provide a durable barrier against corrosion and protection from grime, but don't forget the trailer. Unless it is a galvanized material, apply a coat of a polymer polish to protect it, too. Apply fresh wheel-bearing grease while you are at it.

Rust Is the Enemy of the Trailer Boater

What's the best way to stop rust from ruining your trailer's frame? Brush on two coats of Ospho acid, available at paint, hardware, or marine supply stores. It changes the chemistry of rusting steel from an active to a passive state and stops rust cold.

If rust has already attacked the trailer, use a stainless steel scrubber brush to remove as much of it as you can, and then apply Star brite Rust Converter to the remaining rust. It will convert it to keep it from spreading and prepares the surface for a protective coat of paint. ***NOTE:*** Galvanized surfaces can be painted, too. Most marine stores carry this paint. Premixed and ready to apply, this super-tough coating can be sprayed, brushed, or dabbed onto metal surfaces. It dries to a galvanized color and prevents rust from returning.

The best trick for rust prevention is to thoroughly rinse the trailer, the metal wheels, and all other metal surfaces after use or a road trip.

Limit Tire Cleaner to the Tires

To eliminate the problems associated with overspray of cleaning products onto your tires and wheels when cleaning your boat trailer or tow vehicle, cut a cardboard disc the size of your wheel, with two horizontal slots cut out in the middle to create finger grips. Cover the cardboard disc with a plastic bag or tape to stop any liquid from seeping through the cardboard, and then put the disc over the wheel well to protect it when you're cleaning your tires.

Get More Life from Your Trailer Tires

When you store your trailer, cover the tires, too. Durable tire covers are available at most marine stores or online. Look for covers with reflective outer material and a fleece-type inner lining. Protect your wheels and tires from an early demise from deterioration caused by rust and UV rays.

Horizontal, Not Vertical

Many trailer manufacturers mount the spare tire vertically on the trailer's drawbar, just ahead of the bow post. This is often a bad location, for when you go over a sharp bump, such as a steep driveway or a low curb, the bar goes down and the spare bottoms out, ripping the spare and bracket from the bar. To prevent this, remount the bracket so the spare sits horizontally on the draw bar.

The Versatile Tongue Jack

In a pinch, a trailer tongue jack can be used to change a flat trailer tire. Disengage the coupler from the tow ball and lower the tongue jack all the way to the ground. Next, pile logs, a spare tire—whatever sturdy material is handy—beneath the rear ends of the trailer side frames. Elevate the front of the trailer with the tongue jack. The flat tire should go just high enough to clear the ground.

Slick Ramp Solutions

If you have rear-wheel drive and you're concerned about losing traction on a slippery boat ramp, mount a receiver hitch on the front as well as the back of the truck. Pull the trailered boat from the water using the front hitch, which will keep your drive wheels safely on dry ground. Once on dry land, switch the hitch to the rear receiver for normal road towing.

Sand absorbs excess moisture and provides much-needed traction over slippery grassy growths and on slick ramps. Carpet remnants, old doormats or, in an emergency, your car floor mats provide a nonskid surface for small patches of ramp algae and flotsam. Some narrow cut-to-fit sections of chain-link fence under your wheels also work on a ramp.

Extend the life of your trailer tires by covering them to protect them from deterioration caused by ultraviolet rays.

Carry a small folding camper's shovel to scoop flotsam and washed-up marine growth from under and around your tow vehicle wheels on ill-tended ramps.

Easier Alignment

Having difficulty backing up perfectly to align your receiver hitch and trailer coupling? Instead of shouting at the person who is trying to direct you, place a piece of red or other brightly colored tape on your rear window directly above your receiver hitch. Place another piece of red tape on your trailer winch, directly above the trailer coupling. Line up the two tapes as you back up. Perfect alignment every time.

Having problems lining up your trailer and boat? Mounting a bumper hitch on the front of your tow vehicle, whether it's rear-wheel drive or 4-wheel drive, dramatically improves boat launch and retrieval. You have a clear view of the action from the driver's seat, without looking over your shoulder. It also keeps your rear wheels farther up on dry land. Check with your tow vehicle dealer first; the suspension on some vehicles may not be able to handle the job.

Appropriate Weight Distribution

Is your trailer weight properly distributed? For trailers less than 3,500 pounds total weight, 10 percent of that weight should be on the tongue (hitch point). Trailers ranging from 3,500 to 7,000 pounds should have 7 percent of that weight on the tongue; and trailers over 7,000 pounds (which you probably aren't towing regularly) should have 5 percent of that weight on the tongue. Too little tongue weight will make the trailer fishtail at speeds over 40 miles per hour, and too much tongue weight will reduce the tow vehicle's steering ability. On a tandem trailer, too much weight up front will cause that excessive weight to be placed on the front axle, resulting in accelerated wear on the hub and brakes.

The Effect of Balance on Trailer Brakes

If your trailer brakes are engaging too often, your ball and tongue may be too low, causing gravity to engage the brakes prematurely. If not fixed, you'll find yourself replacing the brakes more often than necessary. You'll also be putting excessive drag on the entire rig.

If your trailer ball is too high, your brakes won't engage quickly enough. To set the ball just right, use a tape measure. For trailers with 14-inch tires, the top of the ball should be 18 to 19 inches above the ground. On trailers with 15-inch tires, make it 21 to 22 inches above the ground. To adjust your receiver hitch, simply flip the ball mount upside down.

Maintaining correct tire pressure is especially important when you think of the weight the tires are supporting.

Only Trailer Tires Are Trailer Tires

Don't use passenger car tires on a trailer. Trailers have stiffly sprung suspensions that require special trailer service tires (ST tires), which have compliant sidewalls to act as shock absorbers. The narrow tread of an ST tire reduces rolling resistance and facilitates turns. ST tires also feature a durable bias-ply and a reinforced bead. In an emergency, your best substitute is a bias-ply truck tire.

Tandem Axle Trailer Inspection

Because tandem axle trailers "scrub" (push and pull) the wheels sideways during a tight turn, you must check the torque on the lug bolts more frequently than on a single-axle trailer. This is especially important before a long haul.

Bearing Suggestions from a Buddy

Don't overpack your bearing buddy. Too much grease can cause it to burst the rear seal and allow water in. When pumping grease into the zerk fitting that leads to the hub chamber, the center disk should begin to move outward. Stop inserting grease when the disk has moved out ⅛ inch. If you see bearing grease on the inside of your wheels, you've overlubed. Replace the rear seal before trailering again.

To get stuck bearing buddies off a boat trailer without damaging them so that you can replace worn seals beneath, hold a block of wood against the bearing and hit it hard with a hammer. Then go to the opposite side of the wheel and repeat. What you are doing is "walking" the bearing out, which should leave it undamaged.

Annual Lug Nut Maintenance

Once a year you must remove, clean, regrease, and tightly retorque your lug nuts. This prevents the graded steel lug nuts from permanently bonding with the trailer's cast-iron hubs.

Protect Your Taillight Wires

During tight turns while trailering your boat, taillight wires can get pinched between the trailer tongue and the bumper. Protect the wires by putting rubber bands around the trailer tongue and then running the wires under them. This keeps the wires off the bumper and away from danger.

The Chef's Wire Stripper

If you find that your wire stripper is too large to use conveniently when rewiring your boat trailer's backup and brake lights, substitute a potato peeler. It works great and can fit into some extremely small spaces.

Trailer Brakes Can Rust Quicker than You Think

Check your trailer's disc or drum brakes every few months for rust. The interior bore of the cylinder is cast iron, and if this rusts, it can rupture the piston seals, which causes leakage and, perhaps, sudden brake failure. A permanently mounted brake drum flush kit is your best preventive measure. While you're at it, check the brake system master cylinder to make sure the fluid level is topped off and that the fluid contains no water from leaks or condensation. If contamination is suspected, flush the entire system.

Extra Trailer Coupler Piece-of-Mind

Putting an appropriately sized bolt or lock through the hole in the trailer coupler helps prevent the latching mechanism from springing open while you're towing.

Make sure your safety chain is properly rated for the job.

Chain It Up Right

What's the sense of having a safety chain if it's going to snap? Make sure yours is right for the job. The specifications of the National Association of Chain Manufacturers require a minimum breaking strength of 3,000 pounds for 3⁄16-inch coil chain and 5,000 pounds for 1⁄4-inch coil chain. Check your boat's weight; if it's over 3,000 pounds, make sure your safety chain is rated for 5,000 pounds, on 1⁄4 inch. Better safe than sorry.

Do-It-Yourself Safety Latch

If your trailer doesn't have a backup safety latch (the latch that holds your boat in place if the winch cable breaks), drill a 1⁄2-inch hole into the winch arm support and attach a turnbuckle into it. Attach the other end of the turnbuckle through the boat's bow eye.

Spare Tow Strap Stowage

If your trailer tow strap is getting on in years, but it's not so far gone that you're ready to replace it, buy a spare tow strap and store it neatly rolled up inside a large cookie tin. This will keep it tangle-free and ready to use whether it's stored on board or in the back of your tow vehicle, plus you get to eat a whole lot of cookies.

A Trailer Boater Can't Be Too Safe

For added trailering security, use a racheting tie-down to secure the boat's bow eye to the trailer, in addition to a gunwale or transom tie-down. This is an area where it is foolish to save money by not using adequate securing straps or trying to make do with a length of dock line.

Getting Back into Position

If your bow eye breaks free on the interstate, your boat may slide back a few feet on the trailer before the tow strap catches it. To get the boat back where it belongs, rig your anchor line to a stern cleat. Run the line through the winch hook and around the opposite side of the boat. Secure it to the other stern cleat and winch away.

Forgot Your Winch Handle?

For a forgotten or misplaced winch handle, pliers, Vise Grips, and a tire iron are all viable substitutes.

Trailer Boater Quick Cleans

To prevent road dust from becoming a permanent part of your boat's glass windshield, mix a capful of fabric softener in a ½ gallon of warm water. Wipe it on the windshield, and then rub dry.

To clean tar and bugs off your boat hull and tow vehicle, dip your boat-cleaning brush in a mixture of equal parts apple cider vinegar and water. The acid in the apple cider vinegar attacks the tar and bugs like an able-bodied assistant (one who doesn't answer back).

To make your apple cider vinegar mixture even more effective, dip a wet sponge in the vinegar mix, and then slip the sponge inside a pair of used stockings or pantyhose. When combined with a little elbow grease, the nylon stocking gives the necessary gentle abrasion to remove the bugs and guts that otherwise seemed a permanent and somewhat dubious bow ornament.

Don't Become a Victim of Theft

Boat trailers are easy to steal. For security, etch or paint your name and phone number where thieves wouldn't expect to find it—underneath the trailer frame. If the police recover your trailer, they'll be able to identify it, even if the thieves have removed the identification number on the tongue.

Use a cable lock threaded through the wheels to secure a trailer parked for storage.

Take the wheels off a trailer parked for storage to further deter thieves.

For a virtually theft-proof coupling, be sure to lock your trailer to your tow vehicle by hooking a padlock through the trailer hitch coupling. Secure the receiver hitch on your tow vehicle by means of a locking pin, such as those sold by U-Haul. Some thieves steal a boat and an unsecured receiver by simply pulling out the receiver pin and taking the whole works.

When parking a trailer attached to a vehicle overnight, back the trailer against something to deny access to it. If possible, position your vehicle so as to block all access to your boat and trailer.

Install an alarm on the tow vehicle to prevent the entire rig from being taken. Some vehicle alarms have motion sensors that can be set sensitive enough to sound if someone climbs on board your trailered boat.

Use a locking wheel nut to secure the trailer's spare tire.

For long towing trips, you may want to consider shrink-wrapping your boat to keep it clean and protected.

Slip-Slidin' on the Turns

To keep your coolers and other objects left on deck during trailering from sliding around as you take sharp corners, stick a piece of self-adhesive foam weather-stripping on all four bottom corners of the movable objects in question.

Rampside Cleanup

Toss a small garden hose in your trunk for cleanups at the dock after a dusty trailering as well as after a day out on the water. If you're billed for water at home, you'll find dock cleanings not only convenient but cost-effective. While you're there, don't forget to flush your motor.

Don't Strain Your Transmission Unnecessarily

Towing in overdrive puts a major strain on your drive train. It heats up and thins out the transmission fluid until it's almost useless. Even in drive the fluid takes a beating, so consider installing an after-market transmission oil cooler and temperature gauge if your new vehicle's towing package didn't come with one.

Buy the Right Trailer for Your Boat

You may have seen a great financial deal on a used trailer that is for a boat larger than yours and be thinking to yourself, "How can I go wrong?" But you can. A trailer that is too large for your boat will bounce your boat around and handle poorly because there is not enough weight on it to counterbalance its heavy-duty capacity. Don't go for a trailer rated for over 20 percent more than your boat weighs (for example, a 2,500-pound boat should be on a trailer rated for no more than 3,000 pounds).

Cheap Maximum Load Increase

Upgrading your tires from 14-inch (B load range) to 15-inch (C-load range) can increase your load capacity up to 20 percent. Check with your trailer manufacturer for more information.

FISHING BOAT TIPS

Drier Fishing

Does your flat-bottom skiff spray you in a chop? Take care of the problem by mounting a 3-inch rubber or plastic mesh guard across the bow at a 90-degree angle. It should be rounded about two-thirds of the way up from the waterline. Solid guards also work, but a mesh one allows air to pass through and won't slow you down.

Reel Renovation

To get at rust in a reel's nooks and crannies, cut a cork to fit the space you need to clean. Then dampen the cork and dip it in metal polish and clean the reel as you would rusty deck metals.

Tarnished metal reel parts? One of the quickest ways to shine them up is by using your finger to wipe on whitening toothpaste.

Shake, Rattle, and Roll

Do your rods rattle and vibrate when they're sitting in the rocket launchers? Get a rubber doorstop and wedge it gently between the rods and the inside of the launcher. That'll keep them rock solid.

The Rod Guide Test

To check your rod guides for abrasion-causing chips or cracks, inspect them visually and pull a piece of pantyhose through each eye. If it snags anywhere, you've found a rough spot.

Does Your Monofilament Feel Right?

Line abrasion can weaken your monofilament quicker than a bluefish with attitude. Test your line for wear by gently running it across your tongue. Your tongue is much more sensitive than your fingers are, and you'll feel any nicks or cuts in the line.

Counteract Rod Bend

If your fiberglass fishing rod has a permanent bend in it from years of fishing, here's how to get it back in shape. Lay it across a desk or table, with the bend facing up and the top third of the rod sticking off the end. Hold it in place by putting a couple heavy books on either side of the largest eye and one across the butt. Then clip a 1-ounce weight to the tip to put pressure in the direction opposite the bend. Take the weight off and check it daily; very heavy rods take up to a week to straighten out.

Real Easy Reel Maintenance

Are the thread guide wraps starting to unfurl on your favorite fishing rod? Cut off loose ends and coat the entire wrap with clear nail polish to hold the wrap firmly.

Does the threaded reel-locking screw on your favorite fishing rod keep coming loose? Back it off a few turns and put a drop or two of clear nail polish on the threads, and then retighten.

Is your rod handle bloodstained from a recent fishing trip? Using 400-grit wet or dry sandpaper on it or scrubbing with an abrasive cleanser will do the trick. Or, if you're careful, paint the handle with diluted bleach to lighten the stain to a uniform color. Use a weak mixture (1:10), and wash it thoroughly afterward.

Be a Big-Game Fisherman with Light Tackle

You're offshore with light gear when you run into a big fish. How do you change your spinning rod into big-game stand-up gear? Push the head of a toilet plunger over the butt of the fishing rod and secure it with a hose clamp, and then wedge the rod against your arm, with the plunger against your back and shoulder. Let's see a fish try to pull that rig out of your hands!

Spooled Reel Storage

Store spooled reels and spools of extra line in the coolest place in your house (but not inside the refrigerator!); heat weakens monofilament.

Are your spooled reels going to be sitting in direct sunlight on board when not in use? Nothing weakens line more than direct sunlight. Slip an old sock with a hole in the toe over the reel. This protects the line, and the toe hole slips right over the rod. This helps keep salt spray off your reels while driving to a great fishing spot with the setups in their rod holders.

The Superbraid Spin

Superbraid fishing lines sometimes spin around the spool when you try to reel in after a long cast. Solution: Spool up 20 or 30 yards of monofilament under the braid.

Keep Those Spoons Shining

If you fish offshore, you probably have corrosion problems with spoons, hooks, and other metal tackle that rinsing alone won't solve. To reduce corrosion after rinsing the tackle, let it dry in a wooden tray or box instead of a plastic one. The wood will draw moisture off the tackle and help it dry more quickly.

Want to shine your spoons, but you don't have any metal polish on board? If you have a cigarette, save the ashes. Mixed the ashes with water to make a fine spoon polish.

Stuck Swivels

Have your bearing swivels stopped spinning freely because they are corroded from salt water? Drop them in a container of 3-IN-ONE oil or Salt Off salt remover for a few minutes, then remove and rinse. They'll spin freely, just like new.

Sick and tired of fishing through bunches of tangled tackle to find a swivel the right size and type? Use a large safety pin as an organizer; clip all the identical swivels to one pin. Works for hooks, too.

You Can't Use Your Pork Rind if You Can't Open the Jar

Rub petroleum jelly around the inside rim of your pork rind or salted bait jar to keep the brine inside from rusting it shut.

The Bucktail Substitute

You're out of pork rind and twister tails, but you want to sweeten your bucktail? Cut a 3-inch strip of skin off a fish you've already caught and slide it on the hook. Leave the scales on: It will give the bucktail extra action and usually holds up through several casts.

Substitute Sinkers

You've run out of sinkers? Crimp down the gapped end of an old spark plug and clip it on your swivel. Count on getting 1 ounce of weight per plug.

Nail Clippers Do More than Clip Nails

Keep an inexpensive pair of fingernail clippers in your tackle box. They're great for trimming off the ends of monofilament leaders when tying on swivels, hooks, or weights.

Make That Lure Dance

You can fill fishing lures that have a hollow interior for weights or noise-making BBs with baking soda to make them jump and spin in the water.

Weedless Poppers

Is your popper picking up weeds on every other cast? Here's a quick fix: Poke a small hole in the body of the popper and drip a drop of fishing knot glue into it. Then insert a small piece of 30- to 40-pound monofilament, about ⅛ inch longer than the hook. When the glue dries, the extra monofilament will keep the weeds at bay.

Make Your Barbless Hooks Bite

You like fishing with catch-and-release barbless hooks, but your bait keeps sliding off the hook? Bite the end off a plastic worm and slide the hook through the plastic chunk until it's in the bend of the hook. It grips the hook and holds your bait in place.

Missing Fishhooks Are Often Found in an Angler's Thumb

To remove a barbed fishhook that has become deeply stuck in a finger, rub ice over the area to numb the finger, and then push the barb through the skin until it comes out the other end. Snip off the barb and withdraw the hook back out. Cleanse and disinfect the area thoroughly before bandaging.

Fish Blood on Your Favorite Tournament Shirt?

Fish blood on your favorite fishing shirt can be removed by rinsing it in cold water and allowing the stain to soak in laundry detergent for 15 minutes before washing. If a yellowish ring remains, use an antirust agent that's safe for clothing.

Easy Cutting Board Cleaning

You can clean wooden bait cutting boards by pouring salt on the cutting board and then rubbing the salty surface down with half a lemon or lime. Follow this up with a quick scrub down with a scrubbing sponge dipped in clean water for an odor-free cutting board.

Don't Miss That Great Shot

You're just about to take a photo of a giant fish that you've just caught and find that your camera batteries are dead. Never fear! Rub a pencil eraser over the ends and replace in the camera. If the batteries aren't completely dead, this will help you get that last bit of life out of them.

WATERSKI BOAT TIPS

A Knotty Problem

Always remove knots from towropes. Why? Chafing occurs near the knot at high speeds. Over time, the rope weakens and a dangerous backlash could occur. A towrope also is vulnerable at the point where it attaches to the boat. If wear is anticipated, cover the end of the ropes with rubber tubing or a rope cover.

Coil Like a Snake

Properly coil and stow your towrope. Right-hand coil it as you would coil a mooring line. When you have 3 feet of rope left, tie a slipknot with the bitter end and stow the rope handle-side down. Nylon towrope has memory, and if it's tied in a figure eight, it will have excess turn and spin.

Ultraviolet Rays Don't Just Cause Sunburn

Ultraviolet rays are the number one enemy of waterski equipment. For that reason, don't leave your gear lying around in the hot sun. Stow all of it—from skis to tow ropes to PFDs—immediately after your last run. Be particularly careful with your ski bindings. They shouldn't be in the sun at all, even for a few moments between runs. Turn them over so the sun hits the bottom of the ski.

Get the Smoothest Ride

Dinks on the bottom of your water skis or wakeboard can create a rougher ride and reduce maneuverability. To keep surfaces smooth, try to store water skis, whether on board or at home, upright and away from other equipment.

Tar Removal

If you ski in dirty, heavily trafficked water, tar could adhere to your skis. Remove it immediately, or it could stain and pit the fiberglass. Spray the tar spot with oven cleaner and wait up to 30 minutes, depending on the amount of tar. Rinse off.

A second effective tar remover that's safe to use on water skis is WD-40. Use as you would the oven cleaner.

Black Scuff Removal

Even when you're careful with your gear, black scuff marks have a tendency to appear. To remove them from fiberglass water skis, gently rub the marks with fine, dry nonsoapy bronze wool until they disappear.

Saltwater Rinse Down

You weren't as diligent about maintaining your skis as you should have been, and now you have saltwater buildup. To remove, simply wash gear with a solution of baking soda and water poured on a damp sponge. Rinse thoroughly, or you'll just be replacing the salt buildup with a baking soda residue.

INFLATABLES

Baking Soda Breathes New Life into Inflatable Boats

To clean inflatable tubes that have become heavily soiled from general use and neglect, make a paste of baking soda and water, apply it to the inflatable tubes, and let set for 1 hour. Wash off with a rough washcloth dipped in a mixture of ½ cup baking soda, ¼ cup soap flakes (which can be shaved off a regular soap bar), and 2 cups warm water. Rinse thoroughly with freshwater.

Oil Stains Be Gone!

To remove oil and grease stains from your boat, whether from waterborne petrochemicals or guests, make a paste out of cornstarch and water, apply to the boat, let set until it's absorbed, and then rinse off. Repeat if necessary.

For difficult oil and grease spots on pontoons, rub borax on the stains. Let set until absorbed and then rinse off. Repeat if necessary.

Be Gentle with Your Inflatable

Never use boat cleaner that contains oil distillates on an inflatable, as such cleaners can eat through fabrics. A damp cloth dipped in vinegar and sprinkled with baking soda should remove most fresh stains. Wash afterward with warm water and liquid dish soap, and then rinse thoroughly.

Hypalon Do's and Don'ts

If your hypalon inflatable has oxidized, spray it with a general-purpose household cleaner such as Formula 409 to renew its good looks. *Do not* use polymer protectant because it is extremely difficult to get off if you need to clean the surface thoroughly to patch the inflatable.

Black Marks Be Gone

As long as they haven't become embedded, black marks on inflatable tubes can come clean with an art gum eraser. Rub lightly at first, and then rub harder as the streaks begin to lift. This works in the vast majority of cases.

Scratches and Chafing of Hypalon Paint

Small scratches in the inflatable tube paint? Buy an indelible marker in a matching shade and fill in the nick.

A Hypalon inflatable that has become chafed should be covered immediately with a Hypalon-based paint. Leaving the spots alone for a moment longer means risking critical damage to the fabric beneath. Buff the areas to be painted first to help form a lasting bond.

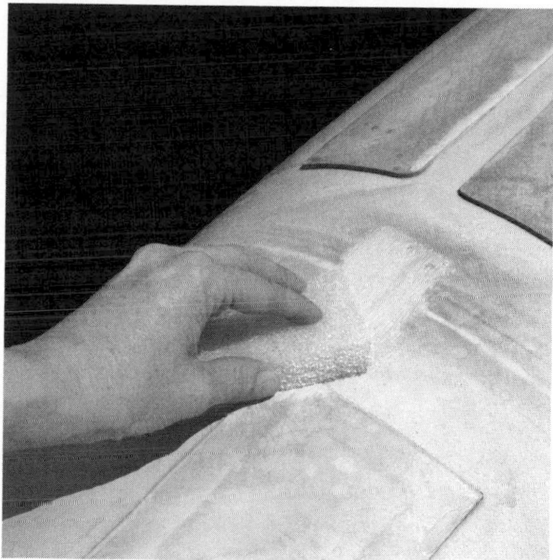

A sponge or cloth dipped in vinegar and sprinkled with baking soda should remove most fresh stains from inflatables.

Sand Versus Inflatables

To prevent the floor of your soft-bottom inflatable from becoming excessively worn, rinse off your feet before entering the inflatable, especially if you're coming from a beach. Sand is very abrasive and chafes both Hypalon floors and pontoons.

The best thing you can do to make your inflatable last longer is to thoroughly rinse off the boat with freshwater after each use. Once a month remove the floorboards, and flush out accumulated sand and grit, which act as an abrasive and wear at the material. Remove the drain plug and clean to ensure a continued tight fit. The best maintenance is to keep a rag on board and clean the dinghy as she gets dirty.

Pressure Gauge Test

You suspect that the pressure gauge on your inflatable is not working properly? Press on the inflatable tubes. Do they give? If so, pump some more. Chances are you haven't pumped up the inflatable as much as you think you have, which is why the pressure gauge isn't registering yet. If the gauge still doesn't work when the tubes appear solid, call the store where purchased and get a new gauge.

Just Like with Boat Guests, Hot Air Expands

Heat causes air to expand, so if you originally filled the inflatable during a cooler part of the day, when the temperature increases, release some air to reduce excessive pressure on the seams.

The Proper Inflation Range

Overinflation is normally not a problem. The tubes on most name-brand inflatables such as Zodiac and Avon can take up to four times the recommended inflation pressure.

Underinflation, however, can be a serious problem, because when the inflatable structure is less than rigid, especially in rough weather, components are more likely to fail.

Sherlock Holmes and the Case of the Leaking Inflatable

If your inflatable is slowly losing air, you can quickly find the leak by covering the inflatable tubes one small area at a time with a coating of soapy water, keeping an eye out for bubbles, which indicate a leak. Don't forget to check the high-chafe areas where floorboards rub against the material for white patches where the fabric shows through. Patch as recommended by the manufacturer.

Proper Patch Procedures

Old patches on your inflatable are beginning to lift. What can you do? For a complete seal, replace the patch, and then apply a top coat of glue after the patch has dried. Round patches are less likely to lift than square ones, so snip the corners. Patches should always be 1 inch larger than the tear on all sides.

If you anticipate trouble getting a patch to conform to the curved surface of a pontoon, tape it to a beer or soda can overnight, and then make the repair. This technique works best if you stow the patch/can combo in a dry place.

To open seams on a badly damaged inflatable so you can repair it, use a hair dryer set on hot. This works well for drying out an area before patching, too. It works whether the repair area is fabric or, in the case of rigid-bottom inflatables, fiberglass.

When patching the bottom of an inflatable, patch both sides (inside and out); otherwise, sand tracked about inside the inflatable can erode the outer patch's seal. Paint a top coat of patch glue over both patches after they dry to ensure a tight, sand- and friction-resistant seal.

Wrap your inflatable patch around a soda can overnight to get it to conform to the curved tube better.

How to Spot Tiny Holes

Does water seem to slowly seep through the bottom of your inflatable, but there are no visible holes? The hole might be too small to see from inside the boat. Empty it and flip it upside down in shallow water. Then get under it and into the air pocket it creates. Now look up; you'll see sunlight streaming through the trouble spots.

Dry Storage

No tarp is completely watertight. Your best bet to keep your boat interior drier during storage is to position the boat with the bow pointing slightly upward so that water drains toward the transom. Add an extra piece of wood to the bow support to achieve the necessary tilt. Leave the drain plug open so that water can run straight out.

Inflatables Need Winterizing, Too

To winterize your inflatable, clean and dry it thoroughly, vacuum up any grit that's dried on, and sprinkle some talcum powder on the deflated vessel before rolling it up for stowage. The powder will absorb moisture and prevent mildew.

Instant Tiller Arm Extension

Need to make a quick extension tiller arm for your inflatable's outboard? Cut a piece of PVC pipe to length and split it in half. Then hose clamp it to the tiller arm.

Outboard CPR

Your inflatable's small outboard seems to have seized up as a result of being stored in that deck box these past few months. Remove the spark plug(s) and squirt rust penetrant into the cylinders. Let it sit for a while, and then try working the flywheel back and forth by hand. This may take some time and several applications. Once you've freed the pistons, squirt lightweight oil into the cylinder(s) and turn the motor over by hand a few times to lubricate the cylinder walls. Only turn the engine clockwise (as viewed from the top) to keep the water pump blades from flipping over the wrong way.

DINGHIES AND TENDERS

Innovative Dinghy Storage

If you'd like to store your small fiberglass or plastic dinghy in the garage, where it's completely protected from the elements, but don't have the space, look to the ceiling. Small and light dinghies and tenders that can be lifted by one or two people can be hung from the ceiling of your garage on two suspended struts that resemble park swings in design (two supporting ropes or chains and a plank "seat"). A piece of plywood or an unused ladder can be placed beneath the boat on the struts to provide additional support and provide space to store gear such as PFDs.

Easy-to-Install Additional Flotation

If you're concerned that your small fiberglass or plastic dinghy might sink if swamped by a wave, add pieces of additional foam flotation and secure it underneath the seats. Even inflatables can use some extra flotation, which will compensate for loss of air in the event of a puncture in the inflatable tube.

Stop Transom Flex

The transom on your fiberglass dinghy is flexing?! First check that you're not overpowered, which puts undue strain on the transom. If you are, exchange your outboard for one of the proper power. You can reinforce your transom by attaching a triangular-shaped piece of fiberglass or marine wood at a 90-degree angle to your mid-transom. Affix the other side of the triangle securely, also at a 90-degree angle, to the dinghy's floor. The longer side of the offset triangle should be attached to the floor for the most support. Epoxy the triangle into place and cover the newly formed joints with fiberglass tape for additional strength.

Perfect Power

If you need to figure out what size outboard to use on your tender, use this rule of thumb: To reach a speed of 25 knots, your boat's weight divided by 40 equals the necessary horsepower. For example, a 500-pound dinghy needs about a 12.5 hp motor to reach 25 knots, and a 1,000-pound boat needs 25 hp.

Seats Aren't Steps

You've used the seats on your fiberglass or wood dinghy as steps to embark and disembark, and now the screws that hold the seats in place have become loose? Remove the loosening screws, drill a slightly larger hole two-thirds of the way into the screw penetration, and then fill the entire cavity with epoxy filler. Replace all screws immediately so that their threads are embedded in the epoxy as it sets. After the epoxy has hardened, remove the screws and replace the seat plank and screws. The threads created in the epoxy mold hold the screws tightly in place.

Bow Eye Installation

Although each dinghy is unique, the basic rule of thumb is to install the bow eye so that the boat can be towed at its normal waterline. Put the bow eye too high, and the dinghy plunges into the water and you have to force it aside, which puts excessive wear and tear on the dinghy and increases fuel consumption on the towing vessel. Put the bow eye too low, and you may find yourself immersing the stern, which also increases towing resistance.

Plug Those Leaks

Your wooden dinghy has taken a beating and has begun to develop small leaks at its joints. The solution is to seal the joints with fiberglass tape. Clean the area thoroughly first, and then apply sufficient resin to the tape and press the tape into place, making sure the tape is pressed flat as you go. Now coat the tape with sufficient resin to soak it. Use short brush-strokes and work from the center outward to avoid bubbles. If needed, add talc to the mixture to thicken the resin. This procedure also serves to reinforce questionable cracks on fiberglass dinghies.

Low-Impact Trailering

The wooden planks on your dinghy trolley (trailer) are scratching the hull. Cover the bare wood with soft plastic tubing or sponges covered with canvas. Make sure the securing nails and screws are placed safely underneath the wood. Never cover trailer bunks or supports with pieces of old tire because stones can get embedded in the treads during normal use and scratch the hull.

MY FIRST WINTERIZING

old the first time I helped win-
mily boat. Looking back, I have
obably didn't do much beyond
ay, but at the time, my parents
n as if the job just wasn't possi-
my help.
es included scouring cabinets and
nything that needed to come out
outtoned up the boat. I bustled all
boat, dragging my teddy bear
sitting him at the helm to oversee
I offered to help lift things (too
ap things with my blanket, empty
(who drank all the Yoo-Hoo's?),
ings up. I loved taping things, but
s knew I'd use the whole roll on
moving slower than a crawl.

Finally the cabin and cockpit were secured for the winter layup and it was time to cover the boat with the huge brown tarp. Because I was the shortest crew member, I was in charge of running the line under the boat. Back and forth I ran, as fast as my little legs would carry me, and in record time we had the boat snug for her winter nap.

That night, sleeping the sleep of an exhausted child, I woke with a start and began screaming like a banshee. When my parents were finally able to understand what I was saying, they sighed, bundled me in a coat, and headed to the car for the long drive to the boatyard.

I'd left my teddy bear sitting at the helm.

the engine for a few minutes to dis-
fresh oil.

tem Changeover

ng sleep over the dreaded thought of
g the fuel system? Don't take
Turn off the fuel line at the tank and
the fuel lines and the carburetor, if
ine has one. (Disconnect the high-
ead to prevent accidental startup.)
he filters and clean them. Remove the
s and replace them with new ones.
t the sediment bowls. Next, remove
an the spark plugs. Spray a small
of valve oil into each cylinder, and then
replacing the plugs, crank over the
by hand to distribute the oil properly.
replace the plugs and fill the fuel tank
conditioning fuel additive or a fuel stabi-
ded to your fresh gas.

Freshwater System Prep

You cut school the day your shop teacher explained how to winterize a freshwater-cooled inboard. Top off the freshwater antifreeze until it is a minimum 35 percent for southern states, and more in cooler climates. If the temperatures will drop below freezing, drain the block of all freshwater, and then follow the manufacturer's instructions. Check the lines for blockage and clean out if necessary. Check the lines for bulges or weak spots and replace if necessary. Grease the plugs to keep them sufficiently lubricated.

Saltwater Line Workup

Many boaters forget the saltwater lines when winterizing a freshwater-cooled inboard. Drain the saltwater lines by locking off the seacocks at the intake and disconnecting the hoses. Drain the water pump. Relax the tension on the water pump belts, and spray down all connections with

WINTERI
AND SP
COMMISSI

WINTERIZING

Basic Fuel Prep

Just before you haul out, add fuel stabilizer to the tanks immediately after topping off, and run your boat for a final few hours of the season. This ensures that the stabilizer is well mixed with the fuel and protects fuel in the filters and lines. While you need to add a fuel treatment with ethanol-blended fuels, do *not* use an additive that is alcohol or contains alcohol! Do not add any additional alcohol to ethanol-blended fuel (E10 or E15) as it will attract moisture into the fuel. Unless stabilized, ethanol-blended fuels begin to degrade in as little as a month, forming gums and other solids that will cause fuel-delivery clogs and result in engine malfunctions. Star Tron is a safe fuel treatment that can be used in all engines with all fuels.

Keep Microbiological Organisms out of Your Tank

Microbioligical organisms are attracted to the condensation that forms in a diesel fuel tank

due to e
winter mo
keep your
in the spri
cides is St
treatment.

The Oil Ne

To eliminate
crankcase, a
do if left un
the engine oi

You've cha
layups, but mo
much differen
your boat out
when the engir
This will remove
lated sludge and
suspended in th
done differently
instruction manu
oil filter with a ne
provide almost in
startup) and refil

I was 6 years
terize our fa
to admit I pr
get in the w
made it seen
ble without

My duti
lockers for a
before we b
around the
with me or
the work.
heavy), wr
the fridge
or tape th
my paren
anything

leaks. Run
tribute the

Easy Sys

You're los
winterizin
Sominex.
drain out
your eng
tension
Remove
cartridge
Wash o
and cle
amount
before
engine
Finally,
with a
lizer ac

a water-repelling lubricant. Seal off the exhaust openings to prevent dampness from sneaking in and undoing all your good work. One of the easiest ways to create a simple exhaust cover is to slice off the bottom of an appropriately sized plastic bottle and duct tape it in place.

WD-40 Buffers Against Winter Dampness

To prevent dampness from sneaking into your exhaust pipe and causing engine corrosion, spray WD-40 into the exhaust pipe immediately before sealing off the exhaust openings.

Don't Leave Exhaust Stains on Until Spring

Transom exhaust stains are unattractive and should not be left to sit over the winter, unless you'd like to risk keeping them permanently. Apply full-strength oxalic acid in liquid or paste form to remove most rust stains from fiberglass surfaces. This is a safe yet very effective acid that is not remotely as dangerous as muriatic acid or other caustic acids. Liquid laundry detergent and elbow grease usually remove fresh black soot. Hand compounding is recommended in drastic cases.

Outboard Treatment

If you dread the task of draining your outboard engine, try this time-tested one-two punch:

1. Flush the engine with freshwater. As you let the engine idle, remove the cowling and turn off the fuel valve. Spray oil into the carburetor intake. Wait until the fuel has just about run out, and then spray more oil, until the motor stalls.
2. Tilt the engine so that it's vertical (it must be out of all water, even a flushing tank). To push remaining water out of the water pump, hand crank the engine.

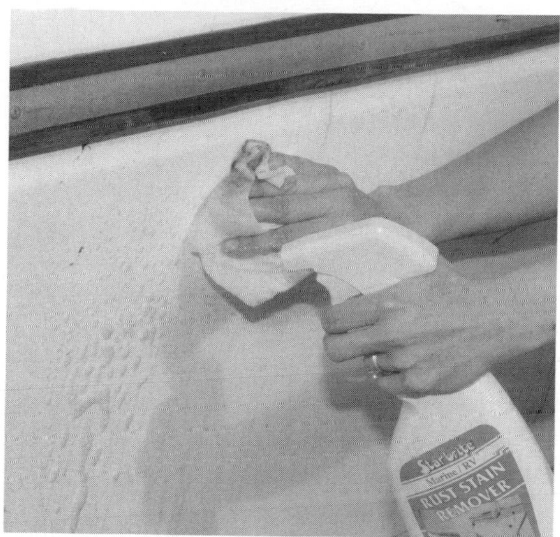

Remove rust stains now so they don't set over the long winter months and make spring commissioning more difficult.

Winterizing Outboard Plugs

Like your inboard-owning brothers and sisters, you'd rather tangle with Freddy Kruger than your outboard's fuel system. After you've drained the fuel tank and all fuel lines, remove the spark plugs, clean them, and spray them with fogging oil. Spray a small amount of fogging oil into each cylinder, and then before reinserting the plugs, crank over the engine by hand to distribute the oil properly. Reinstall the plugs.

Easy Outboard Lubrication

Is there a quick way to lubricate an outboard? Use a grease gun to shoot grease into the zerk fitting on the exhaust housing, until it spurts out the air vent near the top. Next, check the lower unit drive lubricant level as directed in your owner's manual. ***NOTE:*** Disconnect the spark plug wires to prevent unintentional starting.

Prepping an Outdrive

Is winterizing the outdrive of an inboard/outboard similar to laying up a traditional outboard?

Almost. Tilt the outdrive until it's fully down, and flush the engine with freshwater. Pull the flushing and drain plugs, and/or open the petcocks, to allow for complete drainage. (Leave the plugs out when done. Remember to store them where they'll be easily found in the spring—maybe with your boat keys.) Check the oil and lubricant levels and fill as needed. This reduces the chance of moisture damage. While you're at it, why not grease the steering linkage? (Check your owner's manual for the correct lubricant.) Use a nontoxic propylene glycol antifreeze to protect the engine block and water systems from freezing. Make sure to use one with a PVC burst point that is lower than your lowest expected temperatures.

Lubricate, Lubricate, Lubricate

Last winter froze up more than the temperature—it also did in some of the moving parts on your boat. Lubricate your trim and tilt, steering system, throttle linkage, and all other movable parts with oil. Use any excess oil on a rag to wipe unprotected metal surfaces, especially in the engine compartment.

Propeller Fine-Tuning

Your propeller is still in relatively good shape, but it's beginning to show wear. At the end of each season, the propeller should be removed and given a visual inspection. Lightly hammer out the dings and sand the nicks until even. If damaged, what better time to send the propeller out for repair than when you're not going to be using it for a few months? Use bronze wool to scour the propeller.

Let Bleach Scour off the Lower-Unit Growth

An easy way to clean the accumulated growth off a stern drive or outboard lower unit that is left in the water is to tie a heavy plastic bag securely around it. Pour 1 gallon household bleach into the bag, and allow it to work itself around the outdrive. Tie the bag securely so that none of the bleach gets into the water, and let the solution sit overnight. The growth will be gone in the morning.

How Garbage Bags Can Save Hours of Cleaning

You need to keep your now-clean (if you used the previous tip) outdrive or lower unit clean until you next use it, even though it will be sitting in the water all winter. Cover the unit securely with a plastic bag. This will protect it from barnacles and growth. Remember to tape a note somewhere conspicuous on deck, such as on the steering wheel, reminding yourself that the bag is down there and needs to be removed before you start the engine.

Zinc Education

Your boat sits in salt water, but your zincs never wear. Did you accidentally paint or wax them during the season? This is a no-no. Zincs must be left bare to work properly.

If your zincs are installed properly but show no wear, immediately check around them for corrosion, including blistered paint, which indicates corrosion beneath. Strip off all signs of corrosion, and prime and paint with a rust-resistant paint. If in doubt, replace the zincs.

Your zincs seem to erode in no time at all? Each manufacturer uses different blends of metals in its zincs. A generic brand from a marine supply store provides little protection and could even void your warranty. Next time, buy the zincs from your dealer.

Cheap Oil Absorbers

Baby diapers and feminine sanitary napkins work well to soak up engine oil in your bilge. They're inexpensive and may be already at hand.

Check Your Insurance

Many boat insurance policies don't cover ice and freezing-related damage, so always be sure to drain all the lines in your boat and remove any other water, such as that found in forgotten holds.

Freshwater Antifreeze

Freshwater antifreeze keeps the water in your head from freezing and the associated pipes from cracking. First, remove the intake hose at the seacock and lock off the seacock. Fill a 2-gallon bucket with antifreeze and drop the intake hose into it. Flush. The system automatically fills itself with antifreeze. Reattach the hose to the seacock. For boats spending winter on land, open the seacocks for ventilation. Be sure to use a nontoxic propylene glycol antifreeze. Choose one with a PVC burst temperature that is lower than your expected lowest temperature. ***NOTE:*** Some toilets need to be flushed of antifreeze before use. Check your owner's manual.

Winter Glass Repair

It's time to fix that nick in your windshield, mirror, or other glass. A drop of clear nail polish mends a small spot and helps retard further damage. To clean windows and mirrors inexpensively but so that they sparkle, use windshield washer fluid and an old newspaper.

Button up Your Instrument Panel

Winter ages your instrument panel more rapidly than the rest of the boat. To keep the instrument panel looking new, cover it with a light coating of a polymer polish. Do not buff until spring, but leave it as a protective white paste.

Never hose down the instrument panel because it can force water into the gauges. Always wipe down with a wet rag and gentle cleaner. After you're done, toss an old towel across the instruments to wick up any remaining water and the following morning's condensation while providing a protective barrier from ultraviolet rays.

Electronics Connectors Need Attention, Too

Electronics connectors that are left on the boat are especially vulnerable to winter corrosion. To ensure complete protection over the winter, lightly scour the connectors with a piece of fine abrasive material before you spray them with an anticorrosion lubricant. If the connectors are already corroded, scour with bronze wool before spraying lubricant generously.

The Best Place to Keep Your Speed Sensor Is in Your Garage

If your boat has a speedometer, remove the underwater sensor, or you might find it covered in growth next spring. Even if your boat is stored in dry dock, removing the sensor is a good idea because it means there's one more part that can't be damaged during hauling out or bottom cleaning. Install and secure the dummy plug so the boat won't sink if you forget to reinstall the paddle wheel before launching.

A Few Last "Don't Forgets"

The following will take only a few minutes, but completing these few often-forgotten tasks is vital:

- If you want hinges and door latches to work next spring, oil them, and use a graphite lock lubricant in all locks.
- Check your owner's manual to see if your steering system chains and pulleys need an annual layup lubricating.

Deck Antennas

VHF radio and global positioning system antennas are pretty vulnerable when sitting out exposed to the winter elements. The only way

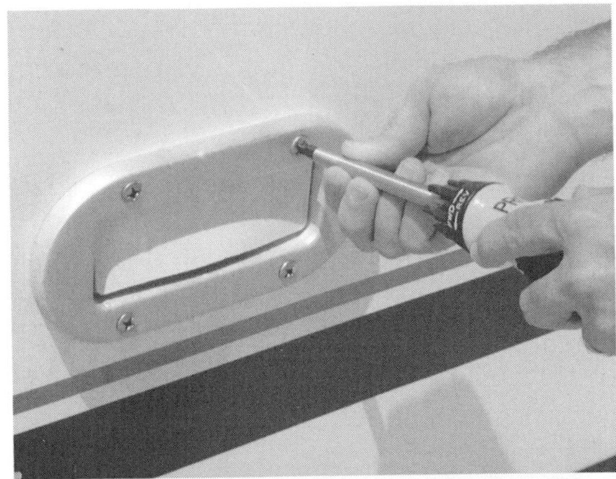

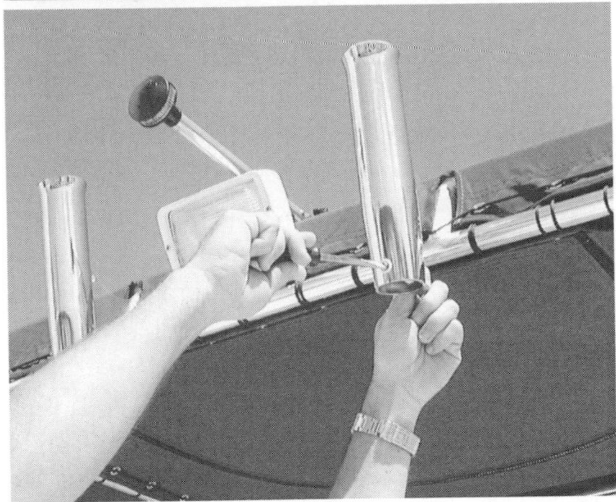

Take a few moments to check for and tighten any screws that have loosened during the boating season.

to really ensure longer life is to remove the antennas and store them indoors or inside the cabin. Thoroughly clean all contacts and mounting points after removal, and protect them with a moisture-resistant lubricant.

Make Nonskid Cleaning Easier

Got a nonskid deck or swim platform that's murder to clean? Don't leave it until the spring, or it will only be worse. Use a little nonabrasive cleanser and a hard-bristle brush. If that, combined with elbow grease, doesn't do the trick, try a tiny amount of acetone.

Remove Scupper Stains Before They Become Permanent

The unsightly stains caused by water runoff from scuppers should be removed in the fall or they may become a permanent hull discoloration in the spring. If the stain is relatively new, a good rust-removal product should remove it. If the stains are worked into the fiberglass, you need to use harsh chemicals such as Lime-A-Way, Naval Jelly, or muriatic acid, which require careful application, goggles, and gloves.

Think of Next Spring

To significantly lessen spring commissioning chores, do a complete washdown to remove the dirt that can otherwise result in a stained boat in the spring. Next, take a moment to polish the hull. Only this time don't buff the polish to a shine, but leave the polish as a protective white paste. Next spring, you can buff your boat to a shine. ***NOTE:*** A second application of polish may be needed in the spring for a complete showroom shine.

Get out the Touchup Paint

If, while cleaning, you notice some nicks and wear in the boat paint, fix them immediately to keep the paint from disintegrating further. Your timely repair will have the added benefit of sealing out potential moisture damage.

Stainless Steel Isn't Indestructible

Stainless steel may be boating's miracle metal, but it can become discolored and pitted. To prevent winter damage, apply polish to stainless steel or spray on a moisture-displacing lubricant such as Corrosion Block. Make all applications thorough but light to lessen the spring cleaning. Don't forget the steering wheel and many small pieces of stainless, such as hinges, on board.

Docklines Need Air over the Winter

If your docklines and anchor line tend to attract mildew like Moldcraft lures attract fish, simply wash and dry the lines *thoroughly* before storage in a dry, well-aired place. Do not store them in the anchor hatch if it leaks (as many do), nor on deck, even if they appear to weather well there during the season.

The Painless Freshwater System Drain

If you'd rather dunk your head in a bucket of bilge water than drain your freshwater system, follow these systematic steps: Disconnect the water line from the water tank and let the water drain. Next, disconnect the water lines leading to the water pump and let them drain. If there are any low points in the system where water can accumulate, don't forget to empty them also. The same holds true for appliance lines and an on-deck freshwater washdown. If you have access to an air compressor, use it to guarantee that the lines are thoroughly cleared.

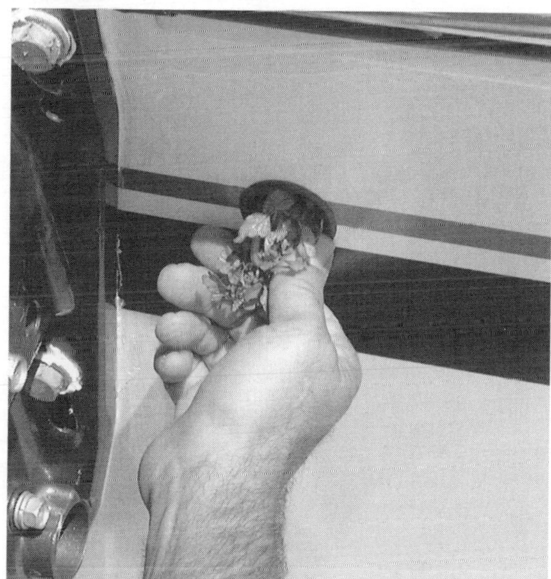

Make sure drains are clear and free flowing before closing up the boat for winter.

When the freshwater system is drained and winterized, why not take the opportunity to take in your water pump for its annual service? After all, you won't be using it for a while.

What's the least complicated way to winterize your freshwater system? Use nontoxic antifreeze formulated especially for freshwater systems. Read all the manufacturer's directions before use. When the water flowing out the system outlets, such as faucets, shows the color of the antifreeze, you've sufficiently flooded the system. ***NOTE:*** Some commercial antifreezes can leave behind a residue you can taste.

Don't Get Locked Out

To keep a cabin hatch padlock from freezing during winter storage, tie a plastic sandwich bag over it.

Winter Air Is Good

Because they don't make Odor Eaters large enough to attack the smells that can accumulate in a sealed cabin, leave some hatches and maybe a window slightly open, making sure that in doing so you're not allowing in rain or snow. Also, prop open all interior doors from the head door to the storage and galley lockers, and leave drawers slightly ajar for increased ventilation. Using a chemical dehumidifier and a chlorine dioxide mold-odor eliminator is the best way to protect against smelly surprises when you open the boat in the spring.

Cabin Cushions and Things

If winter mildew finds your cushions as comfortable a resting place as you do, first vacuum cushions thoroughly, and then prop them at odd angles to the cabin furniture so that air can flow around them. The same holds true for PFDs left on board. This may make your cabin look a mess, but remember that sufficient ventilation prevents mold and mildew.

If you must store clothing, sheets, towels, and so on on board over the winter, put fabric softener sheets in between them to keep them fresh smelling.

Repel Rodents

Mothballs repel most winter pests, including spiders and rodents. Place them inside a sealed container with small ventilation holes (which you can punch yourself) in case you bring curious kids and pets on board in the spring. Another alternative is to mix borax (or boric acid crystals) with powdered sugar and leave about in childproof containers.

Don't Come Back to a Headache

To lessen spring maintenance, apply a polish to the head's fiberglass surfaces (but not the floor!). A rubber shower mat may be needed afterward to keep you from slipping around and perhaps seriously injuring yourself.

Pour a generous amount of sweet pickle juice down the drain to keep a fresh scent throughout the winter. Do not add water. This works in your head sink, shower, and galley drains.

The holding tank can take over the boat during the winter months if not attended to during the fall layup. Flush with freshwater, and repeat as necessary. When done, add 3 to 4 quarts antifreeze to the mixture. Turn on the holding tank pump to fill with antifreeze.

Is the medicine cabinet in the head to be treated like the other cabin cabinetry? You've hit the nail on the "head." Even though the contents are in sealed bottles and tubes, empty the medicine cabinet, clean the shelves, and leave the door ajar for ventilation.

Don't Let Neglect Lead to a Gruesome Galley

You want to leave your canned foods and unopened sodas in the galley over winter.

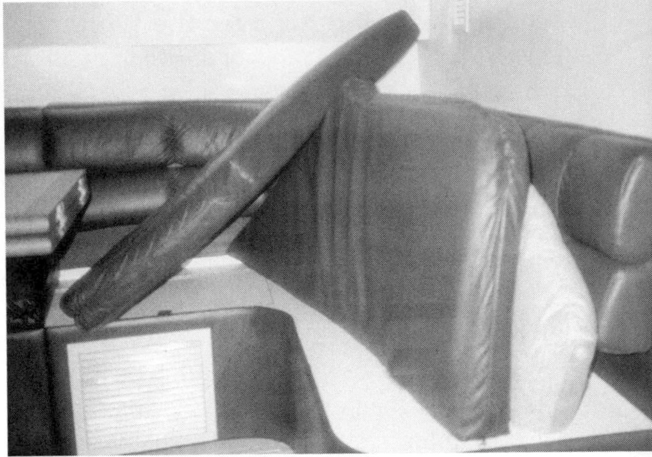

To lessen winter mildew, place cabin cushions at odd angles to the furniture so the air can move around them.

Don't! Cold temperatures can cause liquids and the moisture in food to freeze, and they can make otherwise intact seals rupture. Remove all food and beverages, even if canned, bottled, or in plastic packages.

Help Keep the Energizer Bunny Going

All onboard batteries, from AAA to the starter battery, should be removed and stored in a warm, dry place. Give engine batteries periodic booster charges during the winter months. Clean dirty terminals with baking soda and water and a wire brush, and then lightly coat with petroleum jelly.

Pack So You Can Find Things Later

Sort all the items you remove from your boat, from electronics to PFDs, and put them in labeled boxes for efficient unpacking, just as you would if you were moving to a new house, which in effect you are.

Dink-Free Storage

Last year the electronics you removed from your boat got dinked while in storage? This year, before storing, wrap each piece separately in an old towel to prevent accidental scratching. Next, place them in individual, labeled boxes or wrap them in cardboard to prevent more serious damage.

Canvas Care

Your T-top and other canvas protected you throughout the season. How can you return the favor? Standard canvas really should be removed for proper winter storage, as it's not designed to withstand the harsh elements of winter. Clean all canvas thoroughly, whether on a T-top, Bimini, or boat cover. Grimy canvas is a large "Come Aboard" sign to mold and mildew. Lubricate all zippers with Teflon lubricant prior to storage. If you plan to cover your boat, consider a special heavy-duty, waterproof tarp. Apply a waterproofing product to extend the life of all canvas covers and Bimini or T-tops.

Tarp Technique

Although covering a boat with a tarp will protect the deck from the harsh elements of winter, covering it too tightly will encourage mold, mildew, and unpleasant odors. To ensure suitable ventilation, toss your fenders overboard before covering your boat and tie the cover or tarp over them. This will hold the tarp slightly away from the hull, without leaving the cover dangerously loose.

Boater Versus Winter Winds

Mother Nature is determined to uncover your boat. What can you do to thwart her? A rectangular shaped tarp can work as well as a fitted cover if you run the securing line through all the available grommets. Feel free to use some grommets twice or to add more if necessary. The smallest flaps left blowing in the breeze will soon become a major problem. Also, buy a spool of strong line for a quick tie-down, and you will escape the problems associated with using pieces of scrap line.

Harsh winter winds can cause a tarp to rub and chafe against your boat. To protect your boat from the damage caused by a rubbing tarp, pad the joint and stress areas. Small carpet remnants, foam pads, or a folded towel all work equally well.

Plastic Polish/Protectants

If you leave your boat canvas up, cleaning the vinyl isinglass windows that complete your canvas enclosure isn't enough. If you're going to ask your canvas to act as a winter boat cover, you have to fully protect the isinglass against layup damage, which can range from oxidation due to exposure to the sun to scratches due to the rough winter wind. The easiest way is to coat on a combination plastic polish/protectant. For maximum results, you should do this monthly, or at least as often as weather permits.

Don't Forget Your Boat Over the Winter

It's a good idea to check on your boat at least once a month during winter storage. When tying down the boat cover or tarp, use more than one piece of line, tying the tarp down in such a way that a shorter section of line can be easily untied to form a "doorway" that does not involve removing the entire tarp.

IF YOU CHOOSE TO GO WINTER BOATING . . .

How Low Can the Temperature Go for Your Boat?

To determine the lowest temperature that your boat's oil can withstand, call the oil manufacturer and ask for a copy of the oil's spec sheet. Find its cold performance properties and add 20 degrees to the coldest pour temperature listed. This is the point at which the oil is still liquid enough to move through the system. If it's colder than this outside, keep the boat docked, or you risk scuffing the engine's pistons and rings.

Inboard engines using straight oil shouldn't be run in temperatures lower than 40 to 45 degrees. The oil doesn't flow as readily to the valve train, bearings, and lifters. Multigrade oil works best in cold temperatures; it is more lubricating and less likely to thin. If you're running 10W30, consider switching to the thinner 5W30 in temperatures of 10 degrees and below. But call the engine manufacturer first, because some don't recommend running their engines with certain multigrade oils.

Hot Water Bottles for Boats

To guarantee a quick and easy engine start, set a battery warmer, available at many northern car dealerships, on your boat's battery the night before.

In milder winters, burning a 100-watt lightbulb inside the engine compartment helps keep the temperature up and the engine from freezing.

You Shouldn't Be Able to Ice Skate on Your Bilge

Pouring antifreeze into the bilge will keep any water that accumulates in it from freezing. It's especially important if you forget to drain the bilge for a few days afterward. Star brite's Winter Safe nontoxic, propylene glyclol antifreeze protects against low temperatures, with a Copper burst point of –50F°. ***NOTE:*** Make sure to check the PVC burst point of any antifreeze you use. If your boat's in storage, sprinkle some baking soda into the bilge and leave it there over the winter to prevent foul odors. A little goes a long way, so don't pour in the whole box—too much can clog the limber holes.

Cold Weather Concerns

When anchoring during a winter outing, don't tilt your motor's lower unit out of the water. If you're anchored for a while, water in the lower unit can freeze, causing damage.

Cold weather makes rubber hoses brittle and prone to cracking. Replace questionable hoses (any that are softening, splitting, or more than 2 or 3 years old) when winterizing or at least before taking your boat out on frigid waters.

Winter boating can be an enjoyable pursuit if done properly.

When cruising in the cold, drain any raw water in the engine each night. Don't leave water that does not have antifreeze or is not otherwise protected from below-freezing weather in any of the boat's systems.

Frigid Metal

A cool-looking stainless steel steering wheel becomes untouchably frigid in winter. Wool gloves keep you warm but have no grip; leather gloves grip but not when wet. Wrap the wheel in nylon line. With ¼-inch line, make a clove hitch next to a post. Wrap the line around the rim and tuck it under itself, making a simple overhand knot (half a square knot). Repeat this knotting until you've returned to where you started. Tie the end with a second clove hitch. The knots hold the wrapped line tightly to the wheel and create a spiral ridge for better gripping.

SPRING COMMISSIONING

Octane Drop

You haven't run your boat for months, and now it won't start? Before you call the mechanic, try fresh fuel. Gasoline loses octane quickly, and water can form in your fuel tank in just a few months. Either problem can keep you from cruising. Adding Star Tron fuel treatment can restore octane to old, substandard, or non-spec fuel, saving you money and getting you back out on the water.

Electronics Touchup

Before you plug in your electronics for the new season, touch up the connections with a shot of nonsolvent-based anticorrosive such as Corrosion X or Corrosion Block. The protective lubricant you sprayed on when winterizing has probably, to some extent, dried out. Don't use petroleum jelly because it can also seal in moisture.

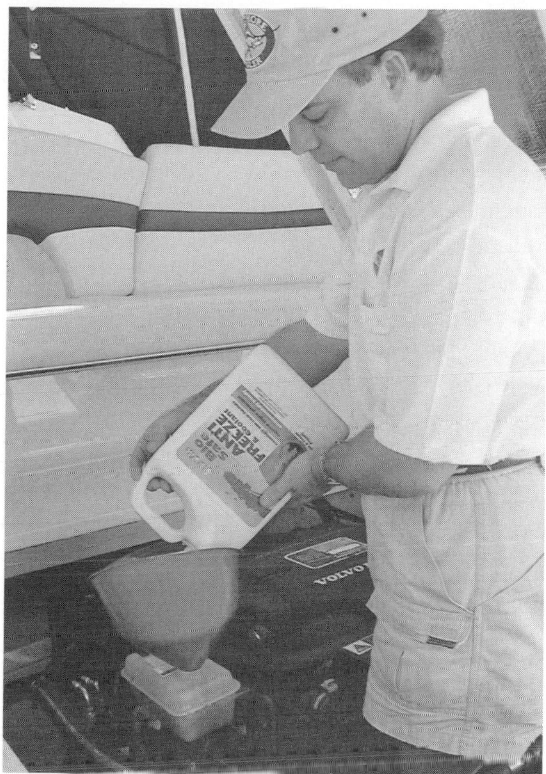

Propylene glycol–based antifreeze is nontoxic and provides excellent year-round protection.

Winter Corrosion Removal

To maintain bright running lights, now is the time to remove the housings. Take out the bulb and clean the contacts in the base with a pencil eraser or fine sandpaper. Do the same to the bulb contacts. Wipe out residue and spray demoisturizer on all contact surfaces. Wipe off any that gets on the bulb after it's locked in the socket. Use a clear plastic cleaner-polish to shine up glass or plastic lenses. If the gasket is damaged, replace or make one out of clear silicone. Grease screws lightly before tightening into the light housing.

Restoring Isinglass

Left your boat canvas up all winter without doing the periodic maintenance that last fall you promised yourself you'd do? Well now you're paying the price. One of the easiest ways to extend the life of your clear vinyl windows is to coat them with furniture polish at the start of every boating season, whether they've been left neglected in the snow and icy wind or not. Furniture polish works well. The polish restores the plasticizers in the vinyl, which leach away from sunlight, salt water, cold weather, and flexing. ***NOTE:*** Be sure to avoid products containing solvents or petroleum distillates. If in doubt, use a specialty product such as Star brite View Guard.

Bring Your Anchor Back up to Snuff

If, over the winter months, your deck-stowed galvanized anchor has become rusted in the places where it chafed against rocks during the season, spiff up its shabby appearance by loosening rust with a wire brush and then applying a rust-conversion coating (available from a hardware store) where needed. Spray these areas with an aerosol cold-galvanizing compound that's at least 65 percent pure zinc by weight (check the label).

Counter Cleanup

When you return to your boat in the spring, you find your Formica or plastic laminate galley counters stained by winter mildew. Squeeze on the juice of a fresh lemon, let set for ½ hour to bleach the stain, and then dust moderately with baking soda and scrub with a clean cloth. Rinse with freshwater. Your galley will smell better, too.

chapter 8

SPECIAL CARE FOR SAILBOATS

Lightweight, often colorful sails such as the spinnaker are usually made of nylon.

SAIL CARE AND MAINTENANCE

What Is Your Sail Made Of?

The rule of thumb is that if a sail is white, it is most likely made of polyester, also commonly referred to by the brand name Dacron. Lightweight, often colorful sails such as the spinnaker and drifters are usually made of nylon. Kevlar—the premiere sail material for racing sailors—is recognized by its golden color. There are other high-tech sailcloth materials on the market, but because they are not commonly found on the average sailboat, we won't go into them here. If you have one of those sails, we expect that you probably already know it.

Important Sail Cleaning Don'ts

Before we get to the do's of sail cleaning, let's start off with some critical don'ts:

- Never wash your sails in a washing machine. Even on the gentlest cycle, damage can occur.
- Never use a pressure washer over 1,100 psi. Sails may appear tough and perform well

If a sail is white, it is most likely made of polyester.

under extreme wind conditions, but they remain vulnerable to these harsh cleaning methods.

- Do *not* clean sails more than once a year. They will be fine as long as you rinse them regularly with freshwater after each day on the ocean or once a week when sailing on lakes or other freshwater.
- Do not use bleach or other caustic agents (see next tip).

The Bleach Controversy

Do not use bleach, solvents, or any other caustic cleaning agents. This is especially important on nylon and Kevlar sails or sails with laminated construction. Some sailmakers say that an extremely diluted bleach mixture (a mere 3 percent to 5 percent bleach to water ratio) is safe on Dacron sails. If you do go this route, rinse the area extremely thoroughly afterward or the bleach may degrade the fabric over time.

A safer alternative for Dacron sails that I recommend before resorting to bleach is a solution of diluted hydrogen peroxide. Hydrogen peroxide is the secret ingredient in some commercially packaged sail washes. Now, you may be thinking of the handy brown bottle in the medicine cabinet, but that's not the one to use. The formulation we are referring to is many times stronger, comes in a powder, and is referred to as sodium percarbonate (often found in common brand names beginning with "Oxy"; check the label). Use as directed.

Petrol Belongs in the Kicker

Beware: Petroleum-based cleaners, waterproofers, and other products can degrade the adhesives on laminated sails. Using them requires a lot of safety precautions to avoid dangerous inhalation of the solution.

Using the Mild Scrub Brush

Eight simple words to clean by: Always scrub in the direction of the seams.

Nylon Sail Bath

Because nylon sails tend to be light and flexible, they can be washed in a large bucket or tub, an oversized storage bin, a kiddie pool, or even your home bathtub. Fill the chosen container with a mild solution of laundry detergent (follow the directions on the bottle or box because each product is different) and allow to soak from 1 to 12 hours depending upon the condition of the sails. Using a soft bristle brush, scrub the sail gently. Rinse thoroughly with freshwater until all soap has been removed. Allow to dry completely.

Gentle Dacron Wash

A mixture of 1½ cups distilled white vinegar and 2 tablespoons Woolite in 1 gallon of water is a gentle yet extremely effective homemade cleaner for Dacron (polyester) sails. Lay out the sail on a flat, clean, nonabrasive surface, or lay a clean tarp over a less-than-pristine flat surface. Gently work in the cleaning mixture with a soft bristle brush. Do not scrub hard; instead, patiently work in the solution carefully one section at a time. Rinse thoroughly with cool water until all the Woolite has been removed. Be sure to allow the sail to dry thoroughly. Any moisture left behind can lead to mildew and worse stains than you had before.

Our Old Enemy, Rust

If you have a sailboat, you will have rust. Eventually, some of that rust may find its way onto your Dacron/polyester sails. If the stain is relatively new and light colored and you'd like to go the homespun route, try lemon juice. Let it soak for 30 minutes and then rinse; repeat as needed.

For stronger stains, use powdered oxalic acid (found in pharmacies and often made from natural ingredients such as rhubarb and spinach). Follow the directions on the container regarding mixing ratio. Allow the sails to soak in this mixture for 10 to 20 minutes and then rinse thoroughly with freshwater. Repeat if needed.

Mildly Mildewed Dacron

The word *mildew* causes shivers down a sailor's spine. However, not all mildew stains are equal. When possible, clean mildew stains on your sails as soon as you discover them and before they have time to set. In those cases a washing down with the Gentle Dacron Wash (see tip on page 118) in *hot* water may be all that is needed. It is worth a try.

Extremely Mildewed Dacron

Although we hesitate to use the "B" word (as in bleach), there are times it may be necessary—such as when nothing else has gotten rid of the stain, even diluted hydrogen peroxide (see "The Bleach Controversy" on page 118). In that case you may want to try a mere 3 percent to 5 percent bleach (often listed on the ingredients as sodium hypochlorite) in a gallon of water. Work on one stain at a time and work quickly. The less time the bleach is on the material, the better. Rinse immediately and thoroughly.

Mildew Mitigator

If you can't clean mildew immediately, spray the affected area with Lysol to destroy existing mold spores and temporarily prevent new growth.

Mildew Migrates

Once you have a mildew problem aboard, you have to be hypervigilant. Keep your newly cleaned sails away from any other mildewed items on the boat, such as sails that have yet to be cleaned, grungy anchor and other lines, sail covers, et cetera. Mildew can spread by contact from spores on a contaminated item to a clean one. Another way that mildew increases is by sending out spores to nearby fresh surfaces that may have sufficient moisture and food on which they can grow. Either way, you want to quarantine your clean sails from sources of remaining mildew.

Oil and Grease Stains

The greases that help the sail system function properly sometimes unfortunately end up on the sail itself. This isn't the nightmare that one might imagine. Simply spray on a general-purpose boat degreaser such as Star brite Super Orange Cleaner/Degreaser to break down the stain. Then follow with the Gentle Dacron Wash (see page 118). Rinse thoroughly afterward.

Prevention Is the Best Maintenance

While you are taking the sails off the boat, take a moment to give them a quick but thorough once-over. Keep an eye out for areas that are worn or corroded, including stitching (both edges and seams), reinforced areas, attachment grommets/rings, and batten pockets, and review the general condition of the sail material (wear spots/chafe, tears, punctures).

Check the slides and headboard on the mainsail, the leech line and its cleat, the roller/furl, and the condition of the sail covers, which provide valuable UV protection. The sun is absolutely the worst enemy of sailcloth.

SAIL REPAIR

Emergency Sail Repairs

Every sailor should have a roll of sail repair tape (or at least some white rigging tape) on board. Do not use duct tape! (More on this later.) These items are invaluable should you get a small hole or a slight tear in your sail. Seemingly minor rips need to be attended to immediately before the wind tears the sail further.

First clean the area thoroughly and allow it to dry completely. This may seem tedious when at sea, but the tape is designed to stick on a clean, dry surface. If the area just won't dry, try dabbing on some rubbing alcohol. You'll be pleased at how quickly this allows the sail to dry.

Next, trim the tape (or several pieces of slightly overlapping tape, if needed) about 2 to 3 inches wider than the area being patched. Securely apply the tape to both sides of the hole, and you're ready to harness the wind again. Depending upon the size of the repaired area, though, you may want to go a bit more carefully until you reach shore.

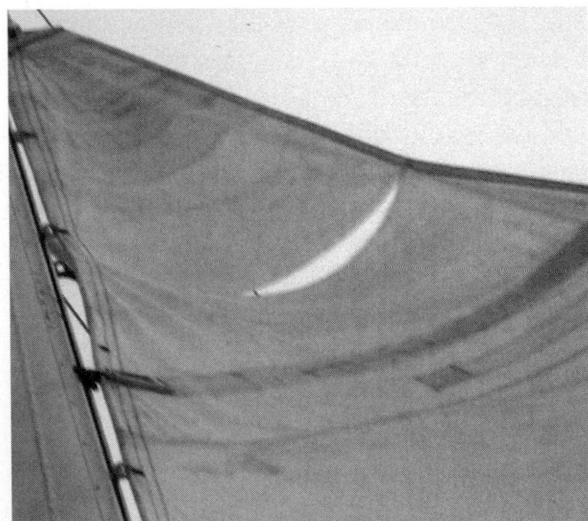

A sail repair kit is an essential piece of safety equipment because you never know when a tear may occur.

Sail Repair Kit

In addition to the sail repair tape already mentioned, your do-it-yourself sail repair kit should contain at the very minimum appropriately sized sewing needles and threads, scissors, spare sail material, and a sailor's palm for pushing the large needles through heavy layers of sailcloth. This basic kit allows you to sew tears that are too large to be repaired with tape.

A more comprehensive kit would include webbing, grommets and a hole cutter/grommet die set, snaps and a snap fastener installation tool, basting or transfer tape for more durable seams, a seam ripper, and a multitool with pliers.

Different Tears, Different Techniques

Before you sew that large tear, strengthen the area to be stitched with sail repair tape. Use it on both sides of the torn sail edge prior to sewing. This tape-stitch method works best on straight-edge tears. Jagged-edge tears or large holes are best fixed by sewing on a repair patch of spare sailcloth.

Step Away from the Duct Tape!

Duct tape is a most marvelous invention, but keep it away from your sails. It doesn't hold as well or as long as tapes made specifically for sailcloth, and it leaves a horrible sticky residue behind. Some sailmakers have been known to refuse to repair sails that have been temporarily fixed with duct tape.

A Word About Sewing Needles

Sewing needles are vulnerable to bending, breaking, falling overboard, and more, so it's a good idea to have more than one (I never go out with fewer than three) of each size you have aboard.

OFF-SEASON SAIL STOWAGE

Nonskid Decks

Nonskid decks have improved deck safety, but although they are friends to your boat shoes, they are not your sail's best friend. Simply put: Don't drag sails over a nonskid deck—it will chafe the material.

Packing Sails

Take the word *crease* out of your vocabulary. Whether you are rolling a sail, flaking it (folding a sail in a loose accordion pattern), or otherwise putting it up for storage, be careful to avoid creases, which can cause the fabric to break down over time. Never ever stuff sails into their bags.

Boat Batteries and Sails Don't Mix

It may seem efficient to store boat equipment together in the off-season, but never store the sails and the boat batteries together. Battery acid has been known to break down sailcloth. Batteries on a trickle charger are the worst because of the corrosive hydrogen gas that is formed during recharging. Hydrogen gas is not only potentially explosive, but it can degrade the sail's metal fittings.

Heat Isn't Any Better

That empty corner in the basement may seem like a great place to leave the sails over the winter months, but be sure to keep them away from any potential heat source, including the furnace, space heaters, even the hot work lights in your home workshop.

FINAL SAIL-CARE TIPS

Here are more tips to help extend the life of your sails.

- Do not flog (allow them to fly/thrash out of control) your sails. Flogging causes the premature breakdown of the sail material, making it more vulnerable to tears.
- Do not exceed the wind range of your sails. Most fabric sails should not be used in more than 30-knot winds. Dacron and other synthetics can withstand higher gusts, but that kind of wind makes for dangerous, uncomfortable sailing conditions, so chances are you'd have lowered the sails by that point.
- Use rigging tape to cover cotter pins, rings, and anything else sharp that can damage the sail. The tape is a cheap and easy preventative that really works. It also protects fingers and toes.
- Rinse your sails often. Clean sails perform better. The salty residue left behind by ocean sailing is abrasive, which can result in premature wear. The salt is also hygroscopic, which means that it absorbs water from the air, which can lead to mildew.
- Remove sails during the off-season and store them inside. Indoor storage can enhance sail life by years.

CARE OF LINES AND RUNNING RIGGING

Convenient Cleaning

The halyards, sheets, preventer, and other rigging lines provide an invaluable service aboard a sailboat, yet they tend to be less thought about than the more high-profile items aboard such as sails. Accumulated dirt, sand, salt, oils, and acid rain can significantly shorten the useful life span of these key players in sail performance. Happily, this is one situation in which your washing machine can do the work for you.

Place lines in pillowcases, mesh wash bags, or—if your wife has trimmed back your sailboat budget too much and you're feeling a bit feisty—her lingerie bags. (Lingerie bags are mesh bags usually with a nylon zipper used to protect delicates from harsh rinse cycles. They are available at some drugstores and grocery stores and online.)

It is important to separate the lines in bags; otherwise, the lines will be a giant tangle at the end of the rinse cycle. Use Woolite, a mild laundry detergent, or a biodegradable boat wash. Set the machine to the gentlest cycle, and use cool water. For especially dirty lines, fill the washer with water and then shut it off for 15 to 30 minutes, which acts as a presoak.

Similarly, if you have a large bucket, tub, or storage bin handy, you can use that as a longer presoak, or just wash the lines by hand if you prefer. If you wash the lines in a bucket, be sure to hose them off until there are no remaining suds to be washed away. Whichever method you prefer, always allow the lines to dry thoroughly after any cleaning.

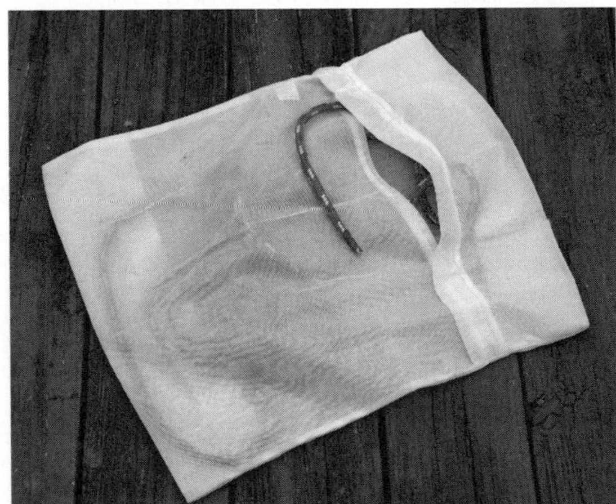

Put lines in a mesh laundry bag to keep them from tangling in the washing machine.

Soft, Flexible Lines

Fabric softener is a simple yet very effective way to keep your lines soft and flexible. Here are two easy ways to accomplish this task.

1. If you wash the lines in your washing machine as mentioned in the previous tip, simply add fabric softener to the washing machine rinse cycle just as you would for a load of laundry. The washing machine will take care of the rest.
2. If you clean your lines using the bucket method cited in the last tip, thoroughly rinse out the bucket, and then prepare a mixture of 6 ounces fabric softener to each gallon of water. Place the newly cleaned lines in the bucket and allow them to soak for 4 to 6 hours or overnight. ***NOTE:*** This method can be used for lines that are already clean but have become stiff. In this case, just skip the cleaning portion.

The bucket unfortunately doesn't give you the washing machine's automated ability to thoroughly rinse out the lines, so you need to hose off the lines thoroughly after the fabric softener soak and then hose out the bucket as well. Refill the bucket with fresh, clear water and put the lines in for a second 4- to 6-hour or overnight soak. Allow the lines to dry thoroughly after removing them from the bucket.

Hard Lines

Lines that have become hard and compacted over time are telling you to give them more than a fabric softener refresher. When rigging lines have become hard and compacted, this is a key indicator that the lines have endured a significant amount of friction and/or have otherwise been subjected to hard use and should be replaced.

Tuck That Pull Back In

A thread pull in an otherwise fine piece of rigging line is no big deal. However, do take the time to tuck the snag back in to keep the line running smoothly and to keep the snag from enlarging into something more serious. If simple hand tucking doesn't work, a small crochet hook can be used from the opposite side of the line to tug the snag back inside.

Dip It

Tattered line ends are a no-no. Not only do they make threading the lines through the running gear difficult if not impossible, they ruin the good looks of an otherwise shipshape sailboat, and they will continue to unravel, making more and more of the line unusable. The solution is a can of line dip such as Dip-It Whip-It from Star brite. [Note: Dip-It Whip-It is the same as Liquid Electrical Tape. Both provide a rubberized coating that is dielectric (won't conduct electricity) and provides a nonslip, durable surface.] Cut the line back to a good, non-frayed portion, cutting off only the bare minimum, and gently dip the line into the can. You don't want to bang the line end around in the can, which will cause the new section of braid to loosen, or you'll end up having to cut the line again for another fresh end. Allow the line whip to dry, and you're ready to go. Line dip lasts considerably longer than simply wrapping the line ends with tape. It works equally well on often-abused dock lines.

The Ultimate Dip It

For those perfectionist sailors, you can hand-wrap the line end with whipping twine before proceeding to the line dip tip just mentioned.

Tattered line ends are difficult to work with and may even jam up the rigging at a critical moment. Trim them back and seal them with line dip.

Select the first usable section of line working back from the frayed edge. Take out one of your sail needles and thread it with whipping line (if you have it, or waxed dental floss if you don't). Thread the whipping twine through the rigging lines braid, creating a loop as you go. Hold the twine and loop in place with your thumb as you remove the needle. Then simply wind the twine around the rigging line, and go over your original excess thread to secure it in place. Keep wrapping in concentric circles until you've got about a half inch of wrapping. Take the remaining twine and slip it through the original loop and tighten until the loop slides under the wrapped portion for a secure, no-bump knot. Trim off excess. Prior to the invention of line dip, sailors stopped here, but a quick dip in Dip-It Whip-It will protect all your hard work and significantly extend the service life of your line even in the harshest conditions such as ocean sailing.

Going from Wire to Rope Halyards

Replacing rope and wire halyard systems with an all-rope option is an idea that is growing in popularity. Before you do, however, a thorough inspection of the running rigging is in order. Grab a piece of sandpaper or three and check for sharp edges along the mast cranes, sheaves, and hounds that the wire halyards were indifferent to but will significantly lessen the life span of your rope line or, worse yet, cause a catastrophic failure. Chafe guards are an option on particularly dangerous areas.

WINCH CARE

The Start

Servicing the winches is perhaps one of the most daunting tasks a sailboater can take on. Yes, you can pay someone to do this for you, but the point of this book is to do it yourself. In addition to the dollar savings, you get the feeling of satisfaction and the sense of confidence that comes from knowing that you have control over the equipment that goes offshore with you, and not the other way around. That said, as with any task that is initially intimidating (not to mention messy), the best way to deal with winch maintenance is to break it down into more manageable parts, the first of which is the list of items you will need to get before you start any work:

- Manufacturer's exploded parts diagram (as close to a "how-to reassemble guide" as you will get), usually available online
- Paper towels (absolutely necessary) and those handy blue Shop Towels (desirable)
- Mineral spirits (acetone or paint thinner) or a serious citrus degreaser for cleaning parts, not to be used while smoking or near sparks, open flame, or high temperatures
- Bucket or other container to clean the parts in
- Box of disposable gloves
- Gear oil
- Winch grease
- Basic spare parts: a pawl and a spring kit
- Comprehensive tool kit that includes the appropriate size Allen wrenches
- 1-inch paintbrush (optional)
- Digital camera (optional)
- Source of hot water

Ready . . . Set . . .

The rule of thumb, no matter what kind of winch you have, is that the connector that holds on the winch handle socket (be it a screw, key, or other form of attachment) is the secret to disassembling the entire winch. After removing the winch handle socket, take out the drum slowly and carefully. Watch out for small parts that may be temporarily stuck in the drum interior; they are just waiting to fall out and disappear as you lift the drum.

Now you've reached the interior parts to be cleaned. Pull out the roller bearings. Take out your Allen wrenches and remove the main housing. Underneath are the gears and ratchets. They will slide out easily.

Cleaning the winches is perhaps one of the most daunting tasks a sailboater can take on.

Making Reassembly Easier

Here is a bit of very good news: On most high-quality modern winches, the parts fit back together only one way, so you really can't reassemble it wrong. That said, I like to take digital photos at critical points along the way of anything I disassemble so that I can refer to them when putting everything back together. This is in addition to the manufacturer's exploded parts diagram. You can't have too many reference points with all these small parts—especially when it comes to the washers, which do not fall under the "can't be reassembled wrong" rule.

Break Out the Mineral Spirits

Place the gears, ratchets, and bearings into the bucket or other container and cover them with mineral spirits. Allow to thoroughly soak. The correct length of time will depend on how long it's been since the winch was last serviced. Some sailors like shop towels, others prefer a 1-inch paintbrush, and some use both for removing remaining grease from the parts, including the gear ring on the drum interior. Place the cleaned parts in the hot water to remove any remaining mineral spirits lest any residue break down the new grease you are going to apply as you reassemble the winch.

Lubrication Rules

As you reassemble the winch, give the pawls a light lubrication with gear oil—never use grease. On the other hand, all the gears, et cetera, do get a thin coating of winch grease. Stainless steel bearings get grease, but plastic bearings do not, as they are in effect self-lubricating.

One trick to making sure things are going along smoothly as you work is to rotate the shaft and the parts you have reinstalled so far to ensure that they are placed properly and spinning freely.

After the unit is reassembled, coat everything with a moderate layer of winch grease. Resist the temptation to overpack. More is *not* better.

If It All Goes Wrong

Despite careful effort, exploded diagrams, and digital reference photos, sometimes parts do not go back as they should. If that's the case, don't panic. You should have aboard an exact mate to the winch you are working on to act as the ultimate guide to where all the little parts go.

CLEANING AND PROTECTING STANDING RIGGING

Quick Rigging Bath

It is essential to wash down the standing rigging after each use. All that is required is a hose and a supply of freshwater, so there is no excuse not to do it after every outing.

Rinse down the standing rigging after every outing. No excuses.

Pay particular attention to the spars, as accumulated salt and dirt can pit and otherwise damage their surface and promote that enemy of all boat owners—galvanic corrosion from the contact between dissimilar metals. All of which can be prevented with regular quick but comprehensive washdowns.

Likewise, keep the boom uber clean. It gets enough abuse from being wrapped in damp sails regularly. You don't want to add the abrasive and corrosive effects of salt and grime to the mix.

Wipe on Protection

At least twice a season, thoroughly saturate a clean cloth with a marine-grade corrosion protectant spray and wipe down all the fittings (stainless steel lifelines and railings, polished metal hardware—hinges, latches, etc.) that you can reach. If there is a light layer of rust, use some elbow grease to remove it and any accumulated salt residue or dirt for a quick yet effective one-step cleaning/protecting of critical equipment.

Turnbuckle Treatment

Screw out the turnbuckles, lubricate the exposed threads with a thin layer of lanolin-based protectant such as Lanacote (yes, it does seem that every part of the boat wants its own particular lube, but there are reasons for this—which in this case is to prevent galling), and screw the turnbuckles back in. Screw in and out a few more times to help work the lubricant in, reapplying lightly as necessary. Do not overlube. While you're at it, check the cotter pins/rings and replace as needed.

Go Pro

Spend the extra money for commercially made turnbuckle covers. They'll repay you by reducing the potential for corrosion instead of the do-it-yourself tape or leather alternatives. Also, periodic inspection is easier with custom covers.

Cleaning the Traveler

The traveler sits so close at the helm, but when was the last time you really paid attention to this handy guy? Clean the track regularly with a mild boat wash and water. The first time you do this, be prepared to do some gentle scrubbing if you have let the dirt build up and are attending to the matter only now that it has become a problem.

The traveler cars should be flushed periodically with that old standby, freshwater. Every now and again go one step further by taking a mild boat soap mixture and squirting it into the center openings. Proceed to roll the car back and forth along the track to work the cleaning solution throughout, and then flush the bearings inside with water as you usually would.

Lubricating the Traveler

Put that can of spray lubricant away—far away from the traveler. Using a spray lube on the

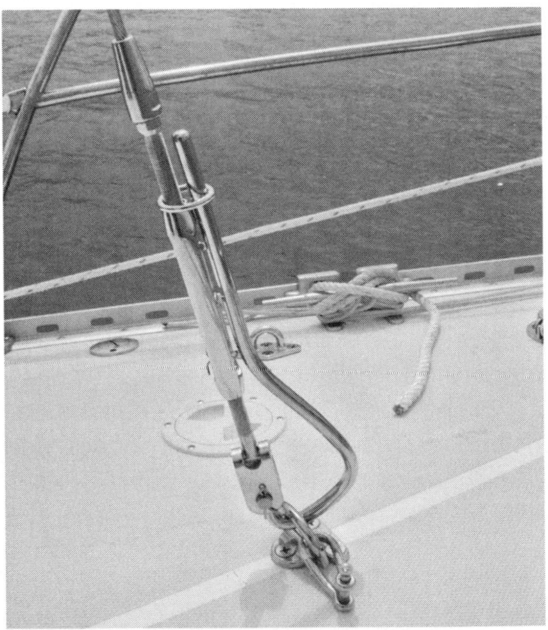

Wipe down fittings at least twice each season with a cloth saturated in corrosion protectant.

traveler car ball bearings can actually make them skid instead of roll, creating a maintenance nightmare. Instead, apply one or two drops of a light machine oil, such as 3-IN-ONE Oil or McLube OneDrop, where the balls make contact with the track. Slide the car back and forth over the area several times so that the lubricant is applied evenly and thoroughly to the bearings. Any lube left on the tracks should be removed with a clean rag.

Clean Up—Lube Down

When it comes to cleaning the mast track, there seem to be no end of suggestions, including one that involves using the metal rod and cleaning pads from a shotgun cleaning kit. A selection of cleaners may be used, from boat wash to acetone. A hardy boat spray cleaner/degreaser is a good midline alternative if you don't know what you're going to find on the way up but don't think you'll need the strength, and unpleasantness, of acetone. You can use a rag or cut up pieces of sponge. Saturate the rag/sponge with cleaner. Stuff a corner of the rag or tip of the sponge into the track and start scrubbing your way up the mast, repeating in sections as needed. Follow with a clean wet rag to remove any excess soaps.

On the way back down, lubricate the track with a dry lubricant. Don't use a grease or an oil, as both will attract and hold dirt and gum up the works once again.

Keep an eye out for dents, bends, burrs, or other rough spots. The cause of a malfunctioning track may not be dirt accumulation but structural damage.

The Furling System

Flush regularly with clean water. Lubrication is not often required, but when it is, use only a marine-grade dry lubricant.

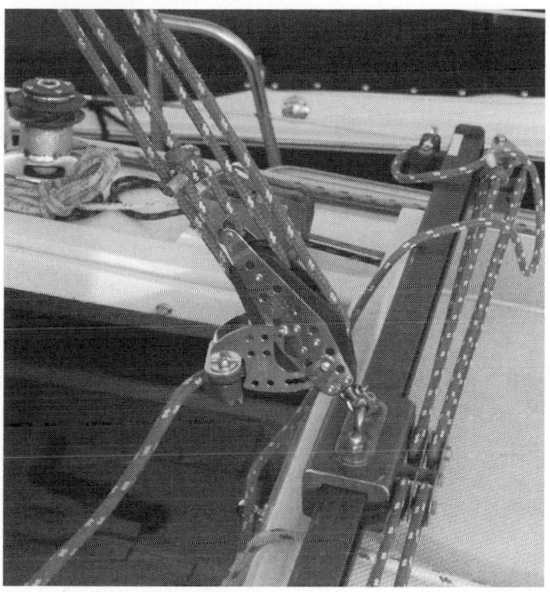

When was the last time you cleaned the traveler? Clean the track regularly with a mild boat wash and water to keep it working smoothly.

Stainless Steel 101

The most corrosion-resistant stainless steel rigging wire is 316; 304 is stronger, at the sacrifice of some of that corrosion resistance.

Stainless Needs to Breathe

Watch what you put on stainless steel. The metal needs to breathe in order to resist corrosion. Even something as simple as tape can restrict the necessary airflow and lead to rust and corrosion.

Rusty Rigging Wire

Despite the word *stainless* in its name, even stainless steel can get rusty. But never fear, no matter how bad it looks, there is more than likely still some good stainless underneath. A stainless or copper wire brush will work well to scour rust from the thin-diameter cables. Better yet, use a marine-grade stainless steel wool, which will allow you to grip completely around the stainless and scour all sides at once as you work. Resist the temptation to clean with household or shop steel wool (note that the word *stainless* does not appear in their name). Traditional steel wool can leave behind tiny pieces of itself that will rust and start your problem all over again.

Keep paper towels handy to wipe down the rigging as you work.

Follow up with a stainless cleaner/polish to remove any remaining rust and give the rigging a Bristol shine.

SOME QUICK RIGGING MAINTENANCE AND INSPECTION TIPS

The Single Clue

A single broken strand of rigging wire *is* a big deal. Yes, you may be right in thinking the remaining strands are more than enough to do the job, but it is more likely a sign of further line failure. Why take chances? Replace the entire section.

While you are at it, check the other sections for cracks, distortions, and additional areas with broken strands. If possible and financially viable, you may want to replace all the associated wire at the same time because once one section starts to go, the rest of them will soon start to go as well if they were all installed at the same time.

The Food Dye Inspection

Problems with wire rigging are not always visible to the naked eye. To do the most comprehensive inspection possible, blend food coloring with that handy can of corrosion protectant you always have on board until you can clearly see the color. Blue is popular. Paint the mixture onto the suspect lines and let it dry for several hours or overnight. Problems will now be visible to the naked eye. This works on metal fittings as well.

Starting at the Top

When you have to go aloft for a repair or your annual inspection, take those handy-dandy cans of corrosion protectant and lithium grease

Look up and check: Do your spreaders tilt slightly upward as they should?

along with you. The wet lube will help break free any stuck fittings you discover. Follow up the fix with a protective coating of lithium grease. You're up there anyway, so give the mast crane, forestay and backstay terminals, and halyard sheaves that are working just fine a protective coating of lithium grease as well.

While You're Up There

Going aloft is tedious, so make the most of your efforts. Don't forget to eyeball the VHF, GPS, satellite TV, and other antennas and their connections. Likewise the radar dome, running lights, et cetera.

Before You Go Aloft

It is a long fall from the mast. So although the shackle on most bosun's chairs is perfectly fine alone, you may want to consider adding a safety line tied via the spliced eye.

Spreading Toward Heaven

Spreaders should have a slight tilt in the upward direction. If not, you need to find out why. Even if they look perfectly fine, check underneath the spreader boots to make sure everything is shipshape on these critical boat parts. Another key area is where the shroud meets the spreader.

Shrouds and Stays

Keep an eye out for rusty areas, cracks, and broken strands in the swages and wire. A neat trick is to run a cotton ball along the wire to see if it snags. When one wire is found to be bad, consider replacing them all, as the others may not be far behind.

Quick Halyard Inspection

Key wear areas to keep track of are where the halyards enter and exit the mast or go beneath a rope stopper, at the bend at a deck fair lead, and at the forward edges of the spreaders.

Shackle Suggestion

When lubricating your shackles, keep an eye out for bent or otherwise marred units. Replace as needed; it's false economy not to replace worn parts as soon as you discover them.

chapter 9

MISCELLANEOUS TIPS EVERY BOATER SHOULD KNOW

THE NEED FOR SPEED

A Blueprint for Speed

Racers "blueprint" the last 6 feet of their boat's bottom by filing and sanding. Lay a straightedge against the hull and shine a light along it to show any irregularities. Another trick is to use wet 1,000-grit sandpaper to polish the lower unit with strokes that follow the water's direction.

Reduce Wind Drag

Aerodynamic drag at speeds over 30 mph becomes an increasingly significant factor in slowing you down. As with water, air likes to flow with a minimum of disturbances. Keep windshields closed, cover the bow cockpit with a tonneau cover, stow fenders, and lower seats to keep the crew out of the wind when making a fast run for it.

Propeller for Speed

An optimized stainless steel replacement to your aluminum propeller is usually worth an extra 2 to 3 mph. Mercury encourages its dealers to stock demo propellers for experimenting. The company also offers adapters for the outboards and stern drives. Try a four-bladed propeller for faster acceleration and a better grip at top speed.

The Higher the Outboard, the Higher the Speed

Raising your outboard on the transom diminishes the amount of gear case being dragged through the water. According to Mercury, rebolting the motor using the lower holes on the engine's transom bracket usually delivers a higher top end, reduces steering torque, and enhances stability.

The Racer's Speed-Enhancing Tips

Speedboat racers in search of top speeds recommend that boaters put in new spark plugs and ignition wires. Use premium gas and try advancing the ignition timing in 2-degree increments. Back off at the first audible hint of detonation. Applying a polymer polish to the hull and the lower unit will reduce drag, thus increasing hull speed.

Synthetics for High-RPM Boating

If you're running her near wide-open throttle often, you may want to consider using synthetic engine oil and gear lubes, which reduce mechanical friction while enhancing maximum-load and high-temperature protection.

Cool Air and Maximum Power

Engines need an unrestricted supply of cool, dense air to produce maximum power. Add a second flame arrestor atop the stock one to double the flow area, says Mercury. Provide extra ports to the motor compartment. Install louvers on your outboard's cowl as well as carbon fiber reed valves and velocity stacks, all of which you can get from Sea Land.

Don't Bring Along What You Don't Need

For absolute maximum speed, jettison excess ballast such as soggy upholstery, spare tools, unused galley gear, extra batteries, and coolers. Drain the water tanks and run with only the fuel you'll need to get you out and back safely.

If you're looking for speed, don't overload your boat with gear you don't need.

A simple zippered bag (or two) is a viable alternative to expensive dry bags.

PROTECTING YOUR ELECTRONIC DEVICES

Tag and Bag It!

A zippered bag is the best and cheapest insurance you can get for your cellular phone, laptop, or tablet device. Drop in a bag of silica gel (these come with new shoes and also are found tucked into the box your phone or other electronics came with), and you're even better protected against accidental splashes of water as well as the high humidity found on a boat. Yes, you can buy expensive dry bags, but a quart-sized zippered bag will work just as well as long as you seal it properly. For maximum protection, put one bag inside another larger bag.

If you want further protection against a phone overboard scenario, tuck a few of the freebie floating keychains you get at the boat show into the zippered bag. These will help keep the bag afloat if dropped overboard.

Dunked Your Phone? Rice to the Rescue!

If your phone, camera, or tablet does get wet—and we're talking a random splash here, not five minutes under 30 feet of water—immediately

Tuck a floating keychain or two into a zippered bag.

Dry out a wet mobile phone in rice.

slide it into a bag of uncooked white rice. This will help absorb the moisture and could help save the device. If you do drop the device overboard and it gets completely waterlogged, pull the SIM card or data card out. There's a fifty-fifty chance your local phone provider can get it to work long enough to transfer your data to a new phone. Many photos were recovered from the data card of a digital camera that was retrieved after a year under 60 feet of salt water. ***NOTE:*** Salt water is much more damaging than freshwater.

Tablets Are for More than Reading Novels

Your iPad or other tablet device can be used to access online navigation sites that feature the latest NOAA charts and other useful information. Keep these important devices in a secure place where they won't slide into the water or fall onto the deck.

TIPS FOR BOATING IN MOSQUITO TERRITORY

Keep the Biters Away

To keep mosquitoes away from your boat, wash the deck area with lemon soap or a mixture of water with lemon juice. The scent will go far to help keep them away!

To lessen the chance of mosquito bites, skip the scented suntan lotions, deodorant soaps, scented deodorant, hair spray, and colognes. All these broadcast your location to mosquitoes.

Eat So You Won't Be Eaten

To further reduce bites, reduce the amount of sugar in your diet (this is no joke!). Sweet-smelling skin attracts mosquitoes.

It isn't just an old wives' tale that eating a healthy dose of garlic or a couple raw onions will keep the bugs at bay. Toss some on your next meal and watch the results.

Vitamin B1 (thiamine), which can be found in brewer's yeast, whole grains, liver, and other organ meats, when taken in sufficient amounts alters a body's skin scent enough to keep the bugs away, yet it remains imperceptible to the human nose.

Some people swear that by taking zinc they alter their body odor to keep away bugs, especially yellow jackets. Amounts up to 60 milligrams per day have been touted. ***NOTE:*** Be sure to check with your doctor before you try this.

Keep Everything Away

When all else fails, rub on some Vicks Vapo-Rub . . . though you might find that you're also keeping your fellow boaters away.

Mosquitoes on the Buffet Line

Mosquitoes like to eat right after dawn through midmorning and 1 or 2 hours after sunset. Wear insect repellent or stay below decks during these hours. Or find a breezy spot that makes it harder for mosquitoes to locate your scent.

Exterior Protection

If the weather is cool, wear long sleeves and pants, shoes, and socks. Avoid bright colors, which attract mosquitoes, and floppy clothing, which can entangle them.

What You Can't See Can Bite You

If no-see-ums are your problem, next time bring along a bottle of vanilla extract. It works as well as most rub on pesticides, with no chemical side effects.

If You Are Bitten

Rub a small amount of ammonia (yes, ammonia) or vinegar on a mosquito bite to stop the itch.

To keep mosquitoes away, wash the deck area with lemon soap or water with lemon juice.

For an unidentified bug bite, rinse the bite with soap and cool water. If there seems to be excessive swelling, elevate the area or apply cold compresses. Calamine lotion will take care of the painful itching. Never give in and scratch a bite, as an infection may result.

One of the oldest tricks in the book is to pack mud on a bug bite. There is no scientific reason why it reduces the stinging pain, but it does.

To neutralize the irritants in the bug venom further, rub a wet aspirin on the spot. ***NOTE:*** If you're allergic to aspirin, do not try this.

A paste made of salt and water is also known to be effective. You can also try a rag dipped in a solution of baking soda and water; leave it on the bite as a compress for 20 minutes.

Swollen Bee Stings

Even people who are not allergic to bees can find themselves with a nasty sting that leaves the area itchy and swollen. To treat, apply ice to keep down the swelling, and then make a paste of baking soda and water and let it sit on for 15 to 20 minutes to reduce itching.

Antihistamine Relief

Over-the-counter antihistamines help lessen bug bite swelling and pain in adults. ***NOTE:*** Antihistamines can cause allergic reactions; if you haven't taken antihistamines before, check with your physician first.

Stop the Sting

To ease a smarting sting, make a paste out of meat tenderizer and water and apply it generously. Repeat in an hour, if necessary. Meat tenderizer contains papain, which breaks down and detoxifies insect venom.

Neutralize Jellyfish Stings

Keep the meat tenderizer around if you find yourself vacationing near the ocean. If you get stung by a man-o'-war or jellyfish, mix ¼ tablespoon meat tenderizer with 2 teaspoons water and apply to the sting. Repeat in 1 hour if necessary. ***NOTE:*** If you are allergic to the stings of these creatures, get medical assistance immediately.

OFFBEAT SUNBURN PREVENTION

Sunburned Through Your Clothes

Skin protection for boaters goes well beyond simply choosing a waterproof high-SPF suntan lotion, applying it once, and believing you're done for the day. Did you know that you can get sunburned through your clothing? A simple test to check how much sun safety your attire offers is to hold the garments up to a light. Loosely woven fabrics, such as gauzy materials, offer minimal protection, and tightly woven cloths, such as denim and canvas, provide an excellent defense.

The Effects of Sun on the Eyes

Have you heard that unprotected eyes can lose up to 50 percent of their night vision after a day on the water? It may take your eyes a full week to recover from a 2-week vacation in the sun. When you purchase sunglasses, make certain they have an SPF of 15 or are designated "A-80.s." Experts advise that for additional protection against sun reflection from the water, get sunglasses with opaque side pieces.

Not Between 10 and 2

The sun's rays are strongest when the sun is directly overhead. They are considerably less hazardous in the early morning and late afternoon. You've probably heard the expression "not between 10 A.M. and 2 P.M." Always try to avoid unprotected exposure, especially during these hours. Remember to adjust for daylight saving time where it is in effect.

Medications That Increase Sunburn

The likelihood that you will get sunburn can be further increased by certain drugs and medications you might be taking, such as tetracycline and other antibiotics, tranquilizers, and diuretics. If you have a surgical, accident, or acne scar, you should cover it with either a minimum 15 SPF lotion or zinc oxide. Otherwise, the scarred tissue may darken permanently after sun exposure and it will look worse than before and increase your risk of skin cancer.

Perfume and Brown Spots

Your chances of acquiring semipermanent brown spots are increased by spraying colognes, perfumes, and after-shave lotions on your skin before or during sun exposure. Ideally you should never apply a scent if you know you're going into the sun. If you must smell perfect, however, you can minimize the potential damage by coating skin where the cologne is to be applied with a thin layer of petroleum jelly. Then apply the scent over the jelly.

The Deodorant Dilemma

Deodorants and deodorant soaps containing hexachlorophene can cause skin disorders when brought into contact with the sun's rays. These can cause an itchy, red rash in sensitive skin.

Photosensitizing Medicines and Foods

Certain antihistamines, antibiotics, or birth control pills may cause skins predisposed toward discoloration to form splotchy, hyperpigmented brown patches after sun exposure.

Pregnancy can cause the same reaction as birth control pills. Most doctors advise staying out of the sun until after the birth.

Photosensitizing foods—which include citrus fruits, celery, figs, parsnips, and vanilla—should not be eaten prior to going out in the sun.

Cataracts

Human eyes are extremely vulnerable to sun damage. Studies have shown that approximately 10 percent of the million cataracts removed each year in the United States are sun related. The thin skin of your eyelids is subject to skin cancer. Sunglasses are an absolute must, but metal frames can become very hot. Leave them home during an extreme heat wave; plastic frames are best for these periods.

Dark Smudges Under the Eyes

You may have already noticed that the sun can cause the delicate oil-free glands in the area under the eyes to become dark and dry-looking after lengthy exposure. Covering the area with eye cream or petroleum jelly before going into the sun considerably lessens your risk of getting dark smudges.

Zinc That Nose

Studies have shown that long-term exposure to the ultraviolet rays of the sun can harm your nose cartilage and, in extreme cases, make the tip droop. Zinc oxide is highly recommended, as is wearing a hat with a peak or brim.

Plastic Tennis Visors Aren't Your Best Bet

Plastic tennis visors may shade your nose, but the plastic doesn't breathe. Visors have been known to cause unbecoming, uncomfortable cases of prickly heat on the forehead. In addition, they offer no protection to the scalp area.

Lip Protection

Petroleum jelly or honey can help to keep your lips moist. Some SPF 15 no-color lip glosses can double as eye protection. For many, the waxy stick is easier to apply than a lotion, which will run into the eyes if applied too close to them.

Scalp Defense

To avoid getting sunburn on your vulnerable scalp, don't forget to put sunscreen over the part lines in your hair and/or wear a hat. Putting conditioner in your hair also prevents the sun from drying and bleaching hair, which is especially necessary in hair that's been chemically processed. Heat also helps conditioner penetrate, giving you a free salon treatment.

A sunscreen of SPF 15—or better yet, a hat—is essential for recent hair transplants. The transplants and surrounding skin should be vigorously protected for up to 6 months after the surgery, recommends Dr. Lawrence Shapiro of Dr. Shapiro's Hair Institute of Delray, Florida.

Sunscreen Doesn't Last All Day

Perspiration and swimming diffuse sunscreen lotion and decrease its potency. The official advice is to apply sunscreen lotion 15 minutes before going outside and reapply it several times during sun exposure. This constant protection allows your skin to start mending the existing ultraviolet damage by building a new network of collagen, elastin fibers, and connective tissue.

Hydrate Your Skin

If you go into salt water for a prolonged period of time, whether to swim, snorkel, or scuba dive, you're not only washing off a large part of even the most waterproof suntan lotion, but you may be severely dehydrating your skin. To keep your face, throat, and other exposed body parts nicely hydrated, first dampen your skin with tap or bottled water. Never use salt or chlorinated water. Then seal in moisture by smoothing on a mixture of half melted petroleum jelly and half melted cocoa butter. The greasy combination forms a protective barrier against excessive moisture loss caused by salt water. (This protection works equally well in chlorinated and nonchlorinated pools and lakes.)

A Quick After-Swim Wash

For a quick body wash after swimming, mix 1 part your favorite shampoo with 6 parts water. Lather and bathe with a sponge. When you're clean, dry yourself with a towel as soon as possible. Skin cells flatten out when they are moist, allowing more of the sun's burning rays to attack a larger amount of tissue.

Aloe Vera Softens Skin

You can enhance any tan that is acquired by applying either aloe vera gel or petroleum jelly afterward. Both make your tan last longer and pamper and sooth the skin.

OFFBEAT SUNBURN FIRST AID

Cheap Sunburn First Aid

First aid supplies for sunburn don't have to be expensive. Did you know that a tube of aloe vera gel (99¢), a jar of honey ($1.59), or a small tub of petroleum jelly ($1.29) can make the entire difference between suffering from sunburn pain and beginning the important task of healing? Three equally inexpensive alternatives are rubbing alcohol, milk, and baking soda. You may already have some of these common, easy-to-store remedies on board.

Free Sunburn Pain Reliever

There is even one free sunburn treatment: Individual mayonnaise packets that come with fish dinners and sandwiches at local eateries can double as a sunburn pain relievers. Sunburned skin hurts when it comes in contact with oxygen.

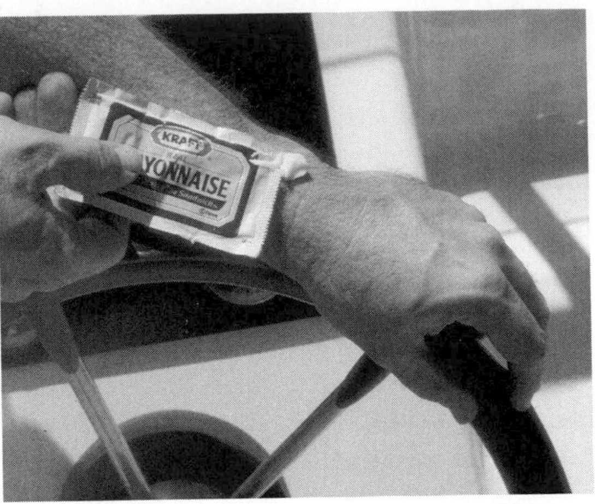

Mayonnaise reduces sunburn pain by creating a protective coating that stops air from reaching the skin.

Simply covering the skin with mayonnaise creates a natural, protective coating to stop air from reaching the burned skin, lessening the suffering.

The Aspirin Connection

If you're certain you've spent too much time in the sun, take two aspirin before you begin to redden. Aspirin helps stop potential damage by slowing down the skin's inflammation-producing machinery. It is also a well-known pain-reliever. However, if you're also dehydrated, bypass the aspirin, drink plenty of cold water, and begin the treatment steps outlined in the following tips.

Speaking of aspirin . . . empty film canisters make great pill holders for aspirins or prescription medicine. They're waterproof, and they're a handy size.

First Step: Cool the Sunburned Skin

The first treatment after becoming sunburned is to cool the heated skin. Splash, smooth, or spray on either of the following liquids: 3 tablespoons baking soda blended in 1 quart water; or 1 tablespoon rubbing alcohol mixed into 2 cups cold water. You can also apply these mixtures as compresses by soaking a towel in them and applying the towel to the sunburned areas.

Saturating a towel with cold milk to create a natural, soothing compress works well, too. The soaked towel should be applied directly to the sunburned areas.

Another effective compress is a towel drenched in a solution of strong cold tea.

After completing the initial cooling process, the sunburned areas need to be covered with a coating that will keep oxygen from coming in contact with the skin. This oxygen-skin contact is what creates the painful burning sensation.

Mother Nature's Sunburn Treatment

Aloe vera gel is a traditional remedy for burns. One of its components is a relative of aspirin, making it a natural painkiller. Aloe vera not only cools and soothes but aids in the healing process.

Aloe Alternatives

Honey has long been acknowledged as one of the best ointments for burns of many types.

Petroleum jelly can be applied directly from the container to skin. If your skin is dehydrated as well as sunburned, you can place a few layers of gauze over the petroleum jelly and wrap with a

Pastes made of honey, petroleum jelly, mayonnaise, and baking soda and water are effective alternatives to aloe vera for sunburn relief.

SEVERE SUNBURN AND HEAT STROKE

Budget home remedies should never be used in the following two situations:

If the sunburn is severe, possibly a second-degree burn, with considerable swelling and blisters, you should immediately seek professional medical attention. In the meantime:

1. Submerge the severely sunburned area under cold water until the pain is alleviated. If you don't have a clean bucket or basin large enough to submerge the area, place cold, wet clothes on the severely burned skin. Do not under any circumstances rub the skin.
2. Keep severely sunburned arms and legs elevated.
3. Place dry, sterile bandages on all severely sunburned areas.
4. *Do not* put medications, antiseptics, sprays, ointments, or even any of the previously-mentioned home remedies on a severe sunburn. *Never* break blisters.
5. Seek medical attention immediately.

Heat stroke, unlike heat exhaustion, is a life-threatening emergency. The symptoms of heat stroke are any or all of the following:

1. An extremely elevated temperature (often 106 degrees and above)
2. Hot, dry, red skin (usually accompanied by a noticeable absence of sweating)
3. A strong and rapid pulse
4. Possible unconsciousness or mental confusion

If you suspect heat stroke, consult a comprehensive first aid book (a *must* on every boat) for the proper procedures for reducing temperature. Then seek prompt medical attention, preferably at the nearest hospital emergency room.

heating pad set on the lowest setting to increase the effectiveness. The heating pad should not be applied for longer than 10 minutes.

Baking soda can be blended with water or milk to make a protective paste to cover the sunburned skin. Do not remove the mixture for at least 1 hour. This mixture soothes the damaged skin while creating a barrier that keeps air, and therefore pain away.

Don't Let Blisters Become Infected

To guard against infection if blisters form on the damaged skin, first cleanse the blistered skin gently with mild soap and water. Blot the sore skin dry. Do not rub with a towel because this will further inflame the skin and may open blisters. Finally, do not attempt to deliberately open a blister.

Start the Healing Now

A protective coating of any of the following substances will speed the healing process: aloe vera gel, petroleum jelly, honey, or vitamin E. You can snip a vitamin E capsule and squeeze the gel drops directly onto the skin.

Lip Treatments

For lips that become dry, chapped, and cracked from sun exposure, a light coating of any of the following healing materials will both protect the lips from further damage and begin to remoisturize the fragile tissue: honey, petroleum jelly, or A&D Ointment. (Doctors prescribe A&D for babies' skin, so you know it's mild.)

The Dehydration Drink

To make a mineral drink that replaces vital body salts lost through dehydration (perhaps from sitting on deck in the hot sun too long), boil a quart of water, and add 1 level teaspoon salt, 1 heaping teaspoon baking soda, and 4 heaping teaspoons sugar. After stirring until everything is completely dissolved, mix in the appropriate amount of powdered fruit drink, if you have any on board. Have the dehydrated person slowly drink 4 to 8 ounces at a time.

Heat Exhaustion

Heat exhaustion, another sun-related malady, has two main symptoms: lightheadedness or nausea caused by fluid loss due to excessive perspiration. A quick revitalizing sugar-free drink can be made by adding ⅛ teaspoon salt and ¼ teaspoon baking soda to an 8-ounce glass of water or lemonade. Have the victim slowly drink half the liquid. The salt and soda quickly replace many of the vital minerals lost through sweat. If the person continues to feel ill, have him or her drink the remaining 4 ounces.

To aid in heat exhaustion recovery, move the victim to the shadiest or coolest spot on the boat. Have the person lie down, if possible. Loosen his or her clothing. Place cool, wet cloths on the person's forehead and body. If symptoms are severe, become worse, or last longer than an hour, seek professional medical attention.

SEAMANSHIP

Windy Day Chart Reading

Keep two rolls of 3M's Blue Long Mask tape onboard—one in the navigation station, the other at the helm. On windy days you can use this tape to keep charts in place without damaging chart paper. This cobalt blue tape sticks just about anywhere. Post a note to yourself on the dash panel or above the windshield. You can remove it up to one week later without any sticky residue.

The Soda Bottle Anchor Float

When you anchor overnight, your anchor line may chafe against underwater objects, even though you have 15 feet of chain at the end. To remedy this, tie a fender, an empty soda bottle (with cap on tightly) or other float to the line 5 to 10 feet from the end of the chain to prevent the line from going slack and chafing dangerously against the bottom.

Garden Tools Are the Answer

If pulling in anchor line is like lifting 100 pounds at the gym, simplify the process by running your line on a conventional garden hose winder. Now all you have to do is crank. The reel can be mounted in the anchor hatch on a larger boat or attached to a wooden plank that is attached to the bow rail on a smaller vessel.

Noah's Depthfinder

Did your depthfinder malfunction while you were navigating a tight channel? To track the channel ahead of you, attach a large bobber to a fishing line and put a weight on the bottom that's large enough to pull the bobber under. Adjust the bobber's height over the weight to match the draft of your boat, plus another foot. Then cast directly off the bow. If the float is pulled under, your heading will keep you in the channel. If the float stays on the surface, the weight is hitting bottom—as will your boat, if you continue on that course.

Compass Deviation Errors

The tried-and true method of checking a compass for deviation errors consists of steering your boat on known courses and noting the difference between these values and those indicated by your compass. Or use a simple variation of this method. Choose a calm day. Steer away from a fixed daymark (or buoy) on a compass heading of 180 degrees for at least a half mile. Drop a small marker over the stern. Turn and come back toward the marker, establishing a new course where the marker lines up with the

You don't need to hire a compass specialist to diagnose your deviation.

daymark; do not steer by the compass. Because you are now on a reciprocal course, the compass should read 0 degrees. If it doesn't, the difference is your error. Adjust out half of this difference. Repeat the procedure—making runs from the daymark to 180 degrees, returning on a reciprocal heading, and making adjustments—until as much error as possible has been eliminated. That takes care of the north/south corrections. Now do the same for east/west (90/270 degrees).

Echo Sounding

If your radar goes bad while you're in pea soup, try this technique to get back to shore. Use a sound signal, such as your air horn, and time the echo. If the echo takes 5 seconds to travel back to you, you're about ½ mile from land; 10 seconds equals about a mile. Cliffs or forested shorelines work best; a flat sandy beach won't reflect the sound as well.

Impress Your Friends

Want to predict the tides? In most cases on the East Coast, if winds are coming out of the south or east, tides will be higher and come later; if winds are coming out of the north or west, tides will be diminished and arrive earlier. The reverse is true for the West Coast.

RULES OF THE ROAD

"Red over red, the captain is dead." As a captain myself, this mnemonic, which explains the light configuration for a boat that is not under command due to an engine malfunction or some other mishap, has always been my least favorite. The following are some lighter phrases to help the average boater recognize some of the more popular night vessel light configurations:

"Red over red, what do you mean my insurance doesn't cover towing, the captain said?!"

"Red over white, if my lines don't get tight, I'll be lying about my catches tonight" (fishing vessel)

"Red over green, the wind is free but the rigging repair costs can be mean" (sailboat under sail)

"White over white, it's the only date I could get tonight" (short tow under 200 meters)

"White over white over white, this tow bill is going to be totally out of sight" (long tow over 200 meters)

"Red over red over red, I can't fit in my wedding dress so I can't wed" (vessel constrained by her draft)

"White over red, he's got friends in the Harbor Patrol so let him go ahead" (pilot boat)

"White behind the boat, don't drive right behind me if you want to continue to float" (partially submerged object being towed astern)

"Red over green over red over green, Santa's reindeer quit so he's traveling by water machine" (just kidding)

The Wind as a Weather Clue

Want to predict the weather? Traditionally, north, northwest, and southwest winds deliver balmy weather; and south, east, and northeast winds carry rain and snow. A damp south wind quietly warns of the approaching storm that will follow its low-pressure tail. A clammy east wind signifies a falling barometer and approaching storm front. In warm weather, these warnings usually mean rain, and in the winter, snow. Shifting winds from the northwest to the northeast, or similarly from the southwest to the southeast, combined with cloud-filled skies, are a forewarning of bad weather moving in. On a seemingly clear day, shifting southwest-to-southeast winds usually bring rain.

The Cloud Connection

Once you've established the direction of the wind, look above you and take note of the clouds. The fluffy white clouds called cumlus, that we see overhead almost every day, when combined with a clear sky, signal a mild day. If they begin to join and form heads, they'll soon become storm clouds. The head will normally flatten into an anvil shape (the clouds are now called cumulonimbus) and the lower cloud darken before the rain begins to fall. Long, wispy clouds that float high in the sky and appear in airbrushed "pony tail" formations (cirrus clouds) are safe, as long as they don't multiply or join. Keep an eye on them though, for once joined, they can bring fierce storms.

Low clouds having no definite shape and often confused with a gray sky without sun indicate a day of on-and-off moderate rain. If the wind is northeast to south, heavy rains could accumulate. Low clouds that look like a gray sky with dark blue or gray patches also signal coming rain. The four basic cloud types often join together to form storm clouds of combination formations, most of which have some dark patches or a dark underside. Add a northeast to south, or east to south wind to the picture, and chances are you're in for a storm soon.

Barometer Reading

If you had the foresight to bring a barometer with you, use it! A falling barometer indicates an approaching storm; a rising barometer, the coming or continuation of already existing fair weather. For further reference, the *U.S. Coast Guard Boating Guide* contains a storm calculation table that predicts weather by using a combination of wind direction and current barometer readings. Contact your local Coast Guard branch to obtain a copy.

Lightning Wisdom

If you find yourself caught in the approach of a lightning storm, count the seconds between the lightning flash and the following thunder. Every 5 seconds is 1 mile of distance between you and the storm.

When Will the Rain Break?

How do you know when a rainstorm is approaching its end? Northeast-to-south winds shifting to the west usually signal a storm's break.

The Answer Is in the Sky

Always keep an eye on the morning and early evening sky. "Red sky at morning, sailor take warning. Red sky at night, sailor's delight," isn't as silly as you might think. Red or deep orange sunrises usually forecast wet weather within the next 24 hours. The cloudier the morning, the closer the storm. However, a red or deep orange sunset often indicates good weather the following day. A golden sunset, with hints of green at the edge, warns of high winds for the next day. A gray sunset means impending rain.

Rainbow Reading

Rainbows also give reliable clues to the coming weather. A morning rainbow indicates an approaching or forming storm. A midday rainbow signifies unsteady weather. An evening rainbow signals that the storm is over. When you see a sun dog (rainbow-like belts circling the sun), know that cold weather will follow.

Has Your Nose Gone into Overdrive?

Sounds and smells are more noticeable as a storm approaches. This is because low-pressure fronts magnify sounds and odors. Low-pressure fronts also magnify aches and pains, especially those related to previously broken bones and torn muscles. Stop for a moment and check out how you're feeling today. The temperature will also take a significant and readily noticed drop as bad weather approaches.

What You See and What It Means

If you're on or near salt water, check the visibility. Extremely clear visibility means that the normal salty haze is being scattered by changing airflows.

Keep an eye on any smoke in the area, such as from a fire on nearby land. Smoke that floats directly upward and disappears quickly signals a mild day; whereas thick smoke that rises only slightly and then levels off and wafts away horizontally indicates a coming storm.

HURRICANE AND OTHER STORM PREPARATION

Find the Best Shelter

If you can't move your boat out of the water and shift it inland, preferably storing it inside a protected shelter, move it to the nearest hurricane hole, and then tie lines to the nearest trees with broad branch systems. Broad-branched trees have widely spaced roots, which support the trees through the coming storm better than thin or young trees.

Two Lines Are Better than One

Doubling docklines and mooring lines in a storm is good seamanship. Go one better by installing extra cleats on your dock. And when you double up your lines, don't put both on the same cleat; instead, make one starboard and one port line fast to the starboard cleats, and one each to the port cleats. That way if your cleat pulls out, you'll still be tied up.

Another trick when tying up for a blow is to lead the bowline from the offshore side of the boat around the stern and then to the dock. That way the boat's hull, rather than the bow cleat, absorbs much of the strain. Wrap an old T-shirt around the line where it crosses the stern to prevent chafing of either part.

Don't forget to set your anchor out and use it to provide additional security.

Read the Fine Print

If your boat is stuck at its marina dockage for the coming storm, read your marina contract carefully; you may have signed away your rights to sue when you signed the dockage contract, even if the marina's roof blows off and karate chops your boat.

What if the storm surge puts *Mom's Mink* on the marina store's roof? Many marinas are shifting liabilities to the boat owner. You may be responsible for any damage your boat does to them, or their equipment does to you. Check before you sign.

Am I covered when cruising south? Many insurers decline to offer coverage on vessels used south of the 22nd Parallel during hurricane season, so don't be surprised if you suddenly find your coverage temporarily dropped midcruise.

Trick phrases used by insurance companies when referring to hurricane and storm exclusionary clauses include coverage lapses during "acts of God" or "named windstorms."

Insurance Companies Can't Pay if They Don't Have the Money

Check the solvency of your insurance company to make sure it has the assets to pay for a large volume of claims that typically follow a hurricane or large storm. Local subsidiaries of larger national companies may not be able to foot the bill. If you have doubts, call your state insurance commissioner.

Secure Your Trailer Boat to the Ground

To secure a trailered boat before a coming storm, use earth augers, available at most home supply stores, as land anchors. Tie the boat tightly to the trailer and then tie the trailer to the augers.

In addition to earth augers, or when the earth auger option isn't available, deflate the trailer's tires by half to make the rig more stable and less likely to roll.

Finally, put water in the bilge of a trailered boat. The additional weight helps keep it in place.

Where's the Blow?

Where are you in relation to a hurricane? If you're facing the wind, it's 10 points or 112 degrees to your right.

PREVENTIVE BOAT MAINTENANCE: PROPER BOAT TOWING

Even Superman Knows When to Say "No"

Although towing a boat in distress may be a heroic gesture, if you're too underpowered to move the object you wish to tow, it may also be a foolish one. Even if you have sufficient engine power, if you don't know how to tow properly, you may end up doing damage to your boat and the boat you are towing, not to mention to both crews. Often the best assistance you can provide, and the one that will prevent you needing more maintenance on your boat, is simply using your VHF to call Sea Tow for the other vessel.

Braided Line Is Best

If you feel completely capable of towing the distressed vessel, remember that braided nylon line is the best towing line. Nylon line stretches, which means that it will work as a shock absorber between the two vessels. Make sure that the line you're using is thick enough to handle the weight you're going to subject it to and is in good, unfrayed condition before you attach it to the boat you intend to tow. Braided nylon is preferred over three-strand nylon because the three-strand variety tends to break under the stress of a heavy tow load. When a line does break, it can ricochet back with tremendous force, aimed at one or possibly both boats, depending on the location of the break. Crew members can easily be seriously injured by a snapping line.

Injury-Free Towing

It is best to keep all nonessential crew members and guests out of harm's way while towing. You may wish to have one person on each boat monitor the towing process, especially on the towing boat, where you will want someone to keep an eye out that the line doesn't get slack and fouled in the prop. Again, keep your sentries clear of any possible line breaks, or have them stay low, near the gunwales.

Balance Is Essential

Never attach a towline to only one side of the tow boat's transom. This severely impairs your ability to steer the boat. It may even force the tow boat onto a heading that is hazardous. To avoid this circumstance, always attach the towline at a point forward of the propeller. This is considerably easier to do on an outboard or a stern drive but must especially be kept in mind on a full inboard.

Bridle Towing: Part 1

The best way to attach the towline to the tow boat properly is to attach it to a bridle. A bridle is a separate piece of heavy nylon line that is attached to both rear or side cleats of the towing boat. Again, if at all possible, choose cleats forward of the propeller. Leave enough slack so that when the towing line is attached to the center of the bridle, the bridle becomes a semi-V shape. If you don't have a spare line to form the bridle, use your bow line. Your stern line will then become the actual towline. If your bow line is longer than your stern line, reverse the procedure, as the object is to keep the towed boat at a safe distance.

Bridle Towing: Part 2

If you're using the bridle method, always attach your towing line to the bridle with a loop so that it can move on the bridle as the towing boat changes heading. Be sure neither the bridle nor the towline crosses over any sharp objects or edges, as either line can become dangerously frayed and increase the possibility that it will break under the strain imposed. Also, make certain that the cleats you've chosen are up to the strain. If you don't trust your cleats, you can attach your bridle to the U-bolts on your transom. This works best if your boat has an outboard mounted on a B-bracket mount that holds the prop further astern. If your boat is an inboard, a stern drive, or an outboard with the propeller too near the transom for maneuverability, your next best alternative is to attach the bridle to the U-bolt at the bow and run it aft along both sides of your boat. ***CAUTION:*** This option is recommended for boats under 25 feet only.

Bridle Towing: Part 3

Attaching the bridle to the U-bolt at the bow isn't as easy as it sounds. If you choose this method, you will need to further secure the lines so that they won't ride up and possibly snap dangerously on the deck area during towing. This can be accomplished by attaching an additional line to one side of the towline at midship. Dive beneath your boat with the additional line, and then come up on the other side of the towing boat to tie the additional line on the opposite towline, again at midship. Once this is accomplished, the lines running around the hull should be tied together approximately 10 to 15 feet behind the transom, depending on the size of the towing boat. The towline should then be attached, with a loop, at this point.

Preparing the Towing Vessel

Once you've secured the towline to the towing boat, the opposite end of the towline should be secured to the bow cleat or forward cleats of the boat to be towed. Remember to run the line so that it comes directly off the vessel's bow. The crew and any other weighty items on board should be shifted aft to keep the bow as light as possible.

Keep an Anchor at the Ready

The anchor of the towed boat should be moved to a handy location before beginning towing. If the towline breaks, the anchor should be tossed overboard to stop the towed vessel from losing control.

High Seas Towing

If you're towing a distressed vessel in moderate to high seas, you'll need to set the length of the towline so that the vessel being towed doesn't come rushing down a wave into the towing vessel as the towing boat works to peak another crest. Another possible problem that may occur if the towing line isn't spaced properly in a choppy sea is that the towing vessel may be running down one wave while the towed boat is climbing up another. This will place the towline under an excessive, often critical, amount of stress.

Rough Water Towing

In rough waters, the tow boat must also take care to keep the towed vessel riding bow-first into the waves. This will keep the towed vessel from being bounced around unnecessarily and possibly broadsided by a high wave, which can cause the towed boat to tilt perilously.

Near the Dock

As you begin to near the dock but are still a bit away, you should begin to slow the towing boat until it comes to a full stop. At this time, the towed vessel should be pulled toward the tow boat. Use the towline to pull the vessels together, alongside each other, with the impaired boat on the dock side. Tie the two boats *securely* together, and then power up slowly and drive the two boats, cautiously, to the dock.

Night Towing

When towing at night, if you have a spotlight on board, shine the light on the towed vessel so that other boats in the vicinity are aware of your relationship, and the towed boat's impaired condition.

Limited Visibility Towing

If visibility is severely limited, such as in a storm or fog, the towing vessel should announce the situation with one long blast, followed by two short blasts approximately every 2 minutes. The towed vessel should signal its presence, if possible, with one prolonged blast and three short blasts directly after the tow boat has finished signaling.

Grounded Vessels: Part 1

Before you attempt to help free a grounded vessel, first make sure that you aren't going to ground yourself in the process. If you can't approach the vessel near enough to toss a line to it, or receive a line tossed from it, and the towing boat is down-current from the stranded vessel, the towline can be floated down to it. The reverse works equally well: If the stranded vessel is down-current, the tow boat can cast off the towline. If for some reason neither transfer can be enacted, and the water isn't dangerously cold, the line can be swum the distance between the two vessels. The swimmer should wear a life jacket no matter what his or her swimming ability. This is not the time to show off any athletic prowess.

Grounded Vessels: Part 2

Once the line is passed to a grounded vessel, both ends of the line should be attached to the most solid portions of both boats. This is not necessarily the easiest spot to tie off on because many cleats aren't up to the pull that will be required to liberate a grounded vessel. If the current is running abeam of the tow boat, the line should be secured just aft of midship on the up-current side. If the current is flowing in any other direction, the towline should be attached to the stern area. If the prevailing direction of the current is so strong that it is likely to force the towing boat aground also, *do not attempt to free the grounded vessel*. In such a case, the towing boat must either wait for more favorable conditions or radio for a stronger, preferably professional, tow boat.

Grounded Vessels: Part 3

Once the line is secured between two grounded vessels, a kedge should be set off the tow boat and a crew member assigned to take up extra line and thereby keep tension on the kedge line as the tow proceeds. If done properly, this guarantees that the towing boat will not be swept aground during the rescue, and the rescued vessel will not be regrounded.

If you have the necessary bodies on board, one person on each boat should watch the towline during a grounding. This should not be the same person assigned to hold the kedge line.

Grounded Vessels: Part 4

During the towing, a slow, consistent forward movement must be maintained by the towing boat until the grounded vessel is freed. Any other action, such as a sudden gunning of the engine, increases the risk of snapping the line and causing severe damage.

TIPS FOR CHOOSING THE RIGHT REPAIR SHOP

Choosing a repair shop for your boat is one of the most important nautical decisions you will have to make. The following guidelines should help:

Make Sure They're Experts About Your Vessel

First, find a repair shop that specializes in boats the size and style of yours. Remember that a great maintenance shop specializing in motor yachts might not know what to do with a 15-foot boat with an outboard.

Find a Specialist

After you've amassed a listing of local facilities (perhaps distilled simply from the local yellow

FIVE THINGS YOU DON'T WANT TO HEAR FROM YOUR BOAT APPRAISER

1. "I've got a cousin who is a faith healer. Want me to call him about your engine?"
2. "Of course teak can get termites."
3. "Stephen King might have an interest in buying this boat."
4. "There are only two words I can think of to say to you: *insurance* and *hurricane*."
5. "Let me put it this way . . . compared to your boat, the *Titanic* is bristol."

pages and a few phone calls), narrow your choices to those who specialize in the type of repair you need. For example, a great engine mechanic might not know the first thing about fiberglass repair.

Check Out the Shop Thoroughly

Next, find out how long the shop has been in business. You're not being paranoid if you ask for references, such as what jobs on a vessel similar to yours they've completed in the past year, or by checking with the Better Business Bureau to see if any complaints have been made against the shop. Thorough research can save you from further damage caused by a boat left in the hands of untrained repair personnel . . . which leads to your next question . . .

What's the Mechanic's Background?

Ask the mechanic about his or her training. What factory schools has he or she attended? Does the repair facility send its staff to regular training seminars? When was the last seminar? On what subject? Check the shop walls for training certificates. Most qualified mechanics are proud of their specialized knowledge.

Is the Shop's Paperwork in Order?

Is the repair shop licensed, insured, and bonded? If not, you may find yourself with faulty repairs and no recourse. This can add up to big bucks.

If All Else Fails . . .

Finally, if you're still at a loss for how to find a safe shop with which you'd trust your seagoing love, or if you'd like to check up on the shop you've located through the prior steps, ask around. Your local dockmasters, marine insurance agents, marine equipment stores such as West Marine, and marine surveyors are professionals who should have a good handle on local mechanics and repair facilities.

A FEW LAST TIPS

A Level Solution

Forgot your level during boat repairs? Fill a jar or old milk container three-quarters full of water. Set it on its side on the area in question. Is the water level? Then your work area is level, too.

Dropped Tools? Not a Problem

To retrieve tools that are dropped overboard, keep a large magnet attached to a long length of line on board and when the time comes, go fishin'.

Repairs at Sea

For quick temporary mends when time is of the essence for anything from leaky hoses to hull punctures, use a cold weld such as waterproof J-B Waterweld (903-885-7696).

Another easy option for quick temporary mends is Star brite's fast-drying general-purpose, aluminum and/or PVC epoxies (the PVC epoxy is great for freshwater system leaks).

To temporarily mend tiny plastic objects that have been broken in half, heat the tip of a screwdriver and touch it to the two broken ends. Then quickly press the ends together while they're tacky.

Don't Throw Away That Empty Soda Bottle

Cut the top off a 2-liter soda bottle to create a disposable emergency funnel.

Cut the bottom off a plastic half-gallon milk jug to form a bailer or scoop.

Screwy Solutions

Stripped screw head? Use a small hacksaw blade to cut a new slot at a 90-degree angle to the old slot.

Stripped Phillips head screw? A dab of 3M's 5200 may be all that's needed to give your screwdriver the needed bite. Allow the 5200 to cure for a few minutes prior to use.

If a rusted screw or bolt breaks off before you can remove it, grind or file down all the remaining parts of the rusted bolt or screw until you reach sturdy metal, and then create a new screwdriver notch with an abrasive wheel.

If a screw turns in its hole but has no bite, try this: Wrap thread, fishing line, or dental floss around the threads and reinsert the screw. If that doesn't work, build up the hole with bits of glue-soaked wood, match sticks, or toothpicks.

Get ready to go boating.

Items Found in a Purse Come in Handy

A woman's purse can be a source of repair materials . . . especially if it holds a nail file, which is great for cleaning fouled spark plugs, or fingernail glue, an excellent emergency adhesive.

Use the Right Tools

For hard-to-reach screws and bolts, try Black & Decker's flexible bit tip holder. It allows you to use a power screwdriver or drill to remove or install those hard-to-reach hardware bits despite the most awkward angles.

Another boater's toolbox luxury from Black & Decker is a multibit screwdriving set that allows you to use your portable drill as a power screwdriver and socket driver—and it even has some regular drill bits, so that you can tackle almost any task on board.

A small waterproof LED flashlight is indispensable to shine light into otherwise impossible-to-reach areas.

Efficient Storage

Separating tools into categorized smaller boxes is often more efficient than having one master box that's too heavy to haul up on deck.

Old eyeglasses cases, especially the clamshell type that snap shut, make excellent tool kits, drill bit holders, and so on and take up little of your valuable storage space on board.

If your pet peeve is a disorganized fiberglass dock box, organize it by attaching inside "shelving." The shelving can be formed of roof gutters, small plastic spice shelves, and so on.

To keep spare onboard lightbulbs from breaking, wrap them in a paper towel and store inside a glass or tumbler.

Snappy Shore Power Connections

Does it take you several seconds of fumbling to get the pins on the end of your shore power cord properly aligned with the receptacle? Plug in the cord and use a felt-tip pen to draw a line on the top of the plug and one on the receptacle. Fumbling will be a dim memory when you can simply line up the lines and plug in the plug.

The Art of Cleaning Boating Attire

If you rub up against a rusty bolt while you're working in the bilge, it'll make a nasty stain on your clothing. Save your favorite boating T-shirt by washing away the rust with a mixture of salt, lemon juice, and vinegar. Once the stain is gone, wash the garment in freshwater so you won't smell like a lemon-head.

Clean beer stains on your boat clothes by dabbing them with a mixture of half water and half isopropyl rubbing alcohol. Wash the item as usual when you return to shore.

To remove serious perspiration stains from your favorite captain's shirt, first try soaking it for 30 minutes in rainwater or distilled water. If the spot remains, prepare a mixture of 3 parts methylated spirits and 1 part ammonia and dab on sparingly. Rinse with clean water and wash the garment as usual. Be sure to keep the material away from open flames.

Spilled your morning coffee when the captain gunned the engine to get away from the dock? If it's a recently made spot, pour salt on it immediately to absorb the coffee and the stain. If the stain is on pure white fabric, rinse the spot in hydrogen peroxide, lemon, or chlorinated water. If the fabric is colored, wash in lukewarm water and rinse in chlorinated water afterward. ***NOTE:*** These tips work only on washable items.

Dock Pick-Me-Ups

Party guests leave half-empty soda cans lying around? Pour that soda on your cement dock or driveway to eat away any oil or grease stains! Then rinse off with a hose.

To remove mold accumulation on a cement dock, fill a bucket with 2 scoops of powdered brand name laundry detergent, 1 cup bleach, and 2 to 3 gallons water, and scrub your dock thoroughly. Then rinse off with a garden hose. It takes the mold right off and keeps it away.

One Last Plug for Baking Soda

Baking soda is a compact, all-around handy item to have on board and can substitute for toothpaste, deodorant, salt, deodorizers for your smelly boat shoes, and laundry detergent. It also works as a sunburn ointment and takes the sting out of bug bites.

No One Is Going to Laugh

When all else fails, take out the engine manual. (You do have one on board, don't you?)

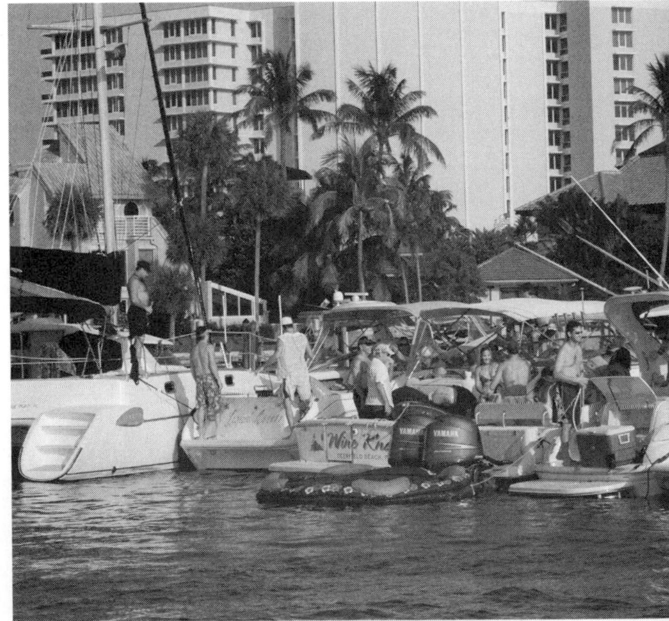

Now it's time to cast off lines and enjoy. We've made boat cleaning and maintenance easier, so there's more time for boating fun.

INDEX